AF361454

Archipelagoes of Longing

Archipelagoes of Longing

Puerto Ricans, Resistance, and Memory

NICOLÁS RAMOS FLORES

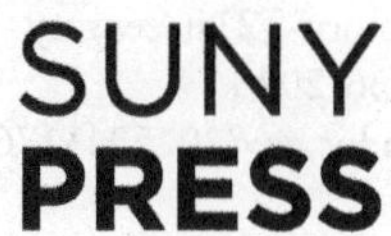

Cover credit: Gamaliel Rodríguez, Correctional Faith, 2022. Acrylic, ink, gold leaf on paper, 72^1/$_8$ × 52^1/$_{16}$ in. (183 × 132 cm). Colby College Museum of Art, Museum purchase from the Museum Art Purchases Fund; 2023.043. Courtesy of Colby College Museum of Art.

Published by State University of New York Press, Albany

EU GPSR Authorised Representative:
Logos Europe, 9 rue Nicolas Poussin, 17000, La Rochelle, France
contact@logoseurope.eu

For information, contact State University of New York Press, Albany, NY
www.sunypress.edu

Library of Congress Cataloging-in-Publication Data

Name: Ramos Flores, Héctor Nicolás, author.
Title: Archipelagoes of longing : Puerto Ricans, resistance, and memory /
    Nicolás Ramos Flores.
Description: Albany : State University of New York Press, [2026]. | Includes
    bibliographical references and index.
Identifiers: LCCN 2025041176 | ISBN 9798855806328 (hardcover : alk. paper) |
    ISBN 9798855806342 (epub) | ISBN 9798855806359 (PDF)
Subjects: LCSH: Arts and society—Puerto Rico—History—20th century. | Arts
    and society—Puerto Rico—History—21st century. | Psychic trauma in art.
Classification: LCC NX528.A1 R36 2026
LC record available at https://lccn.loc.gov/2025041176

A mi familia y a mi pueblo.

Contents

Acknowledgments

Like many projects of this scope, this book emerged from a constellation of curiosities nurtured within various communities. My intellectual interests were shaped and supported by numerous personal and academic spaces. At the University of Minnesota, Twin Cities, I would like to thank Ana Forcinito and Ana Paula Ferreira, who engaged with early versions of this project and offered insightful feedback and reading suggestions. I am deeply grateful to my mentor, Jennifer Gómez Menjívar, at the University of North Texas, who continually encouraged me to think beyond conventional boundaries of what cultural products can and should be studied.

To Israel Reyes-Crespo at Dartmouth University, thank you for reading many versions of these chapters and being a productive thought partner. To Laura Fernandéz at the University of Richmond—who, over the past several years, has read countless iterations not only of this project but of nearly everything I've written—thank you for powering through so many repeated words. I also thank the New England Consortium for Latino Studies, the Global Memories Working Group, and the Works-in-Progress in Latin American Studies group (WIPLA) for your feedback and intellectual support throughout this book's development. To Rebecca Colesworthy, my editor at SUNY Press—thank you for your compassionate and thoughtful guidance throughout this process. To the members of my book workshop—Lawrence La-Fountain-Stokes, Kaitlin Murphy, Yolanda Martínez-San Miguel, and Petra Rivera Rideau—I am forever indebted to your kind, thoughtful, rigorous, and generous comments. Your encouragement deeply shaped this project. Thank you.

At Colby College, I am grateful to my colleagues in the Spanish Department and Latin American Studies Program—Ana Almeyda-Cohen, Sandra Bernal-Heredia, Lola Bollo-Panadero, Ben Fallaw, Patrice Franko,

Lindsay Mayka, José Martínez, Damaris Mayans, Tiffany Miller, Luis Millones-Figueroa, Winifred Tate, and Brett White—for your invaluable support over the past several years. To my friend Dean Allbritton, thank you for the countless hours of conversation, for suggesting cultural producers, and for simply being present during this journey. I also extend my gratitude to Colby College's Provost Margaret McFadden, the Center for Arts and Humanities, and the Lunder Institute for American Art, whose generous support funded several research trips that were vital to this book.

Most importantly, to my family and friends who have supported and nurtured my intellectual pursuits since childhood: To my mom, Lourdes, and my father, Héctor—thank you for always encouraging me to explore, even when the path was unclear. To my sister, Yesenia, thank you for always being a supportive ear, even when the ideas barely made sense. To my late grandfather, Nilo, whose stories and deep knowledge of Puerto Rico inspired many of the foundational questions behind this book. And to my grandmother, Francisca, thank you for always asking (repeatedly!) where the book stood so I could hurry and visit you. To my dear friends Liseth, Aislinn, and Alexandra—thank you for helping me bounce around ideas, pulling me away from self-doubt, and believing in me when I did not believe in myself. And finally, to my loving partner, Nazlı: I will be forever grateful for your steady presence, your challenges that deepened my thinking, and your shoulder when I needed it most. When the project did not make sense to me, it still did to you. And when all I needed was a hug and some *köfte* balls, thank you for being at the ready. This would not have been possible without you.

An earlier version of parts of chapter 2 appeared as the article "Sites of Contestation: Kaleidoscopes of Memory and the Shrouding of Latinx Lives in the Interim National Pulse Memorial," *Latino Studies*, 2024, pp. 254–276.

Introduction

Archipelagoes of Longing and Puerto Ricans

In his series of large-scale drawings, Puerto Rican artist Gamaliel Rodríguez combines inks on canvas to provide a polychromatic yet sinister portrayal of contemporary Puerto Rico. Both finished and unfinished, painted and unpainted space, colorful and colorless, and accented by shimmers of gold, Rodríguez's paintings effectively convey the degradation of Puerto Rican infrastructure. They appear to be photograph-like depictions of the city-scapes, urban decay, and flora of the island, melding bright pinks, oranges, yellows, blues, and greens with black, empty space and incomplete borders. The works give a dystopian feel to contemporary Puerto Rico, but the gold leaf peppered around them points to something more, something not quite definable, depicting the political, environmental, and racial tensions that Puerto Ricans on the island and in the diaspora experience. In many ways Rodríguez's work captures the "affective crisis" facing Puerto Rico today, where the lessons of the past have not fully been learned and are super-imposed on a disastrous present that does not seem to know any bounds (Bonilla, "Postdisaster Futures"). What it also reveals is the possibility of a future in which not all hope is lost, and the colors, while eerie, straddle a thin line between hope and despair, the two emotions sitting side by side, not entirely knowing what to do. Rodríguez compellingly portrays today's Puerto Rico—anxiously waiting for a future that might never come and at a crossroads of various crises, existential anxieties, and emotional registers.

Rodríguez's work is an artistic representation of the catastrophes Puerto Rico has experienced in the last decade. Economic crisis (e.g., the 2007 financial crisis and the debt oversight board), environmental degradation (Hurricanes Maria and Irma along with earthquakes), political upheavals (the 2019 political protest to oust then-Governor Ricardo Roselló), and mass exodus to the United States, counterbalanced by the future possibilities offered by collective action, resistance, and hope, undergird the kaleidoscopic nature of Puerto Rican longing for a different future and reality that is the focus of this book. These continual occurrences reveal a colonial reality that has concrete material consequences for the people of Puerto Rico and their diaspora, who have long been excluded not just existentially but racially, economically, and legally from the broader United States national imagination. Much like Rodríguez's work, longing is neither wholly optimistic nor

Figure I.1. Gamaliel Rodríguez, *Correctional Faith*, 2022. Acrylic, ink, gold leaf on paper, 72¹/₈ × 52¹/₁₆ in. (183 ×132 cm). *Source:* Colby College Museum of Art, Gift of John Marin, Museum purchase from the Museum Art Purchases Fund 2023.043.

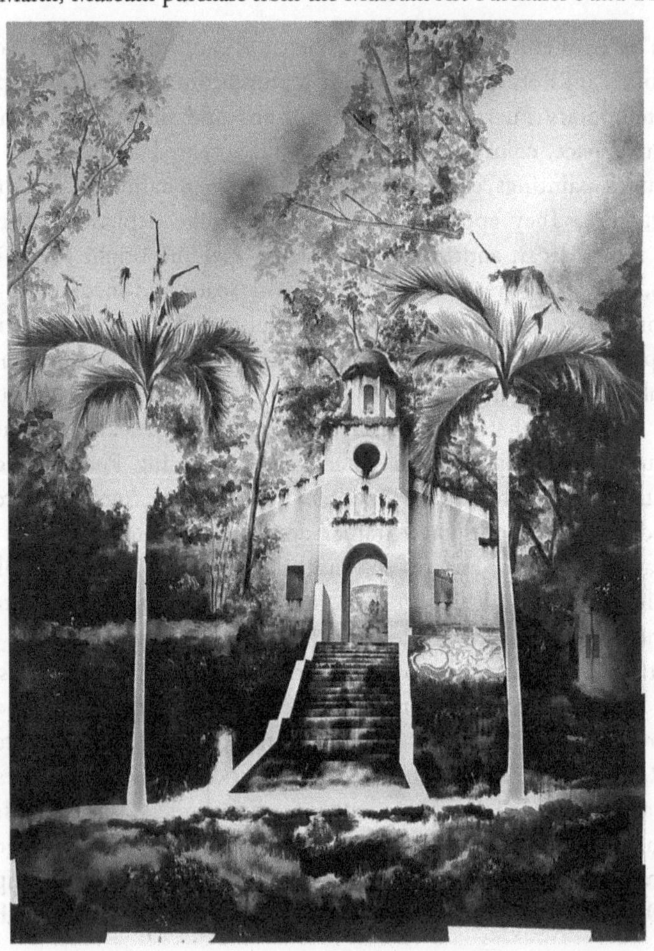

inherently pessimistic; the repeating cycle of collective struggle for Puerto Ricans requires new contemplations of longing that acknowledge the multivalent nature of their experience.

Archipelagoes of Longing: Puerto Ricans, Resistance, and Memory is situated at the intersection of Latino studies and Puerto Rican studies to provide a more holistic understanding of the various manifestations of longing within contemporary Puerto Rico and its diaspora. *Archipelagoes of Longing* is at once a representation of collective political and cultural experience through various visual cultural products and a way to understand the manifold neoliberal and colonial structures that accentuate racial-economic dynamics and exacerbate colonial policies. Issues of colonialism, migration, and identity often dominate the field of Puerto Rican studies. Scholars have highlighted the palimpsestic nature of Puerto Rican studies, deepening the understanding of various intersections such as race and policing (LeBrón, *Policing Life and Death*), nation formation and gender (Moreno, *Family Matters*), and migration and neoliberalism (Reyes), among many others, that demonstrate the inherent dynamism in the study of Puerto Ricans and their diaspora. More recently, scholarship has focused on the effects of disaster and colonialism (Bonilla and LeBrón; Zambrana)—a point I take up in chapters 3 and 4—adding an additional layer of subjugation to the failed administrative policies of the commonwealth. I build on existing Puerto Rican studies scholarship to dissect the complex nature of longing for Puerto Ricans, where multiple nodes are present at once.

Archipelagoes of Longing takes the archipelago as its basis to build out the way longing exists for colonized people by centering the colonial legacy while also acknowledging the inherent fluidity of cultural formations in the Caribbean basin. I define archipelagoes of longing as the continuous, interconnected, fluid, and contradictory collective desire that characterizes Puerto Rican future projections. Akin to the interrelated nature of archipelagic island chains, archipelagoes of longing expose the interlocking racial, environmental, and migratory experiences, past and present, that impact Puerto Ricans and their diaspora. I specifically use archipelagoes of longing in the plural to underscore the multiplicity within longing that nevertheless provides articulations of a dynamic and inclusive whole. My use of archipelagoes as a conceptual framework draws from Edouard Glissant's "archipelagic thinking" and Yolanda Martínez-San Miguel and Michelle Stephens's more recent theorizations of the archipelagic in a more global sense (7). Both scholars use archipelagoes as a hermeneutical lens, a way of thinking and seeing, a method of studying the Caribbean cultural experience. Informed by histories of coerced and voluntary diasporic movements, colonialism and imperialism, racial-sexual formations, and global capitalism, archipelagic thinking allows us to recognize the connectivity and commonalities across distinct locations, on the island, the continent, and the sea that would otherwise go unnoticed if these locations were studied as discrete units. Archipelagoes, in this sense, present an opportunity for rearticulation of the human experience that traverses time and space (Martínez-San Miguel and Stephens 7). In doing so, *Archipelagoes of Longing* brings into view Puerto Rico's colonial history and that history's impacts on island and mainland residents alike, while encompassing the mutability and contradiction of both contexts. By examining Puerto Ricans across the diaspora, *Archipelagoes of Longing* pivots away from location-based longing for Boricuas.

While archipelagoes provide a historical and spatial resonance within these chapters, longing further suspends the fixity of a collective experience, acknowledging contradictory, incongruent, and incomplete desires. Longing is a complex personal and collective experience shaped by memory, colonialism, and the struggles of Puerto Ricans both on the island and in the diaspora. Beyond simply a personal emotion, it is a shared response to the historical and contemporary injustices that define the Puerto Rican collective. Rooted in memory, longing is influenced by the fragmented and incomplete ways colonized peoples remember their past, as studied by Arcadio Díaz Quiñones (1993) and Derek Walcott (1995). Moreover, colonialism warps time and creates what Sandra Ruiz calls a "timelessness" where time is suspended into a continuous loop that challenges temporal linearity, forcing Puerto Ricans to find new forms of liberation. Ruiz analyzes the ways different aesthetic practices help illuminate the Puerto Rican condition that simultaneously endures and resists colonial power relations. Yet, my understanding of longing is also future-oriented. Thus, thinking with José Esteban Muñoz's "queer utopias," I show how longing emerges from a desire for liberation and belonging that is always presently fought for and potentially available for Puerto Ricans even as imperial, colonial, and global forces try to limit it from emerging. Finally, spatial disconnections, caused by colonial and global power structures, further shape this sense of longing, emphasizing the struggle to feel at home, stable, and at peace across different locations and histories. Puerto Ricans on the island and in the diaspora are intricately linked and motivated by the same sense of liberation, regardless of location.

Contributing to this interdisciplinary conversation, my framework, archipelagoes of longing, rearticulates the Puerto Rican experience in terms of its spatial connectedness across diasporic communities and its temporal continuities in colonial, racial, and gendered formations. This experience,

I argue, is best described as longing. Each chapter, accordingly, studies a particular kind of longing by analyzing a cultural product: longing to recuperate a past time, or an idealized version of a past time, to envision just futures (chapter 1); longing to belong, longing to be recognized as an equal member of society (chapter 2); longing for all that is lost or has never been had, longing for political and economic stability (chapter 3); and ultimately longing for liberation for Puerto Ricans on the island and in the diaspora (chapter 4). Each distinct cultural product—murals, memorials, testimonials, documentaries—illuminates a different constitutive aspect of the Puerto Rican experience, and *together* they help explain contemporary Puerto Ricanness. Dispersed yet not disconnected, they allow me to offer an analysis of Puerto Rico and Puerto Ricans in their heterogeneity, historical contingency, multiplicity, and desire—that is, in their archipelagic form.

Longing's Colonial Warp

Puerto Rican longing is a multifarious enterprise. Colonialism is a continued traumatic iteration that seeps into other structural and representational nodes of archipelagoes of longing. Archipelagoes are connected not just through geographic proximity but also by their colonial histories around the world (Martínez-San Miguel and Stephens 3); thus, colonial power relations become the connecting thread of resistance and understanding through this longing. Individual events may occur, but colonial relations are there exclusively to make them worse; in many cases, colonial relations are the direct cause of these events. Puerto Ricans not only challenge nation-state constructs of identity but also inhabit a world reality that intertwines capitalist systems with sociopolitical formations both on and off the archipelago. Puerto Rico is the embodiment of a "modern colony" where global economic forces and United States domestic policy, along with territorial governance, make the colonial administrations of bygone eras obsolete (Grosfoguel 2–5). Within this dichotomy, both colonialism and coloniality emerge simultaneously. Coloniality, as explained by Aníbal Quijano when discussing postcolonial Latin American republics, assumes the continuation of colonial thought, governance, cultural patterns, and social formations that maintain a hierarchy that privileges Eurocentric ways of being, as opposed to the more commonly understood form of colonialism, which involves the metropolitan administration of a land and people for the economic, political, and cultural benefit of the metropole. Puerto Rico is at once in both of these camps but also challenges the formation of these notions over the course of its centuries-long relationship with the United States, in which the dynamic can be seen as that of an "exploitation colony" (Grosfoguel 7). According to this understanding, the United States has long used Puerto Rico to extract economic gain, scientific knowledge, and labor. It extracts and exploits populations without an explicit settler ideal expanding across the archipelago. Colonialism, coloniality, and postcolonialism are folded into one, creating a dizzying understanding of political relations. Puerto Rico's status—maintaining cultural autonomy while still existing under colonial administration and exploitation by the metropole—challenges popular conventions of colonialism and enhances longing's future projections. A desire, in many ways, to be free from these colonial structures.

In its acquisition by the United States in 1898 and the establishment of its commonwealth status in 1952, Puerto Rico as a colony merely changed hands. Colonialism, rather than ending, remains an ever-present menace for Puerto Rico. The current colonial status both exacerbates existing woes and creates its own new problems for Puerto Ricans to solve. Unlike the rest of Spanish-speaking Latin America, Puerto Rico is politically still a colony, enduring both the same postcolonial realities experienced by other Caribbean and Latin American countries and a persistent political stagnation that perpetuates its second-class status. The archipelago's histories, wedded to new and continuing forms of colonialism across the Caribbean, warp the singular understanding of events-based memory formations and force new ways that longing emerges for a colonized people that never ceased to be colonized. Time is thus seen as both unitary and multifold on islands of the archipelago, challenging linear continental time (Thompson 120). In this understanding of the archipelago, colonialism distorts, refracts, and convolutes the representational core of the various cultural products studied in this book. Time, space, and politics are disrupted; what is post- and pre- falls apart for Puerto Rico and Puerto Ricans, requiring new forms of representational examinations to fully encompass and understand the various factors at play. The protests of the Verano Boricua in 2019, the continued environmental devastations in Vieques, Hurricanes Maria and Irma, and United States migration have become so interwoven with colonial remnants that it is difficult to separate the forest from the trees. *Archipelagoes of Longing* centers the muddled and ongoing presence of colonialism by pointing to it but also recognizing the various other factors that contribute to Puerto Ricans' existential malaise.

Puerto Rico's commonwealth status has created a fractured set of results that directly impact both the island's existential malaise and its colonial legacy. After the creation of a new constitution in 1952, Puerto Rico saw intense interest from United States policymakers. No figure has had a greater role in Puerto Rico's current manifestation than Luis Muñoz Marín, a pro-independence politician turned commonwealth creator who chartered the current colonial situation. As the first democratically elected governor of the island, Muñoz Marín occupies an almost mythical place in Puerto Rican history; his impact on current Boricua lives is in constant tension. Initially in favor of independence, Muñoz Marín broke away from the Partido Liberal, which advocated for independence at the time, and created his own political party. In creating the Partido Popular Democrático (PPD), Muñoz Marín's main aim was to combine various social and political alliances under one governing umbrella and forge a beneficial economic relationship with the United States. He made a distinction between cultural nationalism and political nationalism, acknowledging the cultural specificity of Puerto Rico while working toward closer economic relations with the United States (Duany, *The Puerto Rican Nation on the Move* 124–25). He believed that a complete break from the United States would provoke Puerto Rico's economic collapse and lead to poverty in the new republic (Ayala and Bernabe 148–49). Because of Puerto Rico's access to US markets and the American government's sizable contributions to the island, Muñoz Marín did not see independence as an economically viable option for Puerto Rico at the time (150). Though his position was more nuanced than simple economic interest and the PPD platform originally supported some movement toward independence, the lack of support for independence in the US government led him to abandon the cause altogether and create the current commonwealth status, which allowed a form of self-governance with economic support from the metropole (151–52). This economic support came via export-dependent Operation Bootstraps, which provided increased funding for industrialization (Berman Santana 43–44). The main aim of this program, in a pattern also apparent in other economic initiatives for the island, was to focus on external sources of funding and resources while using island-wide cheap labor to produce goods and meet demand from foreign interests, not to fulfill the interests of Puerto Ricans (44). It led many Puerto Ricans to believe their colonial relationship to the United States had, if not completely disappeared, been drastically changed (Jiménez 108). In the program's initial iteration, the archipelago did see economic benefits, such as the development of roads, schools, and health care, but it also led to inequalities that Muñoz Marín, a leftist leader, had wanted to avoid.

I explain this modern colonial story, which centers economic need and political sovereignty, to delineate how Puerto Rico's history informs the contradictions that archipelagoes of longing expose and the historical specificity of Puerto Rico's varied longings. Past and present sit together like the archipelagoes, fluid and stable, connected and detached, whole and particular. Puerto Rico's longing unfolds, linked to the past but conscious of the present. Muñoz Marín and the United States' colonial project saw certain limited material benefits for an impoverished island but also created the twentieth- and twenty-first-century colonial framework that upholds contemporary catastrophe. This framework allows for continued policy initiatives and cultural actions to take hold in the name of progress and democracy, while mass migration to the United States, the Financial Oversight and Management Board, and the commonwealth status are structures-in-tension that actively perpetuate the subjugation of Puerto Ricans. Longing for exits, longing for liberation, and longing for material resources need not compete but sit together, forming part of the various archipelagoes of longing throughout the book.

Most recently this exploitation is seen with the debt crisis that led to the emergence of the fiscal oversight board in 2016. The removal from the tax code of Section 936, which had given companies in Puerto Rico federal tax breaks for manufacturing on the island and kept the Puerto Rican economy afloat until the mid-1990s (E. Morales 80), kicked off the current economic catastrophe. While the plan's ending was announced in 1996 during the administration of then-Governor Ricardo Rosselló, the subsequent administrations of Sila María Calderón and Aníbal Acevedo Vilá did nothing to create a plan for Puerto Rico's future after the end of Section 936 (Meléndez-Badillo 164). This removal precipitated the slow decline of the Puerto Rican economy, leading to the migration of many educated Puerto Ricans to the United States and the accumulation of huge sums of debt to maintain basic government services.[1] Moreover, though many critics point to economic mismanagement by Puerto Rican officials, it is important to note that Wall Street investors saw the new bonds being issued by municipalities on the island as an opportunity for predatory and corrupt lending practices (Morales 110). Finally, because of the spiraling economic situation on the island, in 2016 the United States government set up a Financial Oversight and Management Board, locally known as *la junta*, to handle the archipelago's finances, leading to the slashing of the budget in a bid to improve Puerto Rico's finances (Meléndez-Badillo 174). The economic problems in Puerto Rico have arisen out of a combination of neoliberal fiscal policies that squeeze the few economic resources from the island and a colonial relationship with the United States that does not allow Puerto Rico the financial independence to center its residents' needs. As I will explore in chapter 3, "In Hurricane Maria's Wake: Mourning, Catastrophe, and Consciousness in (Post-)Disaster Puerto Rico," neoliberal economic policies on the island slowly crippled the infrastructure, which led to the collapse of the electrical grid and the prolonged suffering of Puerto Ricans after the hurricane. Here, poor colonial administration and mismanagement, where improvements to the grid were deferred for financial and political reasons, exacerbated the impact of Hurricane Maria and accentuated colonial decay.

This fusion of colonial structures and economic oppressions fuels what Rocio Zambrana calls "colonial debts," which perpetuate Puerto Rico's precarious existence into the present. To Zambrana, debt is the continuation of colonial power relations in the twenty-first century; she highlights how the Financial Oversight and Management Board's focus on creditor repayments rather than basic government services for the residents of the island allows debt to serve as a new coloniality (10). Since, as Mónica Jiménez puts it, "Puerto Rico is a captive space for debt production" (5) and creditors have made and will make billions of dollars in profits, it is important to understand that these debts function as the colonial iteration of neoliberal economic and social policies imposed on the island. Beginning in the late 2000s, austerity measures such as the laying off of thirty thousand public-sector workers, the downgrading of Puerto Rico's credit rating, and the imposition of budget cuts privileged paying off Wall Street creditors at the expense of Puerto Rican daily living standards (Atiles-Osorio 107). Puerto Rico's colonial status does not allow the island to take other measures that sovereign nations normally enact—monetary controls, interest rate regulations, international loans, etc.—to steady the financial ship, hampering economic development and leading to political and social unrest (Morales 108). Owing to a combination of structural limitations in the economy, migration to the United States, and Puerto Rico's twenty-first-century colonial status, the debt crisis led to the implementation of an antidemocratic, unelected fiscal oversight board that took away the island's power to administer its own finances. Colonial administration and predatory economic policies have fused together in a neoliberal colonial dynamic. Which is the true culprit of Puerto Rico's woes? Where do the money problems start and the colonial problems end? They are one and the same, but the delineation has obscured the broader precarity faced by Puerto Ricans, and archipelagoes of longing reveal residents' various longings to escape the multifold tentacles of colonial oppressions. Economic precarity, colonialism, and environmental catastrophes are all the problem, and acknowledging them as such moves us toward a more constructive understanding of the colonial relationship.

The late twentieth and early twenty-first centuries mark a near culmination of this colonial reality that calls into question for many Puerto Ricans the relationship they have with the United States. In the 2021 episode of the podcast *La Brega* "Se acabaron las promesas," political anthropologist Yarimar Bonilla notes that Puerto Ricans have thought of the commonwealth status as "the best of both worlds," with residents receiving a US passport and protections while maintaining their cultural identity, language, and, to a degree, administrative autonomy. This purported autonomy almost forgets to acknowledge how the heavy influence of US policy, cultural norms, and linguistic dominance has shaped the island's self-determination and runs counter to the real material and existential subjugation that Puerto Ricans and Puerto Rico endure. The failed colonial experiment that is the current commonwealth status is the cause of many of the problems that the island faces today. Puerto Rico is an *estado libre asociado*, or "free associated state," of the United States yet continues to not be free from US oppression, is disassociated culturally, and is not a sovereign state. Given this convoluted status, the continuity and discontinuity of the archipelago assists in understanding Puerto Rico's colonial conditions through the distortion of the words. These words point to a muddled status that folds various unrealities into an almost dystopian whole. This disconnect in the term, where Puerto Rico is not free, is culturally disassociated, and is not a state, came out of a broader desire to appease different constituencies on the island and on the US mainland to maintain economic benefits for the colonial power (Bonilla, *Postdisaster Futures* 151). Like Puerto Rico, many other Caribbean protectorates such as French Martinique and the British Virgin Islands also reflect the lingering presence of colonial power (Bonilla, *Non-Sovereign Futures* 10). These protectorates challenge the colonial-postcolonial trajectory by maintaining national identification markers that are not tied to nation-state political formations.

Within these colonial structures, a certain "timelessness," to use Sandra Ruiz's term, occurs in which colonial relations disrupt linear ideas of time to create both excess and depletion of time (25). In *Ricanness: Enduring Time in Anticolonial Performance* (2019), Ruiz dissects the nature of Puerto Ricans through a temporal looping that is defined by colonial relations over time that informs the temporal stagnation and tension within these archipelagoes of longing. To Ruiz, colonialism warps time, generating a sort of timelessness that challenges linear ideas of progress and liberation (3). It is this looping that forces Ricans to endure constantly striving for basic resources and ending up going back and forth in fits and starts of change "under limited self-control in a nonstate state of economic and political impotence" (9). *Ricanness* then also challenges the philosophical underpinning of existence that sees one life in linear time. Looping forces new contemplations and frameworks of the human experience in which there is both not enough and an excess of time (21). Within this endurance, there are both the traditional ideas of revolution and resistance but also experimental acts of living that challenge colonial burdens through aesthetic practices (11). These aesthetic acts that she sees as political endurance are "about laboring to eventually stare past the horizon with apprehension, longing, pain, and pleasure—not feeling invalidated by another in the long pursuit of liberation and continual existence" (12). It is with this looping that acts of resistance emerge in the various temporal performances that "[do] not destroy the futural prospects of the subjects under a looping colonialism" (25). The longing I will examine in the various cultural products similarly sits within this tension, where it at once resists and is bogged down by neoliberal and colonial structures both off and on the archipelago. A Rican longing is at once liberatory and defeatist. As I will explore throughout the book, Puerto Rican resilience has its limits and Puerto Ricans' endurance, while admirable, need not be a defining feature of their experience, but reveals the inherent problems of their second-class status. Like the archipelagoes' historical repetitions, where the past constantly infiltrates the present, in Puerto Rico a looping occurs that repeats and creates new forms of resistance that remain the same and propel longing's shifting articulation. Ultimately Puerto Rican longing is defined by an "arrested future," to use Ann Laurie Stoler's term, a longing trapped in the past as it thinks through the future (21). This temporal confusion arises where the possibilities of a decolonial reality emerge only to be subsumed again by the realities of material deterioration in the archipelago and Puerto Ricans' second-class status on the mainland.

This temporal quagmire informs longing's future projections as co-constituted by memory's past-presentness where historical and contemporary injustices motivate a future sense of liberation and belonging. Debates within the field of memory studies have been engaging with ways the field can better reflect the experiences of non-Western, nondominant peoples.[2] While some scholars have called for the field to be inclusive of minoritized voices, others warn that it must not isolate itself from Western-dominated discourses. Yet within the Caribbean, memory constructions have already been linked to legacies of colonialism and a desire to articulate a fractured understanding of memory. Scholars such as Arcadio Díaz Quiñones and Derek Walcott have rethought the Eurocentric understanding of memory by challenging the intellectual underpinnings of why and how memory is formed.[3] These thinkers inform my understanding of memory in the Caribbean by focusing on the inherent heterogeneity of memory. While I will demonstrate later the way Puerto Rico's colonial status not only distorts time and perception but also forces certain longings to exist, the history of colonialism directly impacts the connection between memory and longing in the Caribbean. As I will show, memory is inherently a fragmented project for Puerto Ricans, requiring new imaginations as to how it is conceived while highlighting that longing is not one-directional or one-dimensional but rather moves out into various nodes.

These various incongruous memory formations are informed by Arcadio Díaz Quiñones's idea of "La memoria rota" (1993), or a broken memory, that helps inform Puerto Rican cultural history. To Díaz Quiñones, the colonial status of Puerto Ricans necessarily impacts the way a nation is formed that moves away from state actors, beginning with the emergence of the Partido Popular Democrático, the pro-commonwealth status party. While I explained earlier how Muñoz Marín and his party were instrumental in formulating the twentieth-century colonial relationship with the United States, it is important to note that Díaz Quiñones claims that this broken memory begins in this earlier historical moment, when utopian nation formation efforts by the first democratically elected governor led to the disjuncture of the collective national memory. Rather than see the state apparatus as the purveyor of a cultural history, Díaz Quiñones performs an excavation of Puerto Rican collective memory in the works of great writers such as Luis Palés Matos, José Luis González, and Luis Rafael Sánchez and Nuyorican authors like Tato Laviera and Esmeralda Santiago, among others. Rather than excluding these cultural producers from nation formation, Díaz Quiñones asserts that is precisely how they write about the tensions, incongruencies, and "ruptures" of the Puerto Rican experience that both goes against colonial nation formation efforts and adequately constructs a representative depiction of Puerto Ricanness. Similarly, Derek Walcott's 1992 Nobel Prize lecture "The Antilles: Fragments of Epic Memory" speaks of the "epic memory" in the Caribbean resulting from the fragmentary and colonialist history of the island. Walcott takes issue with the epic form as a literary genre that defines national formations in the West and demands that more interrogation of the form be carried out for nations not stemming from the sovereign nation-state. Walcott challenges the unitary understanding of what an epic memory could accomplish in the Caribbean because of the various cultures, particularly Asian cultures, that are often not imagined as being part of the Caribbean collective (295). To Walcott, this "epic memory" in the Caribbean thus becomes the collections of fragments that make up the Caribbean imaginary, linking different historical and cultural nodes together.

Understanding memory for colonized peoples in this fragmentary, broken, and incomplete way helps explain its impact on longing for Puerto Ricans. In this sense their history, migrations, and oppressions are often seen in isolation but must be studied together to provide a more inclusive understanding of what they desire. Both Díaz Quiñones and Walcott are instrumental in thinking through how Puerto Rican colonial status complicates traumatic memories, moving beyond the singular traumas that have defined Euro-American discourses and instead acknowledging how traumatic experiences are constantly present. The fragments within Puerto Rican memory are but another element of the colonial saga that challenges a binary and essentialist understanding of memory for colonized people. For both Díaz Quiñones and Walcott, modes of artistic expression, such as literature, become a way to bring about and bring together the various pieces of the Caribbean, much in the same way the various cultural products studied in this book assist in elucidating the longing that Puerto Ricans live and feel. Diaspora-based and island-based experiences become part of the whole of longing. This unification is apparent in the case of Hurricane Maria, during which millions of Puerto Ricans in the United States desperately watched as the Category 5 storm ravaged the island. These Puerto Ricans were not part of the initial event, but their despair along with the ensuing mass migration from the island (Schachter and Bruce) together form part of the collective consciousness. Memory is malleable and adaptable to continual reconstruction (Rothberg 5). This type of constant construction and adaptability influences the longing we see in these chapters, which is constantly being consolidated and dispersed where various structural oppressions (colonial, imperial, environmental) and subjectivities (racial and sexual) that make up the constructions of collective memory for minoritized peoples force longings to shift and change depending on specific sociocultural contexts. For Puerto Ricans, different political movements in Chicago, Philadelphia, and San

Juan; various catastrophic events such as Hurricane Maria; and migration histories fold into a single, yet constantly reimagined, collective longing—a longing to belong, to be seen, and to exist—that is hard to define but part of the communal experience. Longing for a historical representation that adequately represents them, as we will explore in the street art murals of chapter 1, or longing for alternative narratives to official discourses that often understand events in Puerto Rico in binary and isolated formations, a point I will explore through the documentary films of Juan C. Dávila in chapter 4. These official narratives serve to further enhance the colonial relationship on the island by maintaining long-standing neoliberal discourses, racial exclusions, sexual shrouding, and fixed memorial dominance. Thus, with archipelagoes of longing as a framework, experiential inconsistencies within certain desires leave Puerto Ricans unsettled.

A Rican Archipelagic Longing

Archipelagoes of Longing theorizes the archipelago as a multivalent force to complicate longing's varied forms. This framework is heavily influenced by Martinican thinker Edouard Glissant's "archipelagic thinking," in which he provides an analytical lens for thinking through global structures of power. First conceived by Glissant in *Treatise on the Whole-World* (1990), archipelagic thinking assists in decentering continental ways of thought and contemplates the sociohistorical contradictions for understanding Caribbean peoples (18). In his work, Glissant asserts the creolization of the world that centers variety and is brought about through the "trace," or legacy, of global history and through relations that dominate this multiplicity (9–10). These traces and relations lead to a new understanding of identity that emerges through roots, in the plural, rather than a singular root, thus establishing different nodes of origination that do not simply replicate colonial structures of power (12). By thinking through longing in archipelagic terms—such as creolized, hybrid, and multiple terms—we understand longing that eschews Eurocentric constructs and in ways that are relational, rhizomic, and inclusive of experiences. Archipelagic thinking opens up new ways of understanding the world or, as Glissant says, "opens these seas to us" (18). These seas allow for possibilities and relations that have not been thought of and allow archipelagoes to assist in not foreclosing future possibilities. As will be discussed in chapters 3 and 4, political and existential longings push marginalized people forward in a more liberatory sense, even if only in small, incremental ways.

More recently, Yolanda Martínez-San Miguel and Michelle Stephens's take on archipelagic thinking further expanded contemporary interdisciplinary discussions across the Caribbean. Archipelagic thinking not only reflects contemporary power struggles experienced by Caribbean peoples but also challenges colonial relations and discourses that do not completely encompass the various interactions seen in the region. Archipelagic thinking requires an understanding of local contexts and global realities as well as of the connections and differences that exist throughout the Caribbean (Martínez-San Miguel and Stephens 7). Puerto Ricans are impacted by forces—global (climate change and neoliberal economic policies), local (political unrest and governmental mismanagement), and translocal (United States colonial relations)—that straddle various local and global lines of articulation. These lines must be included in the self-formulations and theorizations of and by Puerto Ricans. In contemporary Puerto Rican history, various catastrophic events (Hurricane Maria), social responses (mass migration off the island), and continued colonial administration (the PROMESA Act) have been both distinct forces with immediate impact and also connected to one another. These various moments and events redefine what Puerto Ricans long for yet remain interconnected in their impact on the Rican psyche, and archipelagic thinking as a framework provides a tool to unpack and give meaning. As Martínez-San Miguel and Stephens state, "[T]he archipelagic is conceived, therefore, as a set of relations that articulate cultural and political formations (collectivities, communities, societies), modes of interpreting and inhabiting the world (epistemologies), and symbolic imaginaries (as a poetic but also as habitus)" (13). By encompassing such varied and sometimes disparate relations, a fuller understanding of longing is created, moving away from colonial hierarchies of power that limit minoritized peoples' world-making.

With this multiplicity in mind, Puerto Ricans' cultural products provide a compelling intersection that rethinks collective longing for minoritized peoples. *Archipelagoes of Longing* shows the at-once fragmented and continuous nature of longing that arises from structural perpetuations such as colonialism, race, and gender. There is no doubt that one can extend the analysis of Puerto Rican colonialism under Spanish rule, and of the slave trade before that (Lloréns, "Ruin Nation"); I focus primarily on the ways the United States–centered colonial experiment has failed the people of Puerto Rico on and off the island because of the specific neoliberal realities of the second half of the twentieth century and into the twenty-first century. While I will expand on neoliberalism later in this introduction, I want to assert that neoliberal political structures in the United States and on the island form a broad basis for the continued subjugation of people and exacerbate economic, legal, environmental, racial, and gender structures. The neoliberal global system creates a rhetoric that pretends to extend equality to minoritized and colonized people while maintaining previous systems of oppression. Hence, these structures expose the interrelated oppressions of Puerto Ricans. While a racial-political-economic neoliberalism dominates in the United States and a colonial neoliberalism is exacerbated in Puerto Rico, neoliberal and colonial policies together become the driving forces for unjust practices that feign an exertion of equity only to amplify historical and present hierarchies of power with real material consequences for Puerto Ricans.

Given these various nodes of sociohistorical analysis, archipelagoes connect the varied and parallel forms of longing. Not isolated to one single desire or emerging from a single source, longing takes on many, and interconnected, forms. My thinking on longing is indebted to José Esteban Muñoz's "feeling utopias" and his elaboration of the political and aesthetic power of hope within queer performances. Anchoring his theorization with Ernst Bloch's conceptualization of hope, Muñoz moves away from fantastical understandings of a utopian hope to ones that are not only more affective in nature but also less pinned to concrete ends. Muñoz posits queerness as a future-oriented project that looks to the past to critique the present and build a possible new world. Queerness should not limit itself to the here and now or the practical elements of political motivations but open itself up to new possibilities or potentialities or "to think and feel in a *then* and *there*" (1). Rather than succumb to the present's quagmire, thinking within the present challenges this prison of the present because queerness thinks through possible futures, better pleasures, and new worlds. Much in the same way, Puerto Rican longing feels through a utopian understanding of the future that is open to new engagements with the world. These longings are not foreclosed, concrete, or idealized but rather a mixture of potentialities that are defined as "a certain mode of nonbeing that is eminent, a thing that is present but actually existing in the present tense" (9), and are not limited by contemporary struggles. There is an inherent malleability to this longing that is attuned to the different contexts, histories, and struggles present in the various locations but that still strive for a semblance of something better. In longing for something better, Puerto Ricans are open to the unknown since their current situation is so catastrophic that it requires new imaginations to emerge.

Furthermore, Muñoz critiques the antirelationality, or the rejection of other subjectivities within queerness, of some in queer studies, and insists that queer studies must be collective (10). The power of queerness is precisely the fact that it is on the horizon moving away from the presentism of contemporary political pragmatisms (11). Muñoz disconnects utopianism from being inherently something that must lead to a certain type of liberation or something more concrete, identifying it instead as a "letting loose" and allowing one to *feel* utopia, a proposition of destabilizing one's engagement with the world on one's own terms. In his work Muñoz does not completely negate different notions and rejects the past or present because of its limitations in enacting certain political agendas. Here is where Muñoz's work is a compelling tool for my thinking on longing; he never relegates futurity to a certain fixity but acknowledges, and celebrates, the various temporal, relational, and political tensions that make up these future possibilities of queerness. Past, present, and future are, therefore, key markers of queer utopianism since "the past is a field of possibility in which subjects can act in the present in the service of a new futurity" (16). For Puerto Ricans these future desires are never fixed, constantly changing as the present conditions force new contemplations of future claims to right, as we will see in chapter 1, or future claims of sovereignty, as we will see in chapter 3. Here, when I say "queer utopia," I do not mean it only in terms of its sexual parameters but also in terms of the queering of longing that moves away from hegemonic constructs of what longing should be for colonized peoples. Queering as a verb is a useful tool to think through possibilities for Puerto Rico that build futures not wedded to its colonial present. Thus, queer thinking is a form of archipelagic thinking given the fluidity of the latter in exploring the ever-changing and transforming modes of connectedness in the Caribbean. Archipelagic thinking, as described above, includes and exceeds queer thinking. Ultimately the power of Muñoz's conceptualization of queer utopias is that it straddles various lines of longing; never fully complete nor fully unrooted, longing in this book manifests through various temporal, affective, and existential nodes.

The different longings of the Puerto Rican experience do not exist in isolation, however, and multiple longings manifest simultaneously in the different cultural products. For instance, the longing to belong in Philadelphia and Chicago is linked to the longing for liberation in both political and capitalist terms after protests on the island.[4] Longing, then, by its nature is both affective and utopian, not quite definable in its specific moments but with its presence known even in its contradictory iterations. I dissect how Puerto Ricans often articulate a longing for future projections while not forgetting the way this longing allows them to feel and their desire to move away from past-present struggles. I understand longing as a confluence of emotions, temporalities, and resistances that strives for a better future while being limited by present and historical events. Longing in this book becomes not only a cathartic act but also an act of resistance that attempts to build a new future even within the historical and present realities Puerto Ricans must face. As the chapters will show, longing is at once historical and present, known and unknown, political and affective, concrete and shifting. Boricuas show that through longing's incongruencies, incompatibilities, incoherencies, and indignities, various desires emerge from within and without. Within the heavy emotions, frustrations, and joys that come with being Puerto Rican, and without the political representation, rights, and material needs for survival. As I argue throughout this book, the various visual texts—urban street murals, queer commemorations, *testimonios*, and social documentary films—build parts of the multiplicity of islands of an archipelago that engages various historical traumas and intersectional subjectivities, enriching Puerto Rican studies. This framework provides both a way to visualize longing and a way to read longing that are inclusive of the multiple subjectivities and experiences of a people. Rather than situating idealized pasts or solely utopian futures, I show how these various events are interconnected and will focus on the representational building blocks of longing in literary and visual cultural products to understand the complex nature of longing for Puerto Ricans in the twenty-first century.

Puerto Ricans both on and off the island enact longing's future projections. Neither wholly idealized nor completely pessimistic, the longing I explore in this book straddles a fine line between political immediacy and affective idealism. As I will explore in chapter 4, for instance, Puerto Ricans are aware of the real material and political limitations of their current colonial state, but such limitations should not foreclose progress toward a more equitable future. As we will see as in the two documentaries by Juan C. Dávila, collectively organizing and challenging hegemonic institutions provides a slight future possibility that is grounded in present movements to show the way things can—and should—be in the face of crumbling infrastructure, political malaise, and mass migration. Through this combination of material need and affective desire, I show how Yarimar Bonilla's "hopeful pessimism" is a powerful framework in thinking through a practical way forward. Similarly, as I will show in chapter 1, the restorative nature of street art murals in Chicago and Philadelphia serves as a curative tool for the past in order to build out a more just future. Subjugations endured in the past need not define the narratives of today, and the artists challenge hegemonic narratives both on the island and in their respective cities so as not to be stuck in a repetitive loop of exclusions. In both chapters we see how neoliberal policies and colonialist agendas must be challenged as Puerto Ricans meet the moment. Longing to be a counterweight within these systems, Puerto Ricans are slowly, but effectively, making change that moves them, as a collective both on and off the island, toward a more equitable world.

Moreover, beyond these future projections, longing has an affective core that must be dissected. Throughout the book, emotion provides not only a cathartic tool for Puerto Ricans but also a way to understand the struggles of the present and think through new futures. Sara Ahmed's understanding of feeling in *The Cultural Politics of Emotions* (2014) invigorates my construction of longing. Rather than exploring how emotions define certain bodies, which serves only to think through emotions as part of hegemonic power relations, she asks how emotions stick, examining how they attend to bodies and how bodies react to emotions (4–5). Ahmed asserts that emotions orient bodies and emotions stick to certain objects, demonstrating the "sociality" of emotions (8). Situated neither inside nor outside subjects, emotions rather constitute subjects. It is by orienting and shaping people's emotions that world-making and forms of politics are constructed (12). She tracks the ways that emotions move within a population that then produce effects in a people. What is useful about Ahmed's understanding of emotions is her assertion that the way they connect people leads to transformations of many kinds. The longing within this book is not necessarily a longing for particular version of political freedom that envisions and creates a liberated and sovereign Puerto Rico, but one that strives for an amorphous idea of freedom within colonial structures and calls for a degree of material and existential stability. Through these collections of desires, a Puerto Rican people is constituted both in the diaspora and on the island. Whether sovereignty or freedom happens is just an added result that unfolds from these unmoored notions.

As we will see in chapters 2 and 3, Puerto Rican longing is a much more expansive desire with an end that is somewhat undefined but propels people forward, allowing them to resist and simply wake up every day. For instance, in chapter 3, I show the power of longing to enable effective mourning after Hurricane Maria that forces certain existential questioning for Puerto Ricans both as a people and in their relationship to the United States. By creating a "Rican wake work," I show how a desire to mourn muddles the unidirectional mode of longing through affect. In this chapter, people long to mourn their dead, long for a past that was far from perfect, and long for an uncertain future. Longing's fits and starts come to the fore and challenge our understanding of longing while representing the tensions of the Puerto Rican experience. Much in the same way, the failures of representational inclusivity in the Interim Pulse National Memorial, as will be explored in chapter 2, forces contemplations of mourning and belonging. Through a shrouded presence, I show how intersectional lives—in this case, queer Ricans—are incompatible with the hegemonic structures of commemorations, allowing new modes of memorialization to emerge. In analyzing both the physical site and the digital sites, I reveal the need for more expansive ideas of mourning and representation that do not limit the individual self. In these two chapters, the demands seem basic—electricity, infrastructure, representation—but evince an almost hopeful hopelessness within the colonial and neoliberal structure Puerto Ricans face. Puerto Ricans then endure, to use Sandra Ruiz's understanding, in this longing. Their longing propels them forward even as it acknowledges their stuckness in contemporary failures.

Archipelagoes of Longing points to the multivalent manner in which Puerto Ricans on the island and in the diaspora long together. Anything that occurs on the island is directly linked to Puerto Ricans' experience on the United States mainland, and vice versa. Longing is connected to their colonial reality, and once on the mainland, Puerto Ricans go from racialized colonial subjects to second-class, racialized peoples (Grosfoguel 199). Again, like the islands in an archipelago, disconnected by land but connected by sea, the line between their political subjectivity in Puerto Rico and their political subjectivity in various diasporic communities becomes blurred; they are linked but also different when considering the local contexts. However, the archipelago remains connected historically, culturally, and politically even as people move and certain social structures change. The cultural products studied in this book present a context-specific articulation of collective longing and are linked to one another through the same US imperial power system, allowing the archipelago's fluid connection to take shape. Archipelagoes of longing both disrupt and reproduce the system. For Puerto Ricans, the common system is one of power relations that construct a world in which US colonial dominance is privileged to varying degrees.

And, as I will show, Puerto Ricans are stuck in a continuous cycle of failed promises, incompetent colonial administration, and a capitalist system that creates and maintains inequities.

Longing's Spatial Dispersions

While the temporal variance of past, present, and future defines archipelagoes of longing, spatial discontinuities further open up a more inclusive power of longing that acknowledges the racial, classed, and political struggle of belonging for the diaspora. Archipelagoes' spatial lens allows us to rethink and examine spaces that were once connected but have since been disconnected through global, regional, or colonial power shifts. Or places that have little to no connection historically but are engaged in the same articulation of power (Martínez-San Miguel and Stephens 20). The diaspora helps challenge a singular understanding of collective longing and underscores the colonial aftermath and its persistent vestiges in Puerto Rico. As such, in this book, policies, systems, and social constructs are juxtaposed to better understand the complex dynamics at play when minoritized people express their longing. Puerto Ricans on and off the island experience both the presence of the colonial trauma of the past and the material legacies of the present in a way that cannot, and should not, be fully disentangled. Where one struggle begins and the other ends is so muddled that dissecting them individually fails to do the whole of the suffering justice, thus fracturing Puerto Rican longing. The archipelago provides and expands the understanding of longing for Puerto Ricans, where myriad experiences in various locations are inclusive of the many factors that impact longing's articulation. The Caribbean, and Puerto Ricans specifically, provides a platform for looking at how movement and space come together to create a perpetually shifting notion of identity. In *Poetics of Relation* (1990), Edouard Glissant discusses the need to understand the Caribbean through the lens of movement and space, breaking fixed territorial nation-state formations that are challenged by the diasporic fluidity and in-between nature of Caribbean sovereignty for many islands in the archipelago. What is important to note is how this movement is constantly evolving and has no fixed origin. Glissant argues that movement itself makes up a large part of the Caribbean psyche and that physical location is of little importance; rather, the constant ebbs and flows are what define the Caribbean experience.

Economic precarity and colonial relations continue even when Puerto Ricans move to the US mainland. Financial problems, lack of belonging, and second-class status plague Puerto Ricans once they make the jump to settle in one of the fifty states. Puerto Rican migration has historically been circular in nature, with workers leaving for various United States locations only to return several months later and then go back again. Leading up to the devastation of Hurricane Maria, there was a large net migration out of the island that shuffled traditional settlement locations and reasons for leaving the island (Mora et al. 2019). Yet, while Hurricane Maria produced a massive wave of migration to the United States, a large number of these refugees ended up returning to the island (Schachter and Bruce). This migratory pattern disrupts the delineation of time, space, and solidarity when Puerto Ricans off the island tie themselves directly to events on the island in cultural, economic, and political terms. I will explore in chapter 1 how art murals expand placemaking and challenge historical narratives to recuperate Puerto Ricans' place in Chicago and Philadelphia. *Archipelagoes of Longing* provides a contemplation and inclusion of peoples, stories, and places that are often left at the margins both in the broader United States imagination and in Puerto Rican nation-building efforts. Constantly going between the mainland and the island in search of better opportunities creates a simultaneous longing for home and a desire suspending their sense of belonging. In this sense, the archipelago's sea continues to flow, never allowing Puerto Ricans to settle but constantly challenging them to make do with a system that necessitates their precarity. One economic crisis leads to another, environmental decay makes home precarious, and colonial rule makes life untenable, forcing migration and leaving them in a perpetual state of longing.

Like many other aspects of Puerto Rican culture, this circular migration was impacted by US colonial practices that sought cheap labor for interested capitalists while excluding Puerto Ricans from cultural integration in the United States. As I explained earlier, these neoliberal colonial policies created the conditions in the archipelago that make life unbearable and force thousands of Puerto Ricans to flee the island annually. Diasporicans, or Puerto Ricans in the diaspora, are further marginalized within a neoliberal-economic-racial order in the United States that pretends to extend legal and material equality while actively promoting economic policies that perpetuate their second-class status once on the mainland.[5] Beginning in the 1980s, neoliberalism was no longer solely an economic principle that leaned heavily on markets and the reduction of state intervention but rather an economic-racial order that deployed these forces at the expense of marginalized communities. These economic policies emerged at a time when white resentment of the increasing influence of racial minorities and resource redistribution toward these groups began to shift racist rhetoric into more coded terms that continued the material and racial subjugation of certain groups (Omi and Winant 215). In the 1990s this folded into a colorblind ideology that refused to see racial categorizations and their material impacts but rather used coded terms such as "criminals" and "urban dwellers" to continue the same racialized hierarchies of the pre–civil rights era (216). At the same time, economic initiatives were enacted led by market and private enterprises with a "neutral" ethos that purported to be more efficient than government-run programs (Dawson and Ming Francis 27). By eschewing race-based policies for more colorblind or neutral approaches to resource distribution, the same racial structure persisted in material and legal ways (34). This neoliberal racial order provides a broader context for how Puerto Ricans in the United States engage with governments and suffer continued oppressions on the mainland. As Frances Aparicio has noted, Puerto Ricans are still a racialized other that has become a threat to white middle-class Americans' safety and cultural norms (166). In chapter 1 I will show how mural projects in Chicago and Philadelphia entwine city-backed actors with activists' political desire for material change, and in chapter 2 how the Interim Pulse National Memorial shrouds queer Latinx lives for economic gain; the common thread running through both contexts is how the neoliberal racial order impacts Puerto Rican peoples in insidious and subtle ways. Or, put more directly, as Michael Omi and Howard Winant state, "[n]eoliberalism is premised on racism in many different ways" (228). These "different ways" take on a multitude of forms for the diaspora, such as the displacement of Puerto Ricans in Chicago and Philadelphia, which experience a similar form of instability through very local policies and practices.

Given these structures, Puerto Ricans' representation in the United States has long been one of tension. They form part of the broader United States' "melting pot," yet, excluded from the national US psyche, their place in the United States often remains in doubt. As US citizens, Puerto Ricans straddle an existential line between being legal members of the United States and also sitting on the sidelines of other national constructs regarding race, class, and identity (Silver, *Sunbelt Diaspora*). Their migration to the United States is often defined as a "nation on the move" (Duany, *Puerto Rican Nation*) or "colonial migrants" (Duany, "Transnational Colonial Migration") or using Luis Rafael Sánchez's "flying bus" metaphor, which shows how Puerto Ricans flow between the island and the United States mainland in constant flux. This *vaivén*, according to Jorge Duany, "more ominously" connotes an idea of "unsteadiness, inconstancy, oscillation" (*Puerto Rican Nation* 2). Never fully settling in one location or the other, the *vaivén* has impacts for the archipelago and for Puerto Ricans' sense of belonging and collective longing in the United States. Much of the scholarship has centered on Puerto Ricans migrating to urban centers across the United States, which has been happening in large numbers since the 1940s and 1950s (Laó-Montes and Dávila; Ramos-Zayas; Ricourt and Danta). These early migrations were fueled by economic policies that sought to urbanize the archipelago and provide the United States with cheap labor for its postwar economy. Enclaves in places such as New York and Chicago began to take root, shifting national identification markers and expanding Puerto Rico's definition of nationhood. Since the early 1990s, new destinations such as Orlando, Houston, and Holyoke have become targets of Puerto Rican migration. The chapters in this book will focus on Puerto Ricans in Orlando (chapter 2) and Chicago and Philadelphia (chapter 1) to demonstrate the multivalent nature of archipelagoes of longing, where migration patterns, historical moments, and neoliberal policies directly impact the formation of a collective longing. I open the book with United States–based Puerto Ricans to disrupt the island-to-mainland understanding of the Puerto Rican experience. I specifically explore Puerto Rican sites in Chicago, Philadelphia, and Orlando as they are locations with large numbers of Diasporicans that remain understudied together. Specific historical data will be explored in each chapter, but each individual case illustrates the expanding nature of collective longing, historical inclusion of the island in the diasporic imagination that continues to evolve. The archipelago unsettles time and place, constantly shifting, bringing in new experiences that define Puerto Ricans in the diaspora. United States colonial policies, poor economic conditions on the island, and the promise of better socioeconomic opportunities have contributed to the migration of Puerto Ricans to the mainland United States and in particular to areas beyond the urban hubs of the northeast.

The migration of the past several years, fueled by Hurricanes Maria and Irma in 2017, a series of earthquakes in 2019 and 2020, Hurricane Fiona in 2022, and economic atrophying, constitutes a new chapter in the continuous migration and return that has taken place between the mainland and the island. These more recent phenomena, spurred by an increasingly warming planet, are forcing new contemplations for the island's population. Environmental precarity is now a major factor in the collective longing that sees no easy solution. Like most issues discussed in this book, the recent migration does not have a cohesive narrative. While the initial shock of

Hurricane Maria in 2017 provoked a burst of migration to places such as Orlando and Houston, many Puerto Ricans have since returned. Even so, the steady flow of young professionals off the island continues. These two realities must be faced in order to deepen our understanding of Puerto Rico's relationship to the United States and the formation of national longing. While many Puerto Ricans long to return to their homeland, a reality of no-return sets in that perpetuates an existential malaise. This malaise leads to various longings—a longing for home, a longing for liberation, a longing to belong, and a longing for freedom—that tug at one another and that Puerto Ricans try to articulate.

Thus, while on the archipelago the colonial administration turns to neoliberal policies as solutions that lead to worsening material conditions, in the United States neoliberal racial and economic policies lead to the continued marginalization of Puerto Ricans, who face both tensions at once. As Ramón Grosfoguel, Frances Negrón-Muntaner, and Chloé Georas have noted, Puerto Ricans are racialized and colonized simultaneously, not fitting neatly into nationalist and colonialist discursive dichotomies. I want to be careful not to create a false binary between island-based and United States–based Puerto Rican struggles, because in doing so I would create a fixity of identity that runs counter to this book's broader archipelagic articulation. However, I want to note that the differences that do exist sit together in the broader arc of longing that Puerto Ricans express throughout this book. Ideas of progress are undercut by colonial policies. Fantasies of a new life are undermined by state-backed economic development initiatives that do little to provide material gains for Puerto Ricans across the United States. Combined with environmental degradation, the exclusion of gender identities, the collective will and resistance, and the devastation from natural disasters, these various points, at once connected and disparate, form an archipelago of longing. One crisis impacts another subjectivity, which further exacerbates state ineptitude. The archipelago's historical-social specificity continues to morph into a contemporary neoliberal-racial-economic-colonial structure that knows no bounds.

Chapter Overview

Each chapter of the book explores the tensions that are inherent to archipelagoes of longing. The first chapter, "Puerto Ricans, Radical Nostalgia, and Street Art Murals in Chicago and Philadelphia," tackles the ways Puerto

Ricans in Chicago's Paseo Boricua and Philadelphia's Centro de Oro have reasserted a national history that pushes against hegemonic narratives. In ten murals[6] from the two cities, I show how racial rehabilitation, historical recasting, and political education form a type of radical nostalgia that recuperates past erasures to challenge present-day racial injustices on and off the island. Nostalgia, normally understood as an idealized yearning for the past, is used here not as a tool for essentialist nation formation but rather as an exercise in rehabilitation, challenging racist, exclusive, and idealized hegemonic Puerto Rican narratives. Puerto Rican national narratives, on the island and across the diaspora, often exclude Afro and Indigenous peoples. Historical understandings of political resistance are forgotten. Thus, a sense of place is hard to achieve. In the murals, nostalgia is used radically to recuperate this lost past and enact a political consciousness of the present. Racial formations, material gains, and anticolonial positions are placed in the shadows of the capitalist revitalization efforts that, even as they produce the murals, are the same structures that cause the brutality and exclusions the artists seek to eschew. Ultimately, this chapter reveals the recuperative nature of archipelagoes of longing, as eschewed pasts, rooted in historical specificity, come to life. Longing in this chapter takes the form of being seen, of belonging, of recuperating, and of asserting a presence that has long eluded Puerto Ricans in both cities. These street art murals make it clear that national memories are not a linear narrative but are constituted by irregularities, contradictions, and incongruencies that sit together to form a Diasporican collective longing.

While the murals provide an assertive sense of Puerto Ricanness, the second chapter grapples with the negation of Puerto Ricans in Orlando, Florida. "The Shrouding of Queer Rican Lives in the Interim Pulse National Memorial" examines the memorial and its digital replica and artistic archive as a collective commemoration. Since the 2016 Pulse nightclub massacre, a plethora of artistic and commemorative efforts have been erected in Orlando. While the commemorative sites have brought attention to LGBTQI+ causes and increased visibility in the area, they have also shrouded the presence of queer Latinx lives, which were disproportionately affected by the massacre. With 90% of the victims being Latinx and twenty-three of the forty-nine being Puerto Rican, the shrouded presence of Latinx lives in this commemorative wall has brought attention to the simultaneous visibility and invisibility of Puerto Ricans in the Central Florida region. In the combining of these interwoven yet disparate commemorative products, an archipelago of representation in tension begins to emerge. Through an examination of the physical site, images on the wall, the digital replica's suspension of time and space, and the off-centered recentering of Latinx lives in the artistic archive, I demonstrate how archipelagoes of longing show how tragedies in the diaspora are warped by location-specific politics and form part of the invisible visibility within Puerto Rican representation. Queer Ricans are and are not present; they are flattened and deepened; they progress and stay the same, demonstrating the shifting incongruencies of the archipelago of longing. Rather than examining a commemorative site created by Puerto Ricans for Puerto Ricans, this site creates a photographic negative of sorts that excavates the place of Puerto Ricans, and queer Ricans specifically, within a broader US heteropatriarchal social structure. I emphasize the word *shrouding* because it covers, or envelops, while still acknowledging the presence behind the shroud. Through shrouding, longing takes on a different purpose, becoming almost a cathartic need when representational modes are so absent, as Puerto Ricans, and especially queer Ricans, long for even the slightest acknowledgment of presence. This second chapter bridges various layers of visibility and invisibility with Puerto Rican and Latinx belonging in the United States, recognizing the capitalist forces that seek to warp representational belonging and negate material (and existential) progress within the United States' neoliberal racial-economic order. In the chapter I engage with what is negated and refused but also asserted and represented in ways that are often uncomfortable, incomplete, and irreducible to singular narratives. It reveals an underbelly of longing that remains uncomfortable for many but vital for all.

While the first two chapters engage with the ways archipelagoes of longing can be used to read diasporic longings, the next two explore how they can be used to understand the island-based longings. Chapter 3, "In Hurricane Maria's Wake: Mourning, Catastrophe, and Consciousness in (Post-) Disaster Puerto Rico," examines the way mourning is represented in daily life in *Pa la posteridá: Antología sobre el paso del Huracán María por Puerto Rico* (2018) and *Voces desde Puerto Rico pos-huracán María*, edited by Iris Morales (2019). Since the passage of Hurricane Maria in 2017, Puerto Rican artists and writers have used various artistic forms not only to grapple with the immediate debacle of the hurricane but also to contemplate the myriad structures and decisions that have led to, and continue to cause, devastation on the island. Exhibitions such as *No existe un mundo pos-huracán: Puerto Rican Art in the Wake of Hurricane Maria* at the Whitney Museum of Art, the novel *Velorio* (2022) by Xavier Aquino, and *Aftershocks of Disaster: Puerto Ricans Before and After the Storm* (2019) by Yarimar Bonilla and Marisol

LeBrón have tried to capture the various frustrations, rages, despairs, and regrets that followed the Category 5 storm. In this chapter I examine the collective testimonial works by Puerto Ricans by reading them as a type of "Rican wake work," inspired by Christina Sharpe's "living in the wake," which is understood as a type of mourning, the material vestige of ongoing systems of oppression, and a form of consciousness that is produced in these circumstances. These collections' firsthand accounts, poetry, essays, and short stories detailing the events before, during, and after the hurricane create a collective mnemonic representation through *testimonios*. Straddling the line between creative works and first-person narratives, the *testimonios* utilize mourning to process the colonial, environmental, and political devastation after the passage of the hurricane. Through them, a type of "structure of feeling," à la Raimond Williams, is created that unravels an incomplete yet still emerging longing just after catastrophe. The *testimonios* reveal the collective emotional processing, material devastations, and shared consciousness brought about by Hurricane Maria. Through a close reading of the various texts in these collections, I demonstrate the layers of frustration produced as a result of colonial administration and environmental disaster. The authors convey the collective understanding that ensued, pointing to not just the material loss but also the existential precarity that compels resistance through testimony of the event. In these works, an archipelago of longing is formed through the affective struggle within the writing, which allows for varied emotions, events, and systems to create a collective memorial contemplation of the uncertain Puerto Rican present. Longing in this chapter is at once forward-thinking and haunted by the past. A desire for both a previous time that was imperfect but also a liberatory future that requires material changes. Rather than existing within a singular direction or a fixed desire, longing here is shattered into many directions that require deeper contemplations of completion.

I finish the book with possibilities of present Puerto Rican collective action. Whereas chapter 3 focuses on the overarching despair felt by Puerto Ricans, in "Political Resistance, Collective Action, and Hopeful Pessimism in Puerto Rican Documentary Film" we see the mixing of possible futures that are wedded to ongoing acts of resistance. In this final chapter, I examine two documentaries by Puerto Rican filmmaker Juan C. Dávila and the emergence of what Yarimar Bonilla calls "hopeful pessimism." I excavate *Vieques: Una batalla inconclusa* (2016) and *Simulacros de liberación* (2021) to show how, through political action and collective resistance, Puerto Ricans can achieve an alternative path forward, not one wedded to past idealizations or an impoverished material present but rather one in which the current circumstances can move toward the material gains of a more equitable future. Longing in this chapter presents resistances in order to enact future possibilities. Yet, as Bonilla warns, Puerto Ricans must be cautious not to replicate the mistakes of the past; thus, this longing, while forward-thinking, is arrested by current colonial structures and relationships that must be acknowledged in order to move forward collectively. *Vieques* follows the years after the US Marines were removed from the island of Vieques and focuses on the environmental devastation and colonial injustices that followed. *Simulacros* examines a series of protests between 2016 and 2019 that challenged decisions made by the Financial Oversight and Management Board, the administrative body, established in 2017, that dictates spending for the commonwealth and ensures that its debts to Wall Street firms are repaid. Here, a "simulacrum" of liberation is articulated wherein a rehearsal for a possible independent future is already under way through collective mobilization and mutual aid networks that fill the void of a crumbling administrative state. In both films, mass protests show the will of the people against inept colonial governance as they demand viable living conditions. Longing's present-futureness is exposed and gives hope for real material change. Through archival footage, images, one-on-one interviews, and shots of the island, Dávila weaves an interconnected web of traumas in which government policies, environmental degradation, and geopolitical maneuverers repeat the violence perpetrated by the US government and its colonial counterparts in the archipelago. The documentary style provides an outlet for a people that has historically been marginalized by various forces—the United States military, the Puerto Rican commonwealth government, federal agencies—and challenges the linear understanding of hierarchies of power and the way that trauma is ultimately experienced. But all is not lost, and Dávila shows that people coming together can go a long way in helping the here and now. The films demonstrate how political mobilization and collective action unify the power of the people and show tensions within each context. Dávila in the end challenges Puerto Ricans to think through liberatory possibilities that have long been rejected. Toggling between the structural decay and the ways Puerto Ricans continue to resist, the films build new narratives of Puerto Rican longing of today that point to the possibilities of the future.

Chapter 1

Puerto Ricans, Radical Nostalgia, and Street Art Murals in Chicago and Philadelphia

Public art is the collective expressive aesthetic of a community.

—José E. López

In an interview I conducted with Cristian Roldán Aponte, a Chicago-based Puerto Rican artist and muralist, I asked him the significance of centering Indigenous symbols in his 2017 mural *Taínas* from the Las Puertas del Paseo Boricua/Doors of the Paseo Boricua series.[1] Roldán Aponte explained that Puerto Ricans are not taught about their Indigenous roots and that the little that is taught essentializes their existence. I pressed him further, asking whether there is some type of recuperation of Indigenous peoples in his art, and he said he centers Indigenous women because "es una manera de ponerlo ahí. De lo que no se ve, ponerlo ahí. En el público . . . para que uno sepa de que en una parte está. Aunque sea en su gene" [it is a way of putting it there. That which is not seen, to put it out there. In public . . . so people know that in some way it is there. Even if it's in their genes].[2] Putting it "there," in public, allows for all Puerto Ricans who walk down Division Street in Chicago's Humboldt Park to be reminded of their Indigenous roots. To be reminded of where their people come from. And to be reminded that Chicago is part of the broader Puerto Rican experience. The *Taínas* door captures several of the various themes discussed in this chapter: a sense of home, a recuperation of a past, and an imperfect and incomplete rendition of a people who assert a sense of place while also longing for their island home in the Caribbean.

As one of the most prolific muralists of the Paseo Boricua, Roldán Aponte uses his work to center Indigenous cultural symbols with contemporary political tensions. To Roldán Aponte, murals and public art are key to reeducating a people that has lost knowledge not just of Puerto Rico but also of its Indigenous past. In *Taínas* the artist combines female fertility, Indigenous iconography, and modern Puerto Rico depicted on a door. The women are either fully nude or partially dressed, emphasizing their bodies' reproductive capabilities and paralleling them with the depiction

Figure 1.1. Roldán Aponte's *Taínas*. *Source:* Photo by the author.

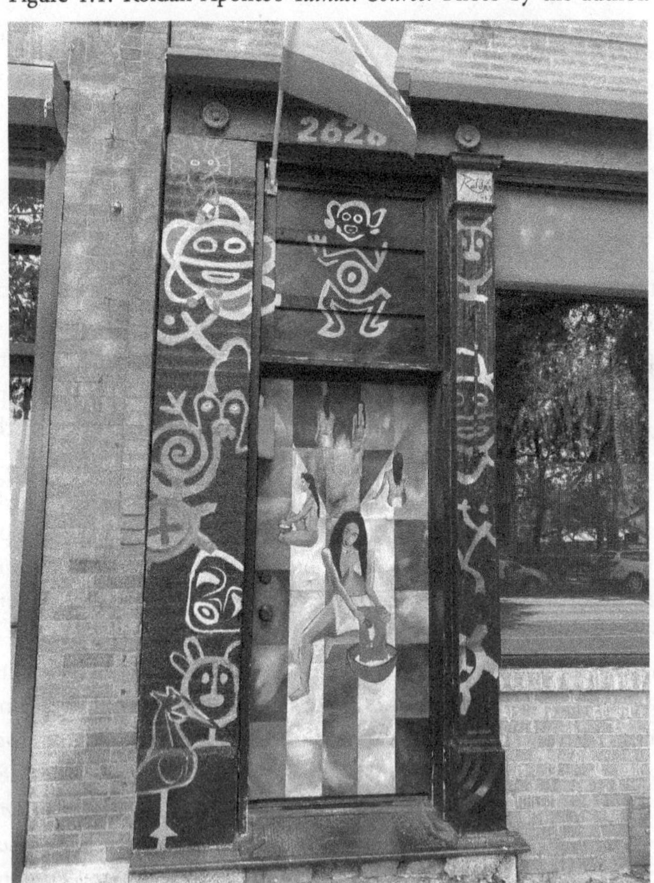

of a *cemí*, or deity, right above them.[3] Roldán Aponte stays away from the regal depictions found in the petroglyphs that point to kings, queens, and high priestesses by eschewing the elaborate headdress found in the original. This petroglyph is associated with the protection of the children of the Taíno elite, as indicated by the modesty of the depiction and the lack of ceremonial headdress (Hayward et al. 133). In representing this female deity on a Chicago door in the twenty-first century, Roldán Aponte links past and present. This *cemí* along with the more commercially identifiable sun deity, coquí, and hurricane serve as stamps of Boricua recognizability. The Puerto Rican flag becomes an almost hazy representation pointing to the unity of the mural but acknowledging the secondary use of a flag to designate community, solidarity, and comradery. Symbols of the nation-state are diminished in favor of an Indigenous past. A recuperation of what is lost. The assertion of who we are even if it is present only in our genes.

I open this chapter with this mural to show the complexities of street art murals and their power within longing.[4] In this chapter I demonstrate how the street art murals of Chicago's Paseo Boricua and Philadelphia's El Centro de Oro recast white, Eurocentric national formations and historical erasures of the past to critique the present marginalization by implementing a radical nostalgia. In these murals various tensions emerge, and Chicago's activist origins and Philadelphia's economic motivations merge into the archipelagoes of longing that at once unsettle and reveal an often-incongruous understanding of the place of Puerto Ricans in the United States. The neoliberal racial order of the United States, in which economic policies serve to reestablish racist social norms through material distribution, causes representational tensions in both Chicago and Philadelphia. Urban redevelopment and anti-gentrification policies that created the Paseo Boricua and El Centro de Oro sit alongside the anticolonial, antiestablishment, and anti-imperial message of the murals even while residents live through unequal access to health care (Han and Rosenfeld; Agrelo et al.) and the constant threat of displacement (Kang; Cintrón Arbasetti). Rather than looking to the past as an idealized era of racial harmony, in this chapter a radical nostalgia seeks to reclaim historical erasures to better understand present material subjugations.

Nostalgia is often understood as a longing for the past, stemming from the Latin words *nostos*, or "return home," and *algia*, or "longing" (Boym xiii). Both time and space are suspended with nostalgia, as the desire for an unretrievable home challenges ideas of space while a temporal malaise of a place that no longer exists, or exists in different forms, disrupts the notion of time that defines the modern (xiv–xv). Nostalgia takes on a central focus in the murals discussed in this chapter because it at once recuperates a (lost) past while also building a (liberatory) present. Similar to the representations of queer Latinx people at the Pulse nightclub commemorative site in the following chapter, here we see how archipelagoes of longing build a collective desire in tension. Rather than contemplating the place of home and its relation to one's present sense of belonging, radical nostalgia breaks away from hegemonic forms of remembrance to excavate the past for answers regarding present political woes, exclusions, and subjugations. Radical nostalgia becomes a way to understand and piece together the material inadequacies of the present to call for effective changes (Robinson). It is radical, in a political sense, in the way it challenges hegemonic actors and moves beyond fixed narratives that serve only to erase marginalized voices.[5] This type of nostalgia is what Svetlana Boym calls a reflective nostalgia, or a nostalgia that demands critical engagement to show how the past "opens up a multitude of potentialities, nonteleological possibilities of historic development" (50). It is in this past-present tension where I situate a radical nostalgia that combines the aspects of the past for recuperative ends, to critique the gaps in the present and build new (just) futures. Puerto Ricans look at a past that has been erased to breathe new life into rejecting the present woes and create more equitable futures. Futures that do not replicate the past and are inclusive of all. Longing here is a corrective for past and present ills. A longing to belong in Chicago and Philadelphia. A longing to correctly represent the myriad ambiguities in Puerto Rico's past, present, and future.

For Puerto Ricans both on the island and in the diaspora, a sense of home is in perpetual limbo. On the island, decades of governmental mismanagement, the junta, and more contemporary environmental catastrophes have created a place that, in many ways, is no longer habitable. Scholars have explored the ways a nostalgic view of the island under contemporary and historical rule complicates the singularity of what it means to be Puerto Rican in the diaspora (Barradas; Flores). The reinvention of the past for a more "positive" future is not new to Puerto Ricans and underscores the various tensions between elites and subaltern groups within the society (Negrón Muntaner, *Boricua Pop* 18). In many of the murals, the trope of an imagined island full of white sand beaches and piña coladas or pristine shots of El Morro Castle search for a sense of home that eludes national belongings, continued economic precarity, and existential displacement once on the mainland. In these formations of home, one sees the perpetual displacement that colonialism continues to inflict on Puerto Ricans, who never feel fully settled on the island but also wonder "what if" on the mainland. Radical nostalgia in this chapter helps to think through archipelagoes of longing, where disparate and often incongruous events construct a collective Puerto Rican longing by forcing the contemplation of an incomplete and imperfect past that is not fully resolved in the present. The murals take on a political agenda of their own that matches the political mission of the various art- ists and organizations that brought about the neighborhoods. It is through this political mission that nostalgia's future projections are exposed within the archipelagoes of longing and expressed in the various murals explored in this chapter. The past, idealized or condemned, helps in understanding the present by demonstrating the genealogy of contemporary social and economic injustices. The multiple pieces and nuances add to the complex nature of longing in Puerto Ricans, and as Sherina Feliciano-Santos notes, "These ambiguities challenge homogenous narratives that rely on colonial logics of erasure, displacement, and replacement to instead consider the multiple historical possibilities of the past as they become materialized in the present and mark the potentiality of the future" (18). These artistic rep- resentations do not necessarily consider a "hopeful pessimism," as discussed in the final chapter, but they do elucidate a *porvenir* (future) that calls into question the past's racial erasures and the present's persistent injustices. In the face of cultural exclusion, economic precarity, and racial prejudice, the murals in this chapter resist hegemonic forces—policies, representation, economics—to help ease the Puerto Rican situational malaise caused by colonialism and migration.

Therefore, through the use of Indigenous and Afro iconography and Puerto Rican revolutionary leaders, I assert the various ways in which these street art murals reconstruct the Puerto Rican imaginary. I analyze how imagery of Taínos and African enslaved peoples, in depicting both iconog- raphy and human figures, challenges white supremacist understandings of the Puerto Rican nation by excavating erased minoritized groups. This is coupled with the glorification of revolutionary heroes, which contests colonial and imperial narratives of the past with heroic figures that challenge power structures, reimagining a world that might have been with individuals who existed. Finally, Puerto Rico and Latin America more broadly are central ideas that emerge throughout the murals through various flora, food, music, and art that are inclusive of the Latinx experience of various cultures in the United States. Depictions of spaces and places important to the Puerto Rican and Latinx communities show a pan-Latinx and Latin American solidarity that echoes the ideas espoused by historical leaders. Through these artistic portrayals of plants, foods, and locations, a sense of place is formed and an assertion of presence is forged. This chapter grapples with many of the uncomfortable truths of national formation on the island and in the diaspora as well as Puerto Ricans' ability to maintain cultural roots, and even complicate said culture, in order to have a more equitable representation. In the end, I show how an archipelago of longing is formed with a radically nostalgic impetus where the liberatory agenda of the artists and the reifying nature of neoliberal policies sit side by side, reflecting the Puerto Rican diasporic experience.

Ricans in Two Cities

Street art murals obtain their meaning through the people who view them and the locations they inhabit. The murals examined in this chapter not only tell the story of resistance, recuperation, and history but also demarcate a sense of place for a people defined by their constant migration in and out of the Puerto Rican archipelago during the twentieth and twenty-first centuries. The introduction to this book noted the migratory patterns that have defined the Puerto Rican experience, impacted by labor needs at US farms and factories that brought migrant workers to the States. This section will focus on Puerto Ricans in Chicago and Philadelphia, specifically the Paseo Boricua and El Centro de Oro in their respective cities. Though political resistance, economic revitalization, and placemaking define the emergence of the Paseo Boricua, it was not immune to the influences of hegemonic actors and capitalistic demands in its creation. Philadelphia's El Centro de Oro emerged out of a need for economic revitalization in a district that had experienced high rates of poverty and economic decline, but that does not mean the murals are devoid of meaning for the area's Puerto Rican and Latinx residents. In both cases, the tensions between neoliberal representational inadequacies and material need impact the radical nostalgia that emerges in each collection of murals.

Puerto Ricans have been arriving in Chicago since the twentieth century, joining an existing community of Mexican Americans in the city. This migration did not come in earnest for factory jobs until Operation Bootstraps, a series of federal and commonwealth economic projects that aimed to industrialize and modernize the Puerto Rican economy (W. Cruz 68). As Gina Pérez reminds us, Puerto Rican migration to Chicago and within the city is conditioned by persistent colonial status and a broader history of exploration, conquest, and empire that defines the Caribbean as a whole (9). In the 1950s and 1960s, hundreds of thousands of unemployed Puerto Ricans arrived and settled in various parts of the city, searching for cheap rents and stable jobs as they could find them (W. Cruz 70–71). Chicago's urban core and surrounding areas were considered prime real estate, forcing Puerto Ricans and Mexicans to reshuffle to various parts of the city as developers and investors moved poor people out and welcomed middle-class white professionals (L. Fernández 92–93). Thus, class-based and racial discrimination practices saw Puerto Ricans displaced as housing projects were dismantled, forcing residents to areas such as West Town, Humboldt Park, and Lakeview (133). By the mid-1960s the Humboldt Park neighborhood, where the Paseo Boricua sits, had become a burgeoning Puerto Rican district where residents could find cheap rents. With this constant moving around, Puerto Ricans' place in Chicago was always ambiguous, and the community never fit in racially or culturally with the whites and African Americans who dominated the city at the time. Active removal turned into more subtle rejections as gentrification made cost of living prohibitive and forced the establishment of a Puerto Rican neighborhood to counter displacement.

By the 1970s and into the 1980s, the Humboldt Park area was known as a Puerto Rican district, though as in times past, gentrification and the removal of Puerto Ricans from this area loomed. In the 1990s, as a new wave of redevelopment swept the city, residents in the neighborhood questioned the timing of certain renewal projects but also welcomed them, remembering the troubles of the past while desiring a more livable district for themselves (Flores-González 11). The desire to assert a sense of place does not occur in a vacuum, and economic revitalization is not anathema to working-class peoples' daily lives. Evidence of Puerto Rican displacement again began taking hold in the 1990s when areas such as West Town, which had previously seen a thriving Puerto Rican population, experienced a huge decline in the Latinx population as artists, studios, and real estate development signs began to appear (12). It was out of this constant fear of being removed from their homes that the desire for an urban redevelopment plan was born in the late 1990s. By this time, Puerto Ricans had more political clout, more professional networks, and more community organization, leading to the formation of the Humboldt Park Empowerment Partnership, which brought together numerous businesses, political leaders, and community organizations to advocate collectively and create the Humboldt Park Empowerment Zone in 1996 (13). The Paseo Boricua and other cultural initiatives form part of this redevelopment plan. The plan was aimed at establishing and enticing business to the area, as had been successful in other ethnic districts across the city (13–14). According to Nilda Flores-González, "Although other business corridors exist within the Puerto Rican community, only *Paseo Boricua* weds economic, political, and cultural into one space" (14). This conglomeration of efforts also fuses various incongruencies where economic, political, and cultural interests do not always align, given that Puerto Ricans still have some of the highest rates of poverty in the city compared to other demographic groups (Cintrón et al.). This disconnect shapes the reality of the Puerto Rican experience and is where the archipelagoes of collective longing emerge, where fears of displacement and the inadequacies of neoliberal redevelopment policies clash.

Similar to Chicago, Puerto Ricans began consolidating their presence in Philadelphia in the interwar years as they came in search of work (Vázquez-Hernández 3–7). The connection between Philadelphia and Puerto Rico can be traced as far back as the late nineteenth century, when pro-independence Puerto Ricans used Philadelphia as a hub to organize with Cubans and other Latin American nationalists for their fight against Spain (2). These ties between the city and the island connected commercial interests such as tobacco, coffee, and sugar, thus forging economic ties prior to the outbreak of the First World War (20–23). These initial economic connections made migration in the interwar and postwar years more frequent, with Puerto Ricans arriving in search of factory and agricultural work at the beginning of the postwar economic boom. Economic changes on the island also led to the increase in migration to the United States, and to Philadelphia in particular, as initiatives to urbanize the island's population forced many to go to Puerto Rico's urban centers and to US cities (Whalen 39–43). This initial wave of migrants was viewed as a source of cheap labor, and Puerto Ricans were willing to do the work since economic conditions on the island were catastrophic compared to the United States. A sort of contract labor system emerged that funneled Puerto Ricans to the States, though not all was an economic Eden; racial and class tensions emerged and, as Carmen Whalen notes, "migrants were wanted for their labor, but not as permanent community members" (49). Philadelphia's postwar economy boomed, combined with its factory infrastructure from the nineteenth century and its farm labor in the city's outlying areas, and Puerto Ricans came to the city because both men and women could find work.

With the rapid increase in the number of Puerto Ricans coming to Philadelphia, racial tensions inevitably began to surface as Puerto Ricans' poor living conditions defined them as having a culture of poverty, with city officials asserting that certain Puerto Rican values and cultural traits perpetuated and caused their precarious economic situation. Similar to Chicago's "urban renewal" efforts of the 1960s and 1970s, Puerto Ricans saw themselves displaced in a city they called home and discriminated against by racist perceptions of their culture. A narrative began to emerge that Puerto Ricans were defective in some way, and government reports and initiatives blamed them for the economic conditions they lived in and that faced the city (Whalen 199). By the late 1960s, Puerto Ricans were seen less as migrant laborers and more as an economic "underclass" (208). Here, as in Chicago, police violence and economic precarity led to the emergence of the Young Lords Party, which organized for better living conditions and education for Puerto Ricans and other minoritized peoples in the city (222). As state actors forgot those in need, organizations such as the Young Lords Party came in to fill the void, and in turn these efforts began to create a place for marginalized peoples.

It is within this context that Philadelphia's "rebranding" efforts to combat the ravages of narratives and the material consequences of poverty demonstrate agency within a failed system. Economic insecurity and the need for material revival set the stage for Philadelphia's rebranding of North Philly's Fairhill neighborhood into El Centro de Oro. This four-block area, currently demarcating a Puerto Rican and Latinx place, stretches from Lehigh Avenue to West Indiana Avenue on Fifth Avenue. The economic zone concentrates mural, street art, and architectural figures that stake a claim in the predominantly Puerto Rican and Latinx district. In the 1990s a rebranding campaign began to change the way the predominantly Latinx area was perceived and to funnel economic resources to a population in need of help. This economic facelift was intended to not just change the perception of the neighborhood but also bring material gains to the area and give people choices as to where they lived (Wherry 17). Like Chicago's Paseo Boricua, El Centro de Oro asserts a claim to the city while also creating a community that brings together images from Puerto Rican, Latin American, and Latinx cultural traditions. Unlike the Paseo Boricua, this area has been seen as a "Latino business corridor" since it was finally opened in 2011 with federal, state, and local funding to revamp the street (Phillips). The story of Philadelphia's Puerto Ricans is uncannily similar to that of Chicago's, with the community having higher rates of poverty than other ethnic groups (Howell). The problems of economic desires fuse capitalism, colonial relations, and racial and class-based discriminations. In both cities, what emerged was the exploitation of a people trying to eke out survival within a system that had set them up to fail.

The history of Puerto Ricans in Chicago and Philadelphia and the emergence of the Paseo Boricua and El Centro de Oro helps to contextualize the tensions present in the various murals discussed throughout the chapter. Political activism and radical nostalgia are marred by neoliberal economic policies that continue to perpetuate the precarity of Puerto Rican placemaking. Longing emerges out of varied interests—a longing to belong, a longing to be seen, a longing for material gains—that have been denied to Puerto Ricans in these cities. Political action to correct historical wrongs, economic initiatives by the same actors that caused the displacements, and cultural narratives that exclude and omit become at once a corrective to and a reification of the past. A barrio thus emerges. Often defined by their relationship to the economic urban decay of the "barrio," Latinxs use the urban space as a place to construct notions of belonging within the broader US psyche (Londoño 9). Yet these urban barrios are not the only places Latinxs inhabit that force new ways of considering the Latinx relationship to the urban space. By moving away from the essentialist nature of urban decay, you create what Londoño calls an "abstraction" that allows for malleability in the understanding of Latinx people's sense of belonging (10). The unclear definition of urban belonging for Latinxs who move away from barrios often hides the broader economic and social troubles that impact the community. By creating and sanctioning street art, many cities across the world, including Chicago and Philadelphia, are using street art to give the postindustrial city a unique *je ne sais quoi* vibe that brings investors, fame, and recognition (Ferrell; Lennon; Wherry). In these initiatives, certain groups are privileged over others, and the Latinx communities in Chicago and Philadelphia are disproportionately negatively affected. The cities of Chicago and Philadelphia are active participants in funding and promoting the art and artists while also promoting neoliberal policies that the artists are trying to combat—that is, policies that promote gentrification, policing practices that hurt the Latinx community, and investment practices that privilege the wealthy. What occurs in these murals is a series of connected images that create an "abstract" sense of place that is in constant tension, perpetually under threat, and forever resistant to the ravages of racial-economic policies that hurt Puerto Ricans.[6]

Thus, in the cases of Chicago and Philadelphia, economic interests and placemaking endeavors need not be mutually exclusive but omit the realities of Puerto Rican longing formations in the United States. One cannot ignore one in favor of the other, and the archipelagoes of longing allow these tensions to coexist. I am not questioning the need for such a space or the importance of art in a community, but what needs to be acknowledged and excavated is how different motivations and desires need not elide each other but sit together in discomfort. El Centro de Oro and the Paseo Boricua create a type of "cartographic memory" that centers the contributions of certain marginalized groups at the expense of hegemonic narratives (Herrera 14). In doing so, "cartographic memories expose the political nature of place-making and the centrality of space in negotiations of power" (15). At their cores, both Chicago and Philadelphia show the multifold power structures that impact the place of Puerto Ricans in the United States, making colonial relations, economic interests, self-representation, and resistance spin together in dizzying ways. The murals in this chapter and the respective cities add additional layers of contemplation to archipelagoes of longing, where a slight shift in power relations impacts Puerto Rican longing.

Solidarities

I opened this chapter by analyzing Cristian Roldán Aponte's door mural *Taínas* to show the various intersections of resistance, representations, and history that can be found in the murals. One of the major images that Roldán Aponte uses is petroglyphs, and walking down the Paseo Boricua and El Centro de Oro, one cannot help noticing these recurring symbols throughout the streetscapes. The designs dot the street from small, innocuous corners to large murals on the pavement. The petroglyphs along with images of Afro–Puerto Ricans recuperate the racialized exclusion of Black and Indigenous peoples within Puerto Rican nation formation efforts. In this section, I examine the ways murals in Chicago and Philadelphia demonstrate the recuperative nature of racial rearticulation that allows for ethnic solidarities to be built. Rather than understanding the Puerto Rican nation in terms of the fabrications of mestizaje that privilege white European lineages and cultural practices, these murals recenter the place of Afro and Indigenous cultural traits in the broader Puerto Rican national psyche. In doing so, they build connections and communities across the Latinx experience in the United States, challenging peoples' perceptions by moving away from colonialist pasts to build new relations that reflect contemporary issues. The murals depict a radical nostalgia in which Indigenous symbols and depictions of Afro–Puerto Ricans recast a historical narrative and critique the exclusionary present.

Indigeneity's place in the broader Puerto Rican national imagination is a contested one. Across the Caribbean, Indigenous cultural traits are often erased, thought to have been wiped out during early colonial expansion. This understanding is what Maximilian Forte calls the "extinction trope," where the dominant narrative across the Caribbean expunges the native even while their relationship to any given nation is much more complex and inconclusive than what is understood in the national imaginary (3–4). Formulations of Indigeneity as an antiestablishment, anticolonial recuperation emerged in the 1990s in Puerto Rico, where left-leaning political leaders looked at Indigenous cultures on the island as a mechanism to resist the present state of colonial decay. Historically the figure of the Indigenous person was seen as docile symbol that had largely been erased from the island (Martínez-San Miguel 200, "Taino Warriors?"). Puerto Ricans in school were taught that the nation had been forged with African, European, and Indigenous ancestry, yet, as in many versions of mestizaje, white hegemonic cultural norms dominated. This is seen most clearly in the creation of the *jíbaro* as a national figure; originally based on a group of Indigenous descendants in the central part of the island, the *jíbaro* was later transformed into a whitened national hero, erasing the figure's Indigenous roots for an elitist whitening of national formation in the mid-twentieth century (Feliciano-Santos 24). More recently Puerto Rican Indigeneity is being excavated within scholarship and political activism to move against colonial discourses that erased the figure. Through these excavations, an effort to establish Indigenous cultural legacy as an original national form that is both anti–North American and anti-Spanish has taken hold (Dávila 17; Jiménez Román, "The Indians Are Coming" 76–77). In these murals Indigeneity is taken a step further and is used to build bonds between new identities that emerge in Chicago, moving away from nation-state formations and toward Indigenous solidarities.

While Roldán Aponte's *Taínas* in the opening of the chapter recovers the Indigenous genesis of Puerto Rico, Sam Kirk uses Indigenous depictions to build solidarities among Latinx communities in Chicago. In Kirk's door from the Las Puertas del Paseo Boricua project, Taíno symbols merge with Mexican Aztec iconography to celebrate the artist's Mexican and Puerto Rican heritage. Rather than solely recuperating a lost past, she forms an intra-Latinx solidarity. The door asserts a connection because of a shared Indigenous legacy and not contemporary racial-ethnic identity markers. Indigeneity becomes the connective marker of our solidarity. In Kirk's door, a Taíno petroglyph female deity sits over a Puerto Rican *vejigante*,[7] a traditional Puerto Rican mask with multiple horns, and a person dressed in traditional Mexican folk costume used during Carnival. The *vejigante* further echoes the combination of Spanish, African, and Caribbean norms to create a unique blend of cultures

(Rodriguez Rabin). The anthropomorphic petroglyph resembles the one found in Caguana, Puerto Rico, and has been identified as a female deity of fertility, as denoted by her headdress, jewelry, and face mask associated with leaders of the Taínos (Hayward et al. 130). Here, Kirk plays with this depiction, adding colors and geometric shapes and seemingly removing the face mask, giving the figure more detailed facial features and using colors to accentuate certain aspects of her body. Her breasts and vulva are present as in the original, gesturing toward the protective and feminine nature of the figure, which was usually placed alongside depictions of the leaders' children as a talisman. Kirk gestures toward the Indigenous connections inherent in

Figure 1.2. Sam Kirk's door from Las Puertas del Paseo Boricua. *Source:* Photo by the author.

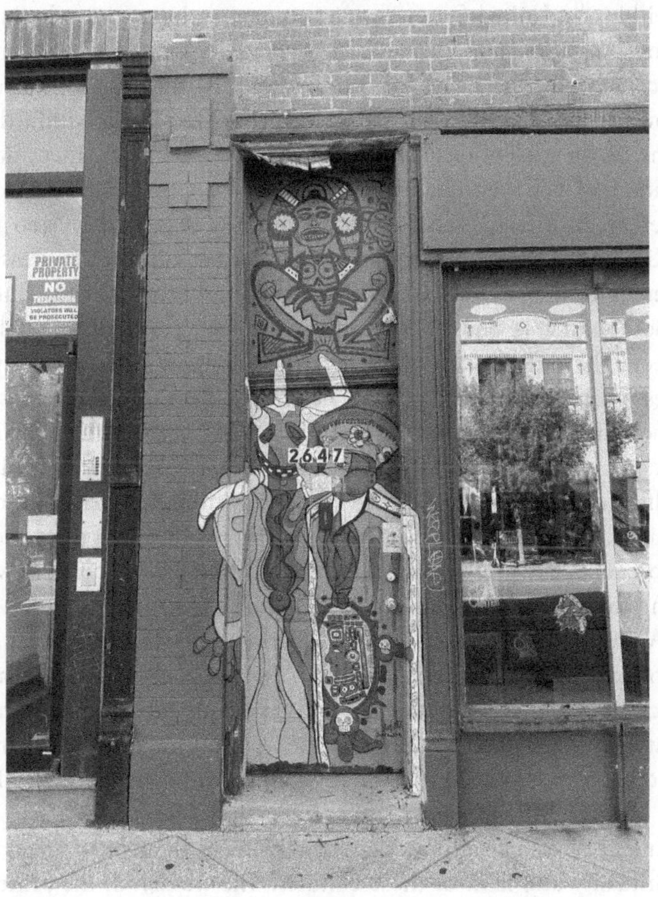

both Mexican and Puerto Rican cultures. This figure will protect all their descendants, elevating the solidarity from political to spiritual, transcending sociohistorical parameters. Behind the female figure are other petroglyphs such as the sun deity, an Aztec god, and the coquí, which serve as a backdrop to the female depiction centered in the frame. The two figures are enmeshed, evenly split over the door. The Puerto Rican flag's red, white, and blue are counterposed with the Mexican flag's red, white, and green. On the Mexican figure, Aztec iconography is combined with skulls, thus balancing Taíno and Aztec imagery. The two figures almost pop out of the door, breaking the strict parameters of the door frame and intruding on the larger building. The two are a symbiosis coming together to underscore the integrated nature of Puerto Rican–Mexican unity in Chicago.

MexiRicans have long challenged the singular understanding of Latinidad within the United States, forcing contemplation of intra-Latinx power relations (Aparicio 160). In Kirk's door we see a type of what Mérida Rúa calls "colando-ing,"[8] where MexiRicans and PortoMex peoples negotiate their own identity, demonstrating agency while also living within the social tensions of their identity (123). To Kirk these doors are, then, at once a declaration of her own duality and also of the city's ability to fold them in together. In a 2017 documentary about Las Puertas del Paseo Boricua, Sam Kirk states, "I've been getting some pushback in certain areas when I do something that reflects a combination of different cultures. But in this neighborhood, it is one of the only places where I've done public work and people haven't asked: why is there mixture? why is there variety?" Kirk declares a sense of belonging with her mixed heritage that grinds against fixed notions of identity. Community belonging and identity mixing push against the neoliberal strategy of dividing minoritized peoples and deepen the self-actualizing nature of these murals within this neighborhood. An expansion of the Puerto Rican identity is affirmed in which diasporic Ricans are also part of the great Puerto Rican family and MexiRicans are welcome. Longing for an inclusive present takes hold.

A similar theme of pan-Latinx solidarity can be found in Betsy Casañas and Ian Pierce's *Sanctuary City, Sanctuary Neighborhood* (2019) in Philadelphia, in which issues of immigration, race, and gender are mixed with Puerto Rican and Latin American iconography to make a powerful statement on unity. The mural centers an ethnically ambiguous woman with a complex afro hairstyle that is covered with flowers, birds, people, and Mexican *calaveras* (skulls), depicting not just the cultures that try to come to the United States but also the spirituality and faith of those cultures. The woman at the center of the mural stares directly out as she parts the US-Mexico border with her arms, allowing migrants to come in. On her left arm, a tattoo reads "Sanctuary" and on her right arm she has a tattoo of the Puerto Rican flag, connecting Puerto Ricans to migrant causes that greatly impact the Latinx community. How a place cares for its people is central to the mural. As Ian Pierce said in 2020 to the Philadelphia newspaper *Al Día*, "[T]he pain of others is our pain"; he then explained, "The mural is about empathy, it's about solidarity, and it's about the incredible pain that people are going through trying to get to the United States" (Neil). A united front is created that pays homage to other solidarities fomented in the community, connecting Puerto Ricans with other marginalized groups, such as African Americans and Mexican Americans, in other parts of the country and Philadelphia. Rather than seeing Puerto Ricans as only part of the United States because of their legal status, the murals assert an allegiance to other Latin American countries and Latinx experiences in the United States.

Moreover, Afro and Indigenous connections become the protective force for these various groups. The woman's face has racially ambiguous features. She is not white. She is not Black. She is not Indigenous. But rather, racially in between. This uncertainty connects to a broad swath of Latin

Figure 1.3. Betsy Casañas and Ian Pierce's *Sanctuary City, Sanctuary Neighborhood*. *Source:* Photo by Steve Weinik. Used with permission.

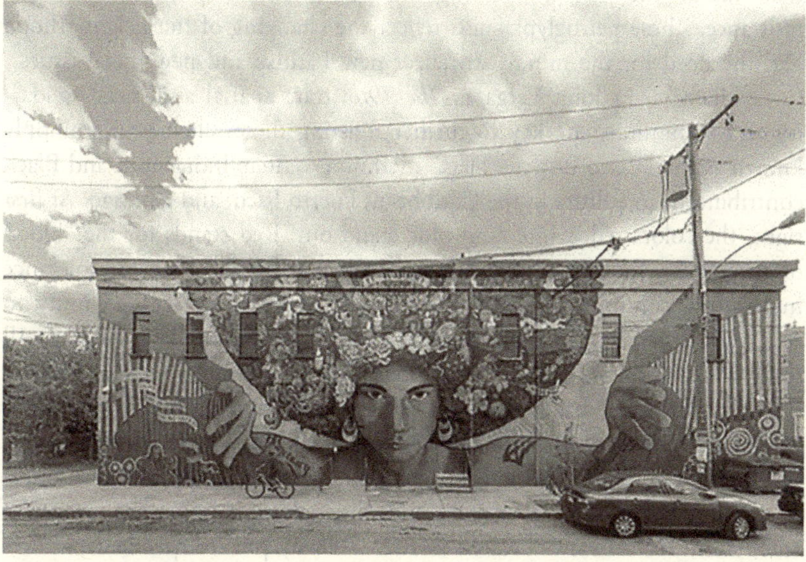

American communities in Philadelphia, creating a sense of place through the mural. The woman's hair is a symbol of unity and resistance. Black hair has long been used to resist white supremacist norms across Latin America (Mercer 115). The large afro overtakes almost two-thirds of the mural and serves as a protective umbrella for all migrants who are trying to enter the United States. Black women's hair is also a site of intimacy and bonding, according to bell hooks, and here the various tentacles of care go beyond the Black community (hooks 232). Various cultural depictions are housed in the woman's hair: Mexican skulls playing music, an Asian dragon breathing fire, lit candles that protect the passage from world to world, and migrants on a boat seeking safe passage to an unknown location. She offers sanctuary for all their journeys, showing how intraracial solidarity is important to combating legal and economic policies for Black and Brown lives. The great Puerto Rican family is transformed once again to include not just Black and Indigenous lives but immigrant statuses and journeys. Her head is slightly tilted forward, with a stern look on her face that asserts a presence for all migrants, all minoritized peoples, and the need to come together in the face of a neoliberal system that seeks their premature death. Border crossing goes from the literal to the more metaphorical, where barriers of all kinds should be combated, even the ones among the Latinx community. Popular Taíno petroglyphs, such as the sun deity and the hurricane, decorate the wall she partitions, both paying homage to the previous Puerto Rican mural that was on the wall and linking Indigenous iconography with forms of resistance. These petroglyphs also reflect the changing of the neighborhood and the need for the murals to reflect new Latinxs and new social issues.

Likewise, in John Vergara's *The 79th*, trans-spatial and racial solidarity and community are key to further resisting these schemes. Commonly known as the "Paseo Boricua Flag," the mural centers Indigenous and Black contributions to culture in the Caribbean, Puerto Rico, and Chicago. At first sight, the colors red, white, and blue stand out. Red stands for the "blood of those who fought and died for collective struggle," blue for tolerance in building community, and white for "the desire for peace and unity to rein [*sic*]," according to the explanation painted on the left of the flag. All three colors form part of the background of the mural, the white being a strip that stretches diagonally from left to right with red on the left lower side and the blue on the top right side. The official Puerto Rican flag is a representation of both political resistance and imperialist oppression, a source of pride and of mourning, a symbol for a people that carries the ravages of colonialism in full view. Created in the 1890s by pro-independence leaders in New York City, the Puerto Rican flag mirrors the Cuban flag to show solidarity with anti-Spanish governmental rule. Originally designed with a sky blue, the flag was later changed to the navy blue of the United States in 1952 to further connect the island to its US colonial rulers. As Marc Zimmerman notes, "The flag has come to embody the diversity of national feelings of the people of Puerto Rico. It is at once a symbol of immense pride—heroic, nostalgic, and otherwise—as well as an unspoken burden" (27). The Puerto Rican flag is not wholly a source of pride or solely a reminder of its colonial reality but rather a mixture of the two. It conjures feelings of belonging and cultural abundance while also being linked to histories of oppression and subjugation. In this tension, the Paseo Boricua flag emerges to retell the story of the Puerto Rican experience in Chicago, acknowledging past pride while pointing toward a location-specific definition of a people. It pays homage even as it breaks away from colonial and imperialist symbols. It is hard to ignore the way *The 79th* makes overtures to the original sky blue, pointing to the emancipatory ideologies the color connotes and the revolutionary desires of the original design. The official

Figure 1.4. John Vergara's *The 79th*. *Source:* Photo by the author.

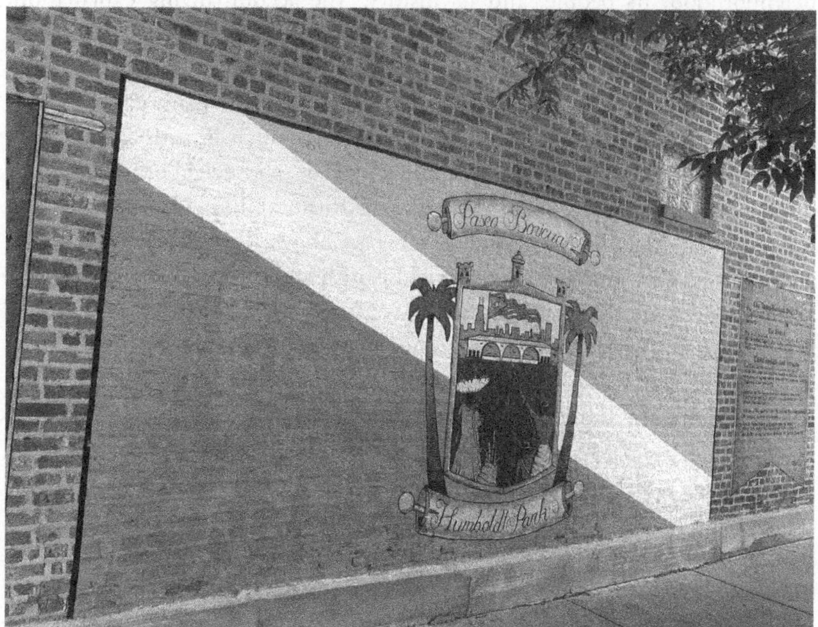

Puerto Rican flag, the *monoestrella*, is stamped all over the Paseo Boricua on storefronts, in stores, on people's cars. It defines the neighborhood as Puerto Rican more than any other symbol used.

In examining the Paseo Boricua flag, Chicago as a place becomes secondary to the Chicago Rican experience. It is their flag that is centered, declaring that their city and their neighborhood—and their version of Puerto Rico—are part of the archipelago too. This flag echoes the official Puerto Rican flag not only through its colors but also by centering the steel flags that demarcate the Paseo Boricua in the middle of the coat of arms. Erected in 1995, these flags have themselves become a symbol of the Chicago Rican people, providing an entrance and exit to the mile-long stretch of the Puerto Rican neighborhood. The reference to the steel flags on the Paseo Boricua flag inserts a particular version of Puerto Ricanness into the flag, simultaneously echoing and recreating meaning. The flag, then, reimagines the Paseo Boricua as a dual place where various histories, peoples, and places are fused together. Not quite Chicago, not quite Puerto Rico, but Chicago Rican—or the 79th municipality of Puerto Rico.

Beyond Chicago-centric depictions, the mural centers Black and Indigenous peoples, echoing other depictions across the neighborhood, but it also fuses Puerto Rican and Chicago iconography to create a static symbol of the neighborhood, its people, and its history. The accompanying explanation, placed on both sides of the flag, allows readers to make connections to other artworks, making the flag a bridge to a broader collective kaleidoscope. The shield is shaped by the colonial architecture of Old San Juan, which frames the Puerto Rican flag atop the Chicago skyline, which in turn sits atop the Humboldt Park boathouse. Architecture, cityscape, and neighborhood become one, making it clear that Chicago is Puerto Rican and Puerto Ricans belong in Chicago. These three physical features are above the image of an African and an Indigenous figure. The colonial Spanish architecture, according to the artist, "represents the Spanish Fort in Viejo San Juan, 'El morro,' and the Spanish legacy." Spanish figures are not used, but the architectural features acknowledge the cultural contributions of former colonial rulers even if the mural centers and embodies Indigenous and Black peoples.

While the Puerto Rican nation can be described as one of mestizaje where racial and cultural mixing come together to provide a harmonious understanding of a people, these national (and colonial) narratives actively whitewash and erase Afro and Indigenous contributions to the nation. The notion of racial democracy dominates in Puerto Rico, where an acknowledgment of Afro and Taíno contributions is present but is overshadowed by a privileging of white European physical traits and cultural traditions (Flores; Jiménez Román, "Looking at that Middle Ground"). Yet, unlike in many Latin American countries, Puerto Rico's nation-defining project has a colonial element that couples classed notions of behaviors with racial understandings to better fit with US dominations in the first half of the twentieth century. Race on the island is implicated with race in the United States. As Jossianna Arroyo notes, "If blacknesss is erased, silenced, and disavowed from public discourse in Puerto Rico, Puerto Ricans in the US mainland have developed complex ways of understanding their relationship to forms of racialization and blackness" (" 'Roots' " 197). Puerto Rican creole elites in the first part of the twentieth century sought to define the Puerto Rican people as a whitened population to not only gain the favor of US officials but also rebut the idea of a backward nation that prevailed in the colonial transition of the time. To Hilda Lloréns, this "obsession" with whiteness ignored the island's more than seventy thousand Black residents whose presence was recorded during the first US census, taken in 1899 (12). White physicality is eschewed for the centering of Black and Indigenous cultural traits in the Chicago Rico of today, enhancing the complications of diasporic race.

Further complicating the matter is the way that Afro and Indigenous markers are included within this mestizaje's whitening project, where the category of *indio* emerges as an anti-Black register of a "intermediate point" between white and Black (Feliciano-Santos 79). The figure of the native becomes a third avenue to reclaim a cultural tradition without reconstituting colonial tropes (Berman Santana, "Indigenous Identity" 213). These reformations are not without their critiques. Indigenous organizations see these excavation efforts as little more than cultural appropriation, and others argue that they are used to exclude the contributions of Afro–Puerto Ricans on the archipelago (Berman Santana, "Indigenous Identity"; Martínez-San Miguel; Feliciano-Santos). I bring these various threads into the fold to show that national cultural formation in Puerto Rico is not settled but rather very much in continual process. The various symbols, peoples, and cultural traditions sit together in tension, like the islands in an archipelago. These islands remind, educate, and reimagine what the Puerto Rican nation is, could be, and will be. The Indigenous figure, then, becomes an unsettled one that takes on a meaning beyond its intended purpose, challenging the viewer to rethink national formations broadly. Indigeneity becomes a recuperative anticolonial imagination that attempts to move away from replicating imperial and colonial discourses around Puerto Rican nationhood. The figure of the native emerges not just to evoke an idealized past that deserves to be salvaged but also as a stand-in for anticolonial movements that the island confronts.

Therefore, the figure of the Black woman and Indigenous man move beyond white-centric views of the Puerto Rican nation. On the Paseo Boricua flag, the Black woman holding an infant on the left carries a basket of goods on her head and a bag of sugarcane at her side. The Indigenous man accompanied by his child points a spear toward Puerto Rican Chicago. Both the Black woman and the Indigenous man and child evoke Caribbean migration to Chicago. Two palm trees flank the shield, and brown-paper scrolls with the words "Paseo Boricua" on top and "Humboldt Park" on the bottom complete the shield. As the text next to the flag indicates, the palm trees "represent the contribution people of the Caribbean have made and continue to make to the rich diversity in our community." The Caribbean, West African, and Indigenous communities are all present on the flag, underscoring the various versions of Puerto Rican culture, its legacy, and its current iteration in contemporary Chicago. US-based racial paradigms clashed with a Puerto Rican racial formation predicated on a mestizaje, in which multiple racial constructs mixed together. This clashing of racial ideologies is seen in the ways census records in the 1910s and 1920s show an increase in identification as white by Puerto Ricans not because of actual changes in racial demographics but because of the reclassification of peoples based both on census demarcations and on individual census workers' categorizations (Loveman and Muñiz).[9] This whitening is less an indication of the racial makeup of Puerto Rico and Puerto Ricans than of the complex narratives and interests that are used in racial formations, particularly for transnational peoples. *The 79th* attempts to disavow these rhetorics, centering and celebrating Black and Indigenous peoples while diminishing white figures. The mural, to a degree, is a corrective to the erased histories that have long plagued the symbolisms of flags, a reminder of a longing to be seen in the way one sees oneself. The mural gives not one meaning but a kaleidoscopic meaning regarding race, representation, and space. It is not one Chicago or one Puerto Rico but a cacophonic Puerto Rican Chicago that acknowledges, recuperates, and rejects all at once. The flag acknowledges the various racial formations and histories inherent in Humboldt Park. It recuperates the buried African legacy and erased Indigenous past that often define Puerto Rican national narratives. And it rejects a Eurocentric view of Puerto Ricans in the United States and Puerto Rico. Symbols take on various meanings, are transformed into new versions, and assert a sense of place on Chicago Rican terms.

Whereas in Vergara's flag Chicago and Puerto Rico become extensions of each other, Danny Torres's *El Centro de Oro* (2007) pays homage to the city of Philadelphia and the broader Latinx community. Solidarities are formed through the city. In this mural the words "Bienvenidos a 'El Centro de Oro'" welcome passersby and demarcate the neighborhood with a title. Similar to the steel Puerto Rican flags in Chicago, this mural begins to assert a Puerto Rican and Latinx presence in the Fairhill neighborhood of northern Philly. Just below these words, shops featuring the neighborhood's nineteenth-century architecture along with the more contemporary skyline delineate the surrounding city. Philadelphia and Latinx identity begin to be forged. Foregrounded over the cityscape are depictions of pineapples, *quenepas*, plantains, and presumably coffee, not only gesturing to the many shops and cafes that serve Puerto Rican and Latin food but also marking

Figure 1.5. Danny Torres's *El Centro de Oro*. *Source:* Photo by the author.

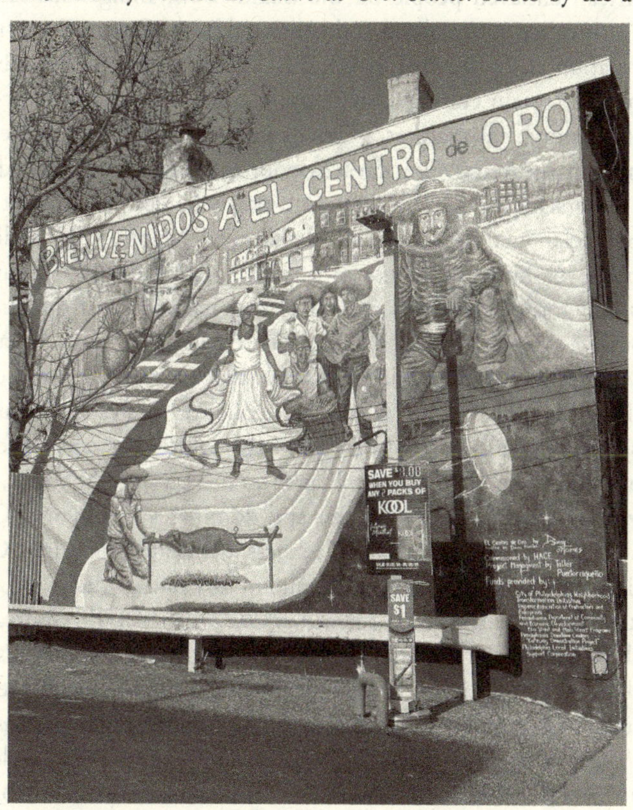

the objects and foods that define a people. Below these foods, the flags of Puerto Rico, Mexico, Colombia, Cuba, Venezuela, Peru, and Argentina form a sidewalk of sorts that morphs into the golden cape of an artist. These nation-state markers on top of the golden cape/sidewalk fusion link city, nation, and Latinx identity together.

On top of this golden street are singers and dancers of *bomba* and *plena* along with a *jíbaro* roasting a suckling pig over an open fire. In a 2022 film about his work, Danny Torres notes, "My murals always have Puerto Rican themes. The *gallos*, the *palmas*, the *lechón asado*, the *bomba*, the *bomba* dancers, the *cuatro*. . . . It's about my culture. It is important keeping the Puerto Rican culture alive" (*I Am Danny Torres*). He continues, detailing how all the murals in the neighborhood have to be related to Puerto Rican culture in some way. Through musical imagery a Puerto Rican identity is established in the mural, not just through the Puerto Rican flag but through cultural forms that are viewed as having been contributed by former African enslaved people on the island. Both Indigenous and Black characterizations are essentialized and contested in the Puerto Rican national racial formation. On the one hand, Blackness in Puerto Rico becomes present only in certain cultural contributions such as music or dance, while the actual phenotypical markers are eschewed in favor of the white "Spanish" population (Pedreira). Blackness is both folklorized and viewed with a nostalgic understanding of a racially pure past whereby the present is then defined by racial mixing (Godreau, "Folkloric 'Others'"). In addition to this temporal marking, Blackness as a spatial definition also occurs, with Blackness being associated with certain coastal regions or urban *caseríos*, or urban housing projects, that demarcate where Blackness exists vis-à-vis the whiteness of the rest of the island even while Blackness is not isolated to any specific place (Rivera-Rideau).[10] Moreover, economic interest and sanitization for tourist dollars is also part and parcel of this whitening venture for many Caribbean nations. By demarcating Blackness in very specific terms, a racial hierarchization occurs where whiteness still dominates ("Folkloric 'Others'" 297). These varied definitions of Blackness delineate what Isar Godreau calls "scripts of blackness," where dominant discourses designate what is Black and what is Puerto Rican (*Scripts of Blackness* 14). To Godreau these scripts allow race to be discussed in public domains "without disrupting the social pacts of cordiality or conviviality that sustain racial hierarchies and the taken-for-granted value placed on whitening or *blanequeamiento*" (19–20). This cherry-picked view of Blackness underscores the complex racial paradigm that Puerto Rico finds itself in. While on the one hand Blackness is celebrated almost in a whisper, the discourse's racist underpinnings reveal colonialist, white supremacist, and economic motivations regarding race.

The mural falls within these racial tensions. The figures are visibly darker in complexion, rejecting the white-centric view of Puerto Rican national formation in a subtle way without directly stating a political intention. Cultural diversity is centered through markers that are more subtle, linking musical traditions with racial multiplicity within this city that has created a Diasporican community. In the United States, Puerto Rican racial formations cannot be placed into the strict black-white binary that dominates US racial views but rather create their own ambiguous racial categories that eschew US-based racial formations (Duany 175). Puerto Ricans in the diaspora neither continue the Puerto Rican–based racial categorizations nor fall within US-based constructs, but prefer their own categorizations that reflect their cultural and racial identity (180). In Torres's mural, this fusion is made clear; the figures are not wholly Puerto Rican or North American but rather their own Philadelphia-based construct that reflects their racial history with the city itself and with other Latinx communities. As with Sam Kirk and John Vergara, here too we see a solidarity that moves beyond specific national affiliations to create a broader connection and identity. A burgeoning pan-Latinx identity is created.

Historical Resistances

In centering Black and Indigenous peoples of Puerto Rico in their murals, these artists recuperate a lost past that has been embedded with a white supremacist rhetoric of exclusion. Much the same way, racial recuperations occur; depictions of political resistance are a central theme in the Chicago's murals. *Oppression and Resistance* (2016) by Cristian Roldán; *La crucifixión de Don Pedro* (1971) by Mario Galán, José Bermudez, and Héctor Rosario; and *La Borinqueña* (2019) by Edgardo Miranda-Rodríguez demonstrate the legacy of resistance and migration that informs key features of Puerto Rican history. These murals look to recenter forgotten stories of heroes and the political consciousness they created, honoring the leaders of the past and educating the public on the accomplishments while simultaneously critiquing the present. The didactic nature of murals becomes salient in these works, which serve as important markers of resistance for the neighborhood. A radical nostalgia here looks to the past for the moments that have been erased and to help change the present. These works show a longing for a historical corrective of political causes from the past into today. US street murals have long centered a history of multiracial solidarity, political consciousness formation, and artistic expression as inherently linked. Influences from Mexican muralist painters had a major impact on the mural paintings of both the United States and Latin America, championing the plight of working-class peoples (Huebner 12). While the specific political moments, peoples, and histories might be different, these Mexican muralist painters demonstrate the power of art in refashioning political narratives for marginalized groups. They not only centered international issues but sought solidarities with various subjugated groups through the subject matter of their murals (Goldman 110–12). Similarly, the street art murals in Chicago and Philadelphia show the intricate link between international and national political causes and their local iterations. By centering patriots such as Lolita Lebrón and Don Pedro Albizu Campos, among others, the murals reestablish Puerto Rican resistance as a key marker of what Sandra Ruiz calls "Ricanness," which she sees as being "animated by acts of political and aesthetic endurance, those

Figure 1.6. Mario Galán, José Bermudez, and Héctor Rosario's *La crucifixión de Don Pedro. Source:* Photo by the author.

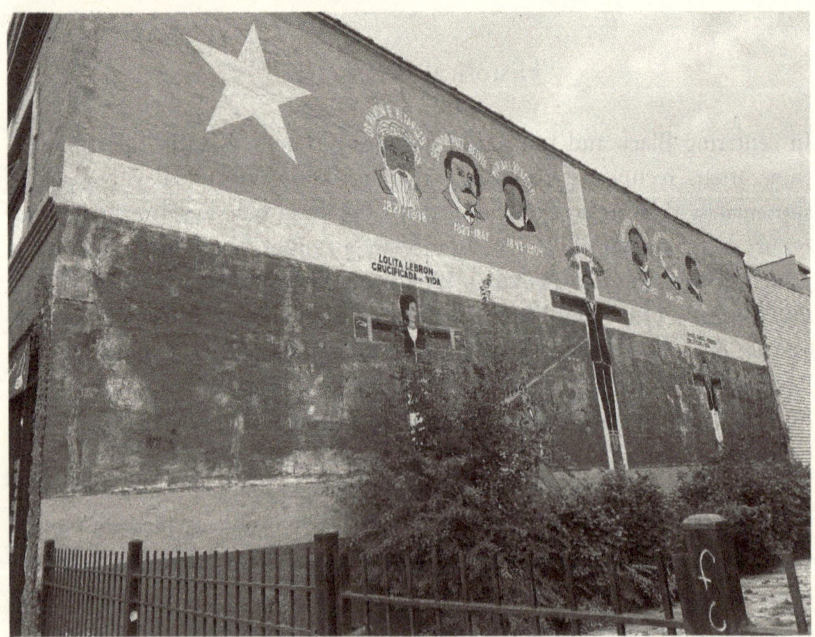

moments of staying power in the face of cultural, personal, and national subjection" (10). While these specific people have gone or are in their final days, the murals remind the community of the principles that leaders of the past fought for, and which should be fought for today. They show the endurance of a struggle that is not over.

La crucifixión de Don Pedro (1971) centers the revolutionary causes of different pasts. Originally created in 1971 and restored in 2010, the mural commemorates Puerto Rican pro-independence leaders of the twentieth century while also critiquing those seen as traitors to the independence cause. Sprawling across the entire side of a nineteenth-century building and facing a vacant lot turned public park, the Lares revolutionary flag sits in the background, dominating the visual aspect of the mural. At the center appears a crucified Don Pedro Albizu Campos, the twentieth-century Afro–Puerto Rican who advocated for independence from the United States. His name, birth year, and death year give the life cycle of a man who is the symbol of not only revolution but also the Puerto Rican spirit. He is flanked to his left by Lolita Lebrón and Rafael Cancel Miranda, who were "crucified in life," a reference to their decades-long imprisonment for terrorist acts against the United States House of Representatives in 1954. Both Lebrón's and Cancel Miranda's faces are directed toward Albizu Campos, signaling the importance of his words to the two revolutionaries. Between Lebrón and Albizu Campos is the figure of Luis Muñoz Marín, the first democratically elected governor of Puerto Rico, as he impales Albizu Campos with a spear. His is the only figure that is almost smiling as he mutilates Albizu Campos, a critique of colonial relations and of the political structures that Muñoz Marín created. Above these four individuals are the names of poets and revolutionaries of the nineteenth century; appearing from left to right: Dr. Ramón E. Betances, Segundo Ruiz Belvis, Mariana Bracetti, Eugenio María de Hostos, Rosendo Matienzo Cintrón, and José de Diego. As art professor John Weber has noted, the aesthetic style is Byzantine-like, with simple facial features (Mitchell). The depictions also show how the historical figures' politics was informed by their Catholic faith; Lebrón and Albizu Campos saw the nation as being inherently linked to Catholicism (Muñoz; Jiménez de Wagenheim). Form and aesthetics are not the main goal; instead, meaning, education, intellectual trajectory, and historical recuperation become the central impetus of the mural. The mere fact of having these figures present, in the simplistic style, is important. It is the impact that declares this space Puerto Rican. Together these figures form part of a broader educational goal and intellectual underpinning of the murals.

These individuals were not just activists in the Puerto Rican independence movement but covered a variety of areas needed for a successful campaign. The didactic nature of murals is at the core of their depictions. The mural does not just delineate a space for Puerto Ricans but also offers an intellectual assertion of resistance. These leaders, poets, attorneys, educators, and designer of the revolutionary flag are a reminder of the activist spirit of the neighborhood and Puerto Rico. This is echoed through the restoration efforts that took nearly a decade to complete and were spurred by the same gentrification threats that inspired the mural's original creation. In the early 2000s a real estate developer planned to build condos on the lot that the mural faces, blocking the view of the mural and erasing the representation of Puerto Rican history in the area. Local leaders came together to negotiate with the developer, only to be rebuffed; this sparked protests and a sit-in to prevent the construction from moving forward. The city eventually took control of the lot, and the restoration was completed in 2010 with the help of the Puerto Rican Cultural Center, which provided both logistic and economic support in coordination with the city (Mitchell; Molina).[11] Not only did the mural become a site of present-day restorative efforts, but a certain antiestablishment poetic justice has also resulted. The leaders on this wall, I believe, would be proud. Local Puerto Ricans are coming together to reassert their heritage, their history, their legacy. The mural's meaning-making turns into action.

Murals such as *La crucificixión de Don Pedro* exemplify the multifarious political nature of mural paintings, with the organized placemaking inspiration of street art underscoring the archipelagic nature of the radical nostalgia they create. Like the murals from the Mexican muralist era of the early twentieth century, the artworks in Chicago and Philadelphia are marred by incongruous political agendas that that combine clashing representations of Puerto Ricans. Viewing the murals through the prism of archipelagoes of longing allows for an interrelated malleability to be read in the artworks' meanings. As political issues change, so do the murals' meanings, allowing for the political events of today to be linked to the political agendas of the past. Some artworks, such as those by Cristian Roldán and Sam Kirk in Chicago, are city-backed, Puerto Rican Cultural Center–sponsored murals that become a type of state-sanctioned art, demarcating a space for Puerto Ricans in the broader cityscape. And here is where the tensions arise: What happens to anti-hegemonic meaning-making when the cultural actors are backed by the various organizations they are trying to topple? The works are situated at once as a hegemonic force for social change and as bottom-up acts of resistance by those deemed to be from the outside. Together they build the broad narrative of the neighborhoods.

Whereas *Crucifixión* centers the contributions of Don Pedro Albizu Campos in Philadelphia, the mural *La Borinqueña* takes a similar approach by centering the contributions of women in the Puerto Rican imaginary. Female leaders and nature along with the fictional superhero of La Borinqueña come together to commemorate leaders from the past and gesture toward a more just future. La Borinqueña is a comic book superhero created by Edgardo Miranda-Rodriguez that celebrates both Puerto Rican Indigenous and African cultural formations and diasporic racialized identities in a Brooklyn-based Nuyorican named Marisol Rios de la Cruz. Her interest in environmental studies takes her to Puerto Rico, where she is given superpowers by the Taíno deity Atabex. As La Borinqueña, she helps with environmental devastations and other colonial aftermaths the archipelago faces. The mural echoes the character's backstory by depicting various Indigenous flora and fauna from Puerto Rico such as the *coqui*, anole (a Puerto Rican crested lizard), *ceiba* (Puerto Rico's national tree), and *flor de maga* (Puerto Rico's national flower), among others. La Borinqueña watches over these creatures, and one cannot help noticing the bright greens, blues, reds, and pinks that stand in stark contrast to the urban setting where the mural sits.

The mural of La Borinqueña connects a diasporic heroine with Puerto Rican women leaders, creating what Ivonne García calls a "diasporic intersectionality" that focuses on the Puerto Rican migrant experience and challenges heteropatriarchal, classed cultures by centering gendered, classed, and racialized subjectivities in the figure of La Borinqueña (72). In doing so, according to García, this character "writes back" to Puerto Rico's colonial history. However, most passersby would not know this story inherently, only seeing a nonwhite Puerto Rican woman wearing a Puerto Rican jumpsuit and cape and proudly carrying the Puerto Rican flag. A warping occurs in which a commercially successful graphic novel character is placed on the same plane as greats such as Julia de Burgos, Marianna Bracetti, and Lola Rodríguez de Tió. The meaning behind La Borinqueña is lost in the visual, and one cannot help contemplating the economic interests and marketing rationale behind the mural. Neoliberal racial-political structures at their best.

The bright colors of *La Borinqueña* obscure the six women arrayed on the right side of the mural. Depicted in an almost sepia color palette, the six women from right to left are Pura Belpré, Julia de Burgos, Celestina and Gregoria Cordero y Molina, Mariana Bracetti, and Lola Rodríguez de Tió. The sign just below the mural explains who these six women were and

Figure 1.7. Edgardo Miranda-Rodriguez's La Borinqueña. *Source:* Photo by the author.

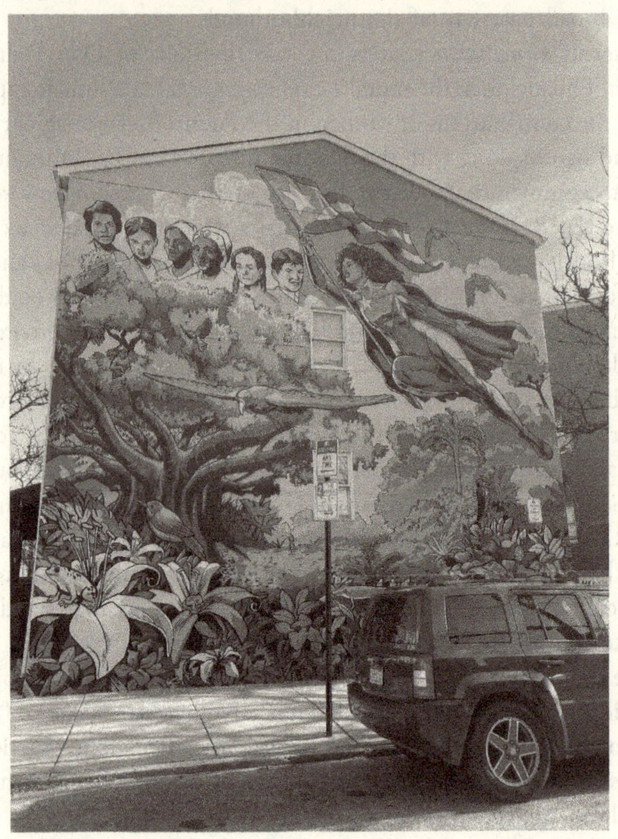

their importance to Puerto Rican history both politically and culturally. The women are almost an echo of *Crucifixión*'s six great figures; here, we see the centering of women and their contribution to the nation. As in *Crucifixión*, the women look down at the flora and fauna of Puerto Rico as if from the skies, commanding passersby to protect this land just as they did the nation. Education, nationalism, and poetry were a prevailing theme in these women's lives, emphasizing the interconnected nature and importance of educating oneself for the nation. The didactic nature of a mural is once again highlighted. But unlike in *Crucifixión*, where the leaders of yester-year look down on a revolutionary figure, in *La Borinqueña* the fictional character takes up much of the attention, placing her on the same plane as these pioneering women. Political agendas are softened; an expansion into new topics such as environmentalism is viewed as the new iteration of the cause these women fought for. The mural makes subtle gestures to the link between environmental causes and colonialism, an issue I discuss further in chapter 4 in relation to Vieques. In connecting political leaders with the country's flora and fauna, we begin to see a more all-encompassing radical nostalgia that thinks through the various tentacles of colonialism's debacles and builds a world that is inclusive of all life.

While *La Borinqueña* highlights representational strains by mixing an economically successful graphic novel character with revolutionary women, in *Oppression and Resistance* (2016) by Cristian Roldán Aponte we see the relaying of Puerto Rican history from colonization to the 1966 Division Street riots. Chicago becomes another part of the long arc of Puerto Rican historical resistance. Beginning with the arrival of Spanish colonizers, national formation, political resistance, migration, and then the 1966 riots, the mural's didactic purpose reinscribes Puerto Rico's troubled history: the suffering, the racism, but also the joy, creativity, love, and resistance. Affective incongruencies emerge. In each block a theme is centered that mixes and blends various tensions and resistances. They celebrate Black and Brown contributions. In the colonial block, Indigenous and Black peoples are foregrounded and caricatures of colonizers remain in the background. The Indigenous and Black figures have the most details, showing facial expressions and body composition. The bodies echo the cubist paintings of the twentieth century, where abstract shapes come together to form a figure. Here the figures are more defined, but the block colors allow for various shades of black and brown coloring to be emphasized, demonstrating the racial mosaic. The white colonizer looks like a cartoon where even as generic facial features acknowledge the presence of a face, the exaggerated nose diminishes their contribution and pulls attention to the detailed figures of Indigenous and Black roots. But the Spaniards' buffoonery does not absolve them of responsibility for the violence inflicted. A depiction of a Spanish colonizer stabbing an abstract Indigenous person reminds passersby of colonial violence, the devaluing of life, and the forging of a nation.

As pedestrians move to the right, new figures emerge. The descendants of the earlier colonization efforts morph into new people who make up a new era in Puerto Rican history. Land becomes key to this block, where the rising sun is a petroglyph with the Puerto Rican flag asserting that Puerto Rico is an Indigenous nation. By using the nation-state symbol of the flag and fusing it to the petroglyph sun deity, Indigeneity and nation become one. The sun deity rises over the iconic mountain peaks Las Piedras del

Collado, more familiarly known to Puerto Ricans as Las Tetas de Cayey for their close resemblance to female breasts. The figures of a *jíbaro* on horseback, a woman in traditional dress dancing, a Black man playing drums, another farmer in the fields, and two Black lovers are depicted here. Art and culture, at least the emergence of them in the Puerto Rican nation, are at the core. Racial nuances and connections to the land become one. Dance and music are depicted. One woman's arms are a deep blue but her face merges into the land, showing that she is part of the land, that her dance is Puerto Rican—no longer demarcating any specific racial category but rather a more land-based affiliation. The woman is accompanied by a man playing drums, evoking the African legacy in music but also emphasizing a figure behind the music, not just a generic trope. The *jíbaro* appears again, now not on horseback but as a farmer, further emphasizing the importance of land and nature as cultural markers in Puerto Rican identity.

National cultural formations give way to political consciousness on the island. The flag of Lares, known as the revolutionary flag of Puerto Rico, is flown by another *jíbaro*-like figure sporting the traditional hat that campesinos wear. A traditional Puerto Rican single-room wooden house is filled with *macheteros*, members of the Puerto Rican nationalist organization that used the machete as the symbol for their cause. Known officially as the Partido Revolucionario de los Trabajadores Puertorriqueños-Ejercito Popular Boricua (PRTP-EPB), it advocated for the rights of workers and "asserted the right to armed struggle for national liberation" (González-Cruz 152). The machete pays homage to the physically intense labor of working in the fields, echoing the hammer and sickle of the Soviets. Land, workers, and national liberation reflect the history of the struggle, equating the past *Grito de Lares* with later twentieth-century struggles for freedom. Similar to Lebrón and Cancel Miranda in *La Crucifixión*, who were jailed for terrorist activities, the *macheteros* are celebrated for their cause. Oscar López, in particular, is paid tribute in this scene, as the young man in the middle with glasses. López, who is depicted throughout the Paseo Boricua, is shown here in a more youthful version; the mural acknowledges his influence within the organization and the continued struggle for liberation. One man's terrorist is another man's hero.

Revolutionary movements give way to migration to Chicago, evoked via a skyscraper of luggage in the form of steps similar to the Willis Tower, a prominent feature of Chicago's skyline. Two polychromatic figures go up the stairs, alluding to the new life they are about to lead in Chicago, demonstrating the hardship of getting to the city and leaving behind their native land. Mountains with petroglyphs on them almost look as if they are weeping as these Puerto Ricans leave. Indigeneity becomes an affective cry of the island to its people. The tower of suitcases and the Willis Tower form a barrier to the depiction of the Division Street riots. A woman hangs off the side of the Willis Tower, looking at the riots, while another female figure, pregnant, on top of the building, looks back at the mountains, as if longing to stay but recognizing the need to leave. The child within her is the future of Puerto Rico, and like many Puerto Ricans, the woman contemplates whether to leave. Whether her choice is the correct one. The buildings, the journey, and the distance show the precarious reality that Puerto Ricans find themselves in in Chicago.

Figure 1.8. Section of Roldán Aponte's *Oppression and Resistance*. *Source:* Photo by the author.

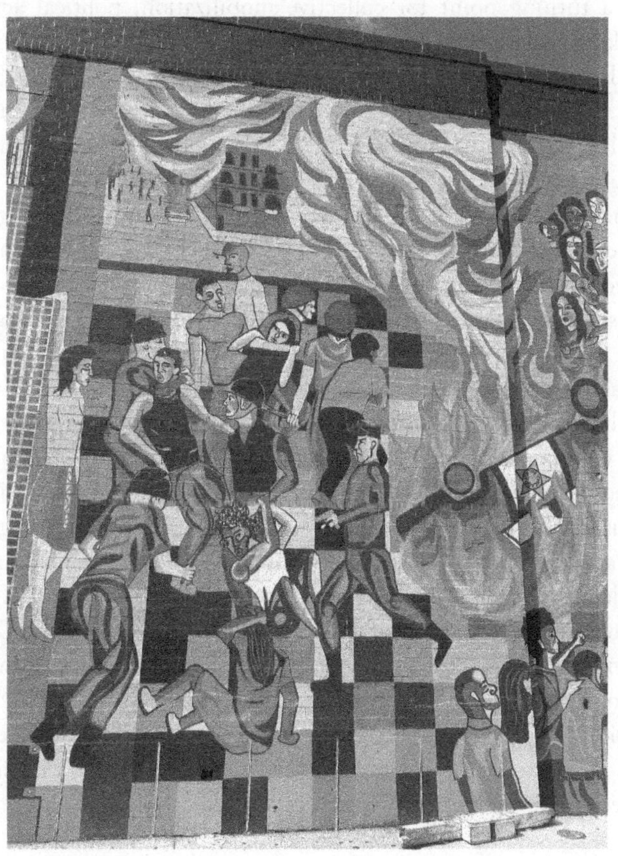

The Division Street riots are depicted with a melee of police officers and rioters. Police officers grabbing the rioters, bodies, shapes, and facial images jumble together, turning into a glob of chaos reminding the viewers of the violence of that summer. Off to the side is a police vehicle in flames. Protesters and Young Lords in their distinctive berets complete this section of the mural. This part of the mural declares that out of these ashes a people is born. Puerto Ricans were never fully visible in the city's dynamics, and it was not until the 1966 Division Street Riots[12] that a Puerto Rican consciousness in the city and political activism was cemented (L. Fernández 134–35).[13] The riots are credited with leading to a political consciousness for the Puerto Rican diaspora (Fernández). The riots "interrupted," according to Michael Rodriguez-Muñiz, the normal flow of the city and the fraught relationship with the police. He states, "[T]hey resisted their internal colonial reality, and began to assert themselves as equals" (209). The riots marked a turning point for collective mobilization, political action, and placemaking against these forced displacements. Similar to the didactic nature of murals centering revolutionary leaders, here we see how the history of resistance is not new and that Puerto Ricans have forged different ways to be seen in the city. Resistances of the past should be used as models in the present.

The mural closes with a series of flags: the Puerto Rican flag with sky blue, the Chicago flag with petroglyphs instead of stars, and in between these two, smaller Paseo Boricua flags and the revolutionary flag of Puerto Rico. A small figure of a *jíbaro* with plantains becomes key to gesture toward progress and fixity at once. While the flags denote the place of Puerto Ricans in Chicago today, the latest chapter in a long history of Puerto Rico, the *jíbaro* alludes to progress and continuation beyond the flags by linking past struggle with contemporary issues in Chicago. To the *jíbaro* Chicago is part of his home too. The *jíbaro*'s ubiquity in both cities signals Disaporican consciousness of their history, both troubled and inclusive, but regardless of their location, the *jíbaro*, like them, belongs. Where it takes Chicago Ricans is not defined beyond knowing that there is more to come. The mural points to future possibilities of Puerto Ricans, who should see Chicago as their own place they can call home, whichever version they deem fit. The mural touches on many themes seen throughout this chapter, depicting the tensions, movements, and inconsistencies that define archipelagoes of longing. In the end the mural shows who we are, where we came from, and where we are going.

Conclusion

As the epigraph to this chapter notes, public art is the collective expression of a community. The street art murals in Chicago's Paseo Boricua and Philadelphia's El Centro de Oro collectively express the history, resistance, and force of a people. In both cities the artists take from the past to reassert a present that is more racially, economically, and politically just. They use art to imagine a new world. These murals take from a racist past that has actively excluded Indigenous and Black peoples and their contributions to Puerto Rican culture and place racialized peoples at the forefront of contemporary racial justice experiences. In asserting their presence not as a footnote in history, new self-actualization and relations to others begin to unfold. Challenges to the status quo appear. Through historical figures, often forgotten by (or hidden from) Puerto Ricans in the diaspora, the art opens up new contemplations on the will to combat colonial and racist oppressions in the United States. By presenting these historical figures, the art educates some Puerto Ricans and reminds others of the collective will to resist. But Puerto Ricans are not the only second-class people in the United States, and throughout the art, solidarities with Mexican and other Latinx groups forge a new way forward. In building these representational solidarities, the murals acknowledge both the specificity of the US experience and also the lasting legacy of US imperial and colonial pursuits in the Americas more broadly. A radical nostalgia is used to reimagine the future.

With these various anti-imperialist goals, there is the constant backdrop of the continued neoliberal and colonial structures that plague Puerto Ricans on the island and in the diaspora. Similarly, since the passage of the 2012 Ley 22, which created a tax exception on investments in Puerto Rico and the establishment of an economic development zone in 2017, monied interests have been flocking to Puerto Rico to flip houses (Graulau 2021). With these economic incentives for foreigners, housing prices are increasing to the point that local Puerto Ricans can no longer afford to live on the island, thanks to the same neoliberal thinking that displacements in Chicago and Philadelphia are predicated on. Island and mainland policies might look different but have the same detrimental effect on Boricuas. Hegemonic forces—federal and municipal—that enact policies hurt working-class peoples and communities of color both on the island and on the mainland. Yet the artists in this chapter resist through murals that build consciousness, represent the resistance, and assert a sense of belonging for Puerto Ricans in Chicago and Philadelphia. Here, the murals show a longing to belong and correct the narratives of the past to build a better future for generations to come. Much in the same way, in the next chapter we will see how economic forces and representational nuances clash in the Interim Pulse National Memorial. While in this chapter the liberatory intent of street art murals comes face to face with the continued reality of being both colonized and racialized peoples, the Pulse commemorative site and its digital iterations show the complexities of queer Puerto Rican representation. The commemorative wall limits intersectional depictions by shrouding the Latinx identities, yet the digital replica and artistic archive open up new ways to imagine commemorations that are less space-centric. Similar to the murals, the Pulse wall sits within these contradictions formed by archipelago of longing. Contradictions, incongruencies, and incompatibilities sit together. Within these disconnects, the archipelagoes of representation act in concert to form a whole. Ultimately the murals show a desire for the past that does not quite satisfy the present, revealing an archipelago of longing within the Puerto Rican diaspora.

Chapter 2

The Shrouding of Queer Rican Life in the Interim National Pulse Memorial

When you're brown & gay you're always dying twice

—Roy Guzman, "Restored Mural for Orlando"

On June 25, 2021, President Joseph R. Biden signed into law the creation of the Interim National Pulse Memorial, which designated the former Pulse nightclub, the site of a mass shooting in 2016, as a national memorial site. This legislative and executive action five years after the deadly attack acknowledged the increased visibility and recognition of members of the queer community within broader US society. The Interim National Pulse Memorial and the accompanying archive of Pulse-related art add to the growing list of other commemorative sites for the LGBTQI+ community, such as New York City's Stonewall Inn, San Francisco's Castro Theatre, and the AIDS memorial quilt, as locations that make important contributions to cementing and maintaining the representation of queer lives. These sites also offer ways for the community to heal and grieve the lives lost in the ongoing struggle for better resources to combat the oppressions that still ravage it today. Currently, an impromptu commemorative wall sits as a placeholder commemoration, intended to be a place of mourning, solidarity, and healing. Yet, the shrouding[1] of the mostly Latinx and Puerto Rican victims,[2] where their presence is acknowledged while attempting to obscure their existence, calls into question the status of intersectional identities that sit outside hegemonic narratives of subjectivity. This further challenges the

65

place of Latinxs and Puerto Ricans in the broader US imagination. The Interim National Pulse Memorial and archived artistic productions created after the massacre sit between these poles that at once celebrate the visibility of the queer community while also acknowledging the limitations imposed by the ongoing struggles for concrete rights and multifaceted representation.

With this collective commemoration at its core, in this chapter I argue that the collective cultural products—the physical commemorative site, the virtual replica, and the artistic archive—constitute an archipelago of queer Puerto Rican longing. Rather than understand these as products of idealized queer futures or fabricated queer pasts, I depart from an essentialist and utopian analysis to develop an archipelago of longing that brings together the often-disparate reality of queer Puerto Rican lives, which includes their contradictory iterations. Representations of queer pasts, heteronormative pressures, and intersectional lived experiences come together to push against singular depictions. These commemorations open up new, diverse, layered, and multifaceted realities within the Latinx world, forcing complex contemplation of intersectional subjects. While the previous chapter examined murals' representation of longing to recuperate the past to fix the present, this chapter contemplates the absence of representation, forcing a different type of longing. Here, these commemorative sites become a photographic negative of sorts where Puerto Rican and Latinx lives are shrouded in the attempt to memorialize a catastrophic event. In doing so, this chapter deepens queer Rican longing by excavating obfuscated senses of representation that are part and parcel of the broader archipelago of longing for Puerto Ricans. Longing in this chapter is to be seen and loved. Represented and celebrated. And accepted for your whole Puerto Ricannness in all its versions. This chapter asks: How can commemorative sites at once recuperate and perpetuate erasures of multiple subjectivities? How do digital commemorative sites open up new, more inclusive narratives around mourning? What does the negation of representation inform us about the broader Puerto Rican longing?

Queer commemorations reveal the conflicts inherent within the broad spectrum of the LGBTQI+ community. The Interim National Pulse Memorial and the digital artistic archive expose how intersections of race, class, gender, and immigration status that often emerge in tandem with sites of memory are overlooked. Events following the Pulse nightclub shooting in 2016 show how queerness and Latinidad are incomprehensible to a news media and national discourse that are keen on placing people in limiting (singular) subjectivities by erasing the complexities of intersectional identities

(Zaezae; Randall-Moon). The exclusion of queer and Latinx lives in the US national imaginary underscores the layers of marginalization and shrouding within a white, heteropatriarchal society. The shrouding occurs in many forms, through their place in the city, their representation on the commemoration, and their place in the Puerto Rican community that reflects their political, cultural, and existential shrouding. Scholars and thinkers have pointed to the constant identity elimination imposed on queer and Latinx lives after the Pulse nightclub massacre (Acosta; La Fountain-Stokes and Martínez-San Miguel; Ramirez et al.). Others have critiqued the monied interests that plague the commemoration's parent organization, the onePULSE Foundation (Blair, "More Than onePULSE"), and the government negligence that exacerbated deaths due to faulty zoning permits (Blair, "Pulse"). More recently scholars have looked at mediated collective mourning through new organizations (Morse) and examined how local Puerto Ricans have asserted themselves in the face of expansive obfuscation from the broader society, asserting their own suffering that was largely ignored (Torres). This scholarship underscores the intersections of mixed representations of Latinxs and the neoliberal inadequacies that shroud Latinxs from being effectively memorialized.

In studying the way intersectional representations have served to limit minoritized people in the national discourse, scholars such as Acosta, La Fountain-Stokes and Martínez-San Miguel, and Ramirez et al. suggest that these erasures stem from a double marginalization that at its core contests white, heteropatriarchal hegemonic cultural dominance in the United States—a dominance that Puerto Rican and queer peoples actively challenge. Queer Puerto Ricans challenge what Jasbir Puar calls a homonationalism or the national inclusion of "homosexual jargon" at the active exclusive of racial and sexual others (2). To Puar, United States exceptionalism is marked by who is allowed in within the national imagination, be that morally, sexually, and culturally, that defines both international and domestic self-definition (4). Following the massacre, news media sought to flatten the shooter, Omar Mateen, as solely linked to terrorism[3] and the victims as only gay, underscoring a homonationalism—and is telling of who is allowed in and who is not within the United States national imagination. The Interim National Pulse Memorial, digital replica, and archived artistic productions created after the massacre move against these types of homonationalist discourses of queer Ricans by pulling back the curtain, so to speak, and exposing subjectivities that are often obfuscated—in this case, shrouded—from the broader public.

As I explained in the introduction, memory's past-presentness informs archipelagoes of longing by being inclusive of a fragmented sense of memory for Caribbean peoples. This fragmentation requires a more inclusive representational mode that takes into account systemic oppressions such as colonial, neoliberal, and heteropatriarchal subjugations. In these commemorations, the representations of queer Puerto Rican and Latinx lives grind against capitalist desires, much the same way street art murals do in Chicago and Philadelphia, creating incomplete visions of the event. The incongruencies, fissures, and discontinuities of this archipelago of longing emerge. While the creators and curators of both the Pulse memorial and the archives of art and artifacts have been clear in underscoring the eradication of hate, the physical, digital, and artistic archive destabilizes established narratives on queer Puerto Rican and Latinx lives. Currently, the Interim National Pulse Memorial includes a provisional wall that wraps around two-thirds of the former Pulse nightclub and features photographs of the commemorations and events held after the massacre of June 12, 2016.[4] The images have been meticulously curated, ranging in size, shape, and depiction to capture a kaleidoscopic view of various parts of the city, mourners, and resistance. The pictures show scenes of not only solidarity but also compassion, love, celebration, mourning, and contemplation that encompass the inherent tensions of a commemorative site. Viewed from a distance, the rainbow flag, groups of people, and the city of Orlando play a prominent role in the images associated with the massacre. In certain areas, the wooden structures and the images are interrupted by sections of glass that reveal the physical building where the shooting took place. The gray industrial building retains not only the bullet holes from the infamous night but also the names of forty-eight of the victims.[5] This site folds hegemonic narratives, existential assertions, and intersectional subjectivity together in repeating, erasing, and polemical ways. These images center a commercial sorrow that supersedes the Puerto Rican and Latinxs lives that were lost. The digital replica takes this point further by interrupting time and space to enter the global sphere of collective mourning while also creating the fixed idea of the wall. The replica maps the same images, the same location, and the same tragedy for an online (global) audience. Frozen in a crisp, clean dusk, with an idealized image of the city in the background, this digital replica halts the slow deterioration of flowers, flags, and the wooden structure itself under the brutal onslaught of the Florida sun. Temporal-spatial tensions extend the archipelagoes of longing by linking this hyperlocal event to broader neoliberal structures that arrest changes to the commemoration, allowing the shrouding to continue.

In addition to the wall and its digital replica, I examine the digital artistic archive to reveal the shrouded presence of Latinx and Puerto Rican lives. The art removes the shroud ever so slightly, allowing a Latinx visualization to poke through. Housed in the Orange County Regional History Museum and digitally archived, an almost secondary memorial was erected through these artistic productions that echoes the physicality of the Pulse nightclub wall. Archiving over ten thousand artifacts, the One Orlando Collection stores a plethora of images, photos, trinkets, and other pieces of memory that members of the community have placed in various locations around Central Florida. Thus, an incongruous depiction emerges of queer Puerto Rican lives that remain present, albeit in minimized ways. In analyzing the commemorative wall, digital replica, and archived artist works, I demonstrate the ways longing for queer Puerto Ricans and Latinxs is a multifaceted enterprise that folds hegemonic narratives, existential assertions, and intersectional subjectivity together in repeating, shrouding, and emergent ways. The longing in this chapter takes the form of being adequately represented, of being inclusive of multiple subjectivities, but also a longing to adequately mourn the lives lost. These longings have no clear solutions and are shrouded both by systemic oppressions and hegemonic actors that actively move away from intersectional lives. Thus, an incongruous depiction of queer Puerto Rican and Latinx builds an additional archipelago of longing that reveals the quotidian obfuscation of their reality.

Figure 2.1. Main entrance of the Interim National Pulse Memorial. *Source:* Photo by the author.

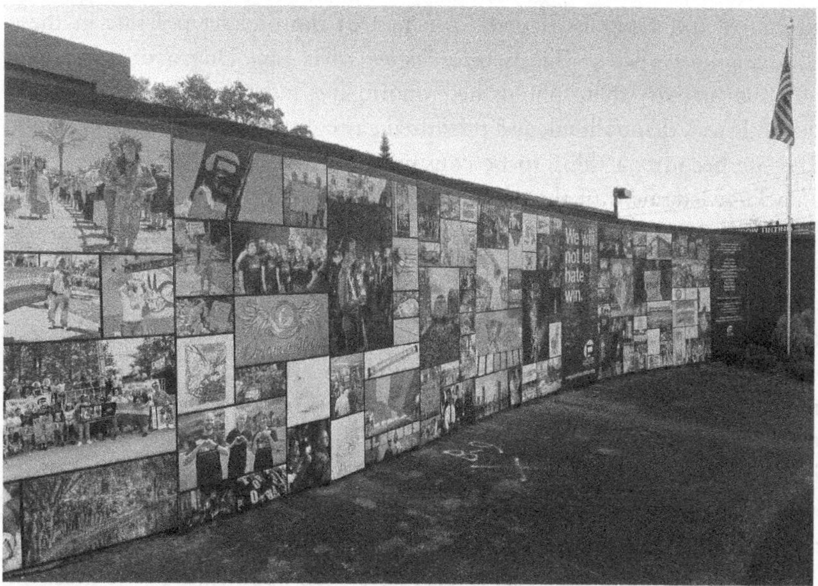

Pulse Background

Like many other sites of tragedy, the Pulse memorial has been marred by competing interests, juxtaposing economic desires, and inadequate representation. Shortly after the shooting, Barbara Poma established the onePULSE Foundation, dedicated to the construction of a permanent memorial (Dineen). Following the public outpouring of support that saw the placement of flowers, photos, and artwork around the Pulse nightclub, a quest to create a permanent space of commemoration began, with Poma becoming the face of the campaign. In 2017 Poma began raising funds through a combination of requesting donor contributions, lobbying the state, and crowdsourcing to reach the $45 million goal. This campaign culminated with a global design competition for the memorial and museum that drew architecture firms with no connections to the local community to design a commemorative site. Ultimately, Orlando-based HHCP and Lille-based Coldefy & Associates were chosen for the final design, combining a local firm with an international one to create the winning concept (Santich). The site has become a type of "trauma tourism," to use Laurie Beth Clark's concept, where moneyed interests are combined with mourning and community engagement to create a complex (and contested) tourist experience.[6] The combination of government support with moneyed interests and global perspectives complicates the local nature of this queer Puerto Rican and Latinx tragedy.

The details around the erection of the site show how neoliberal political structures and capitalist desires form part of the broader polemic in these commemorative sites. This is to a degree what Lisa Dugan calls the new homonormativity that upholds heteronormative institutions by promising a depoliticized, demobilized, and privatized gay culture for consumption (179). The site becomes a thing to be consumed for a mass audience rather than an acknowledgment of the complex subjectivities and lives lost on June 12, 2016. Hence, the concept of archipelagoes of longing helps describe the interrelated oppressions of queer Puerto Rican life depicted in this interim commemoration, where economic interests and representational inadequacies fold into each other like the individual islands and various oceans and seas of an archipelago. These incompatible interests are one way that Latinx representations have been shrouded in the commemorative wall, underscoring the interconnected nature of various factors that erase Puerto Ricans in the broader US consciousness. This erasure has not been lost on local residents, and Poma's efforts have been met with protest from local leaders and family and friends of survivors who believe the memorial and museum are being coopted for profit. These local leaders have been opponents of the museum and memorial as well as the temporary commemorative wall. These protests demonstrate how the neoliberal policies that led to the shooting are connected to the same erasures that the wall now represents (Blair, "The Pulse Nightclub Shooting"; Blair, "More Than onePULSE"; Blair, "Reimagining a Public Pulse Memorial"). Government mismanagement and antigay bias are culprits in the events of the shooting. For instance, during the shooting local officials failed to secure the space, and prior to the shooting Poma directly failed to comply with the safety codes that would have helped people trying to escape as the shooting occurred (Blair, "Pulse"). I explain the context of this commemorative site to illustrate the ways that commemorations are by their nature a contested space. The combination of neoliberal, economic, identity, and political tensions undergird the broader issues related to archipelagoes of longing that tug at each other and create, destroy, and then recreate the same tensions. Poma and her work show the varied interests in the commemorative site, but so do the archival practices that help recenter queer Rican lives in this commemorative site.

While this context helps situate the various tensions at play in these commemorations, it is important to affirm that I am not critiquing the push for the memorial, the organization's goals, or the intentions of the onePULSE Foundation. What I am attempting to provide in this chapter is a critical analysis of how incongruous desires lead to the shrouding of Puerto Rican and Latinx identity in a memorialization of an attack that took the lives of forty-nine people. Even as the memorials honor the victims, they also decenter their Puerto Rican and Latinx identities for mixed political and economic agendas. My analysis stays within the bounds of the narrative relayed by the images on the wall, the digital replica, and the artworks, irrespective of other political or ideological considerations of the memorial wall itself. While I understand that the attack was not perpetrated solely against the queer Latinx community, it did disproportionately take their lives, contesting the place of queer Latinx representation and Puerto Ricans' relationship to the broader US nation.[7] Archipelagoes of longing opens a space where multiple subjectivities are involved, inviting a contemplation that is additive, encompassing multiple communities, peoples, and traumas.

Brief View of Latinxs in Orlando

Up to this point I have delineated what it is at stake when examining the place of Puerto Ricans and Latinxs in the commemorative sites studied in this chapter. It is imperative that I situate the Puerto Rican and Latinx community of Orlando in the broader US context. Puerto Ricans have been arriving in Florida in earnest since the 1990s, when programs both on the island and in the state of Florida began promoting migration to the state, specifically new housing developments in Buenaventura Lakes in Central Florida (Delerme 22). Between 1990 and 2000 Orange County, where Orlando sits, saw the largest increase of Puerto Ricans stateside (Duany, *Blurred Borders* 106). Puerto Ricans in Orlando tend to be more educated, have higher incomes, and more often identify racially as white than counterparts in other parts of the United States (Duany 108–09). These demographic differences impact the way they engage with both Orlando and Puerto Rico, shaping ideas of belonging and nationhood in both locations. As Jorge Duany notes, "Mickey Ricans' could follow a different path from other Puerto Ricans diaspora communities" (Duany, "Mickey Ricans?" 237). Barreneche et al. have noted the "sticky" nature of the migration to Orlando, challenging the revolving door construct that saw Puerto Ricans ebb and flow between the island and the mainland during the second half of the twentieth century. Most recently, with the devastation of the 2017 Hurricane Maria and the subsequent earthquake that rocked the island in 2019, a massive migration to Florida has also impacted the notion of place and belonging for many Puerto Ricans (Alvarez). After Hurricane Maria, Puerto Ricans saw the same type of out migration as before the Hurricane only in larger numbers to Central Florida (Mora et al. 210). But even before the Hurricane, Florida has received a full third of all migrants since 2006 (Mora et al. 217) more than any other single location. Unlike in the migratory waves to New York and Chicago, Puerto Ricans in Florida have decided to stay, challenging the demographic makeup and politics of the Central Florida region and the state as a whole. Thus, in Orlando Puerto Ricans integrate politically, culturally, and economically, which calls into question identity formation and belonging for Puerto Ricans. Their integration into the community has been fraught with additional ambiguities by both the community at large and Latinxs in the area (Silver, "Asking as a Citizen"). Orlando Ricans at once straddle belonging and unbelonging, with their participation in local and state politics differing substantially from that of their Cuban counterparts in Miami, who hold great sway in local, state, and national politics.

Orlando Ricans who have historically navigated the United States' binary racial tensions have struggled to be categorized in racial labels that moved away from the white-black divide. In more contemporary times, Puerto Ricans struggle with being represented accurately as members of the broader Central Florida community and its increasing diversity with other

Hispanic communities from Colombia, Venezuela, the Dominican Republic, and other Latin American countries. Issues of race, class, and national origin become competing categories for political mobilization (Silver, "Asking as a Citizen" 126–27). While Puerto Ricans experience the same immigration trajectory as many other Latin American immigrants, their status as US citizens sets them apart and adds to tensions within the Latinx community. Puerto Ricans thus sit at the nexus of several subjectivities in relation to visibility in the Orlando area. They are simultaneously second-class citizens, racially minoritized, and culturally othered within both the hegemonic US culture and the Latinx community of Central Florida. As Patricia Silver notes, these tensions merge a sort of invisibility, with pressure to assimilate into the broader US construct, and a hypervisibility in regard to the US colonial relationship across the Americas ("You Don't Look Puerto Rican" 406). This fact adds to the broader question of the at-once erasure and centrality of Puerto Ricans and Latinx subjects in the commemorations of the Pulse nightclub massacre. Unlike in the previous chapter, where an assertive Puerto Ricanness is claimed through murals and the centering of previously erased lives, here we see a different Puerto Rican experience, but one that is nevertheless integral to their second-class status in the United States. Thinking of these sites as an archipelago allows for further contemplation by allowing these tensions to sit side by side, a reality that might reveal social tensions to some but exposes the lived experience of Puerto Ricans and Latinxs. Already a community that struggles to find a firm footing in the regional representation, this massacre adds a layer of contemplation of the place of minoritized peoples that do not fit neatly into either-or narratives that actively omit varied subjectivities.

Commemorative (Dis)Continuities

Tensions between history and memory are embedded in the National Pulse Memorial, which often emphasizes commemorations of and by the LGBTQI+ community. The images that make up the current commemorative wall provide a historicization of this event and encourage further critical engagement with the site. Memorializing an event requires creating a narrative that excludes and emphasizes certain occurrences, peoples, and subjectivities. The Pulse nightclub commemoration sits on a plane that at once points toward an idealized future of equality while also highlighting the actual subjugation present within the queer and Latinx communities today. Commemorations are important community-building tools that draw attention to the events, causes, and meaning that a society holds dear. On this wall one sees the creation of a hegemonic narrative that shrouds Latinx lives through a folding of temporal and spatial strains, elucidating the obfuscated intersections of a queer Latinx subjectivity. Through these tensions, the incongruencies of archipelagoes of longing are revealed; it is through this continually forming and repeating commemorative site that the shrouding becomes highlighted, forcing one to ponder the place of Puerto Ricans and Latinxs at the site. Thus, Puerto Ricans and Latinxs in Orlando are at once folded into and omitted from this representation via the fixity of the photographs used and the overabundance of the city of Orlando as a place.

Through various panes of glass, the actual nightclub is revealed throughout the commemorative wall, peeking out between the images of the pride flag, mourners, and celebrations of LGBTQI+ life. The ominous gray building stands as a haunting reminder of the tragedy of June 12, 2016. As one walks around the wall, the glass panes provide a time-lapse explanation of the events; ideas of time are affixed to a physical space. The building takes on a presence of its own, accentuating the story and revealing itself as a site worthy of remembrance. The written words serve almost as the voice for the building, a voice of the past that sits in the present. Above the top right corner of one window, a text reads in Spanish and English, "First responders breached this wall at 5:02 a.m." Just behind the glass pane, spectators can see acrylic plastic over the penetrated building, allowing a silhouette of the ruins to become visible. Moving along the wall, observers see a waterfall on the building just behind the glass, a feature of the building that marked its vibrancy to clubgoers in the club's past. The wall reads, "The iconic glass fountain wall was destroyed at 2:08 a.m. The fountain has been restored." The fountain's flowing water resists the grim reality that took place inside. Water as life becomes a powerful message to spectators, reminding them of the people who enjoyed the club. Moving ever so slightly to the right, one can see the bullet holes from the night's massacre, juxtaposing life with the material reminder of death. Time as progress and space as place are folded into a palimpsestic formation, allowing the archipelagic nature of longing to take root.

The glass windows that reveal the gray building echo how queer monuments have long been sites that disrupt, attempting to effectively make sense of the events of the past while underscoring the ambivalence of the present. The narrative constructed within the queer community requires their monuments to represent an inadequate queer past while also reflecting on

Figure 2.2. Pane of glass with view of the Pulse fountain. *Source:* Photo by the author.

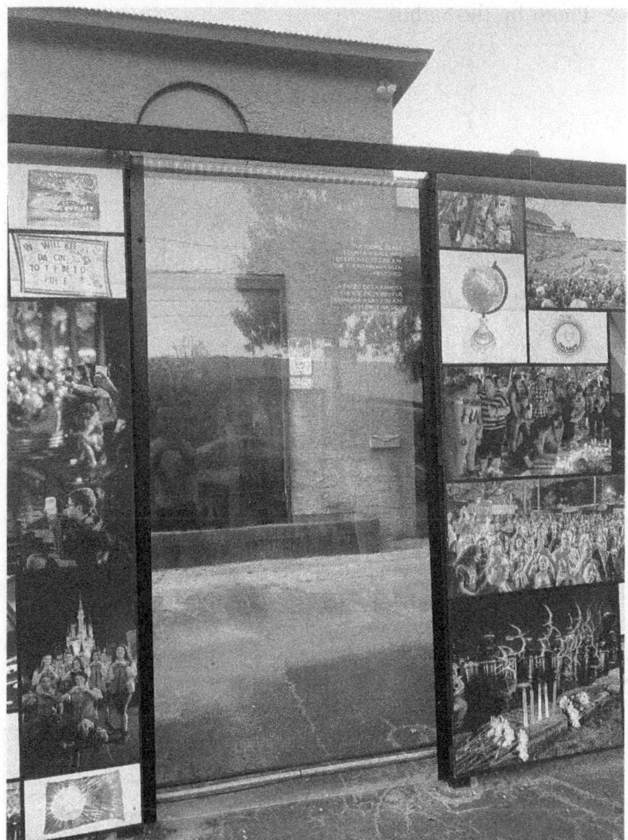

the ambiguous queer present. Past queer self-narrativization assists in constructing contemporary identities (Bravmann 4). The need for monuments in the queer historical landscape and the queer material reality is a contested one. Queer monuments, like any commemorative site for minoritized lives, grapple with how to effectively tell their story in the face of hegemonic cultural norms that aim to erase their existence. When monuments are accepted by hegemonic cultural arbiters, a transformation (or mediation?) occurs that calls into question how a group is presented and by whom. The Pulse National Memorial decenters minoritized peoples' lives for economic, political, or nefarious agendas that have negative existential effects on the lives they are trying to represent. Or, put another way, as Thomas Dunn

Figure 2.3. Pane of glass detailing the night's events with view of the former night-club. *Source:* Photo by the author.

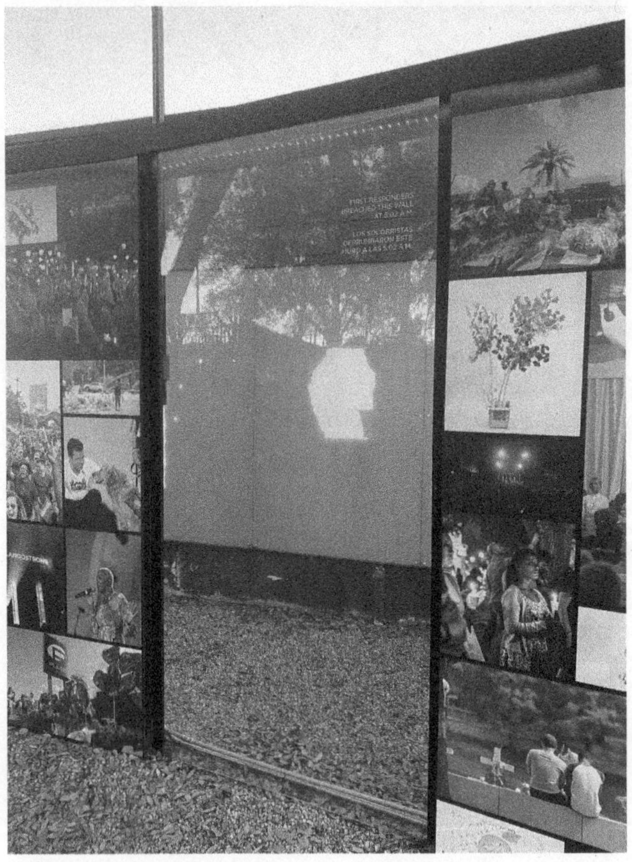

notes in speaking on a LGBTQI+ monument by the National Park Service, "national institutions cannot be trusted to take GLBTQ memories seriously" (172). The onePULSE Foundation cannot be trusted either. The narration of the night's events glosses over specific peoples' lives. Chronicling the event, establishing temporal nodes, and nodding to spatial wounds creates a botched "queer utopian memory" that serves as a white-centered mural in which Latinx identities are shrouded. Instead of showing the possibilities of the future—as José Esteban Muñoz (2009) proposes queer utopias can achieve (38)—the commemorative wall shows an inability to understand multiple identities at once. The Pulse commemorative site demonstrates the layers of meaning and understanding that break temporal and spatial parameters and reveal an absent presence that undergirds the Puerto Rican relationship to the United States.

The chronicling of the events in relation to the physical space is not the only way a botched queer memory is created; a mosaic of images from the citywide mourning becomes a further tool of shrouding, demonstrating the various layers of meaning in the images. In these images viewers see Orlando's queer community, the tributes left at the site by local and national leaders and residents, and objects left by mourners around the city after the massacre. The images remove the specificity of the location and the people who died to create a monolithic commercial mourning site that universalizes the events to global cosmopolitan spectators. As Zachary Blair comments on first seeing the wall, "I was looking at a serpentine billboard advertisement, where high-definition rainbows and smiling faces were being used to sell the nonprofit's misleading slogan" ("More Than onePULSE" 3).[8] The images shroud the queer Latinx experience and center the act of mourning rather than the lives lost, creating what Roland Barthes calls a "third meaning," or a meaning that cannot be understood at first glance. Barthes dissects the meaning of an image into three layers. To Barthes this third meaning is filled with an "obtuse" signifier because it blunts and rounds the more direct meaning by going beyond the literal meaning and is difficult to define as it sits in a space that is infinite (320). The wall, then, has an infinite number of meanings, including obfuscated and varied identities that move away from essentialist tropes. Even as it is the idealized memory of the queer community, it also omits the Puerto Rican and Latinx lives that were disproportionately lost in the event. This mosaic is important. Representation does matter. I want to make clear: But at what cost? Who is excluded? And what realities are omitted in the pursuit of national (or even international) attention?

It is within this desired ideal that Barthes's third meaning emerges in these images. The pictures tell a story in Barthes's first meaning: a community that is mourning and coming together. Photographs of mourning crowds with the backdrop of Orlando's skyline or candlelight vigils that home in on some of the attendees as they contemplate the events that have transpired give spectators the initial understanding of the gravity of the event and the purpose of the memorial. Barthes's second level, where the pride flag plays a prominent role, emerges quickly through the images. The flag waving in the wind at dusk next to two palm trees, the pride flag being held by attendees of a pride parade, and the bows of several pride flag pins all emphasize the main subjects in the image. The pride flag on other objects plays a major role also, giving members outside the community the seal of approval. Flag-bedecked objects such as the jerseys of the Orlando Football Club team, the pavilion now colored by the rainbow flag in Lake Eola, and the skyline lit up in the rainbow lights all come together to flood the city with a cacophony of queer life. The rainbow flag asserts the event's connection to the LGBTQI+ community and has a long history of asserting presence and providing hope in the face of heteronormative social structures that negate queer lives. Created in 1978 by Gilbert Baker, the flag originally had eight stripes symbolizing "pink for sex, red for life, orange for healing, yellow for the sun, green for nature, turquoise for magic, blue for serenity, and purple for the spirit" ("Gilbert Baker"). While prior to the flag the community often used the triangle, which referenced the yellow triangles Nazis utilized to mark gay men in concentration camps, this flag underscores the variety within the community that it represents. Pictures of people wearing the flag, a teddy bear with the flag colors, and pride flag ribbons seep into every crevasse of the physical wall, inundating the site and declaring it a queer site.

While the first and second meanings of the flag are clear, the third meaning is more muddled, nuanced, and somber. The flag is internationally recognized as a symbol of the community, and while the original eight stripes have been changed to a commercialized six, the notions of solidarity and diversity within the community still dominate. Other flags have emerged to recognize the spectrum of identities in the LGBTQI+ community such as the trans flag and the bi flag, both of which make cameo appearances along the wall. The third meaning of the pride flag obscures the presence of the Puerto Rican and Latinx community this tragedy impacted the most. In moving from the literal and symbolic meanings of the various images on the wall, the third meaning is less direct and open to an amorphous and blurred revelation. It is what is not present in these images that speaks to the third meaning: the obfuscation of the Puerto Ricans and Latinxs. Pride does not inherently inspire a sense of belonging for queer Latinx peoples. Discussing New York City, Larry La Fountain-Stokes notes the uneven participation of Puerto Ricans in the Pride Parade and of queer Puerto Ricans in the Puerto Rican Day Parade, reflecting the struggle of queer Puerto Ricans to "gain a space in their national ethnic imaginary" (71–72). LaFountain-Stokes criticizes the overwhelming whiteness in queer theory and in popular culture, noting that the tensions of belonging to both the queer and Puerto Rican national imaginaries can be fraught with negation and shame (56–57). These expressive tensions further emphasize the incongruencies in representative politics by revealing the contradictions in queer and Puerto Rican notions of belonging. I am not claiming that the onePULSE Foundation purposefully, at a macro level, obfuscates the Puerto Rican and Latinx experience. Yet the shrouding of the Latinx community underscores the invisibility of intersectional identities, the flattening of Latinx subjectivity. The flag becomes a symbol that should be celebrated but also a symbol that is used to whitewash the commemorative site. Narrative tensions emerge and representational lack persists.

The pride flag is not the only prominent flag displayed, but the US flag imagery throughout the physical mural also asserts the place of the queer community within the broader national psyche. The US flag allows for a connection between the hegemonic society and the minoritized group by declaring that the massacre did not only happen to the LGTBQ+ community but was also an attack on all Americans. Words such as "peace," "hope," "love," and "strength," embedded in the images, on people's shirts, in signs, and on other public facing surfaces, pepper the wall, subliminally telling the

Figure 2.4. Images of the pride flag on the Interim National Pulse Memorial wall. *Source:* Photo by the author.

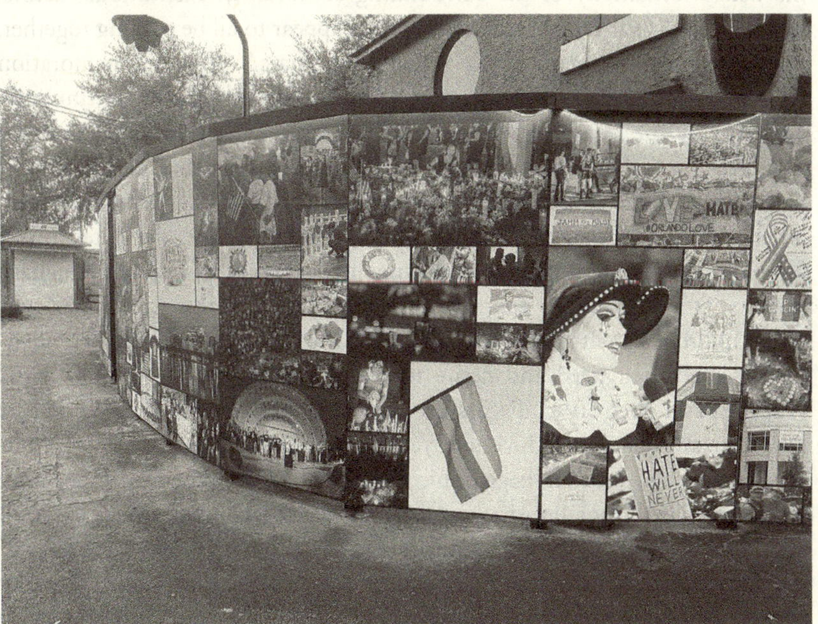

spectator what they should be feeling or reading into the images. The faces that emerge throughout are mostly joyful in nature, showing smiling men, women, and children at an individual level. These people as a collective come together to push against the pain of the night of June 12, and the words "We will not let hate win" guide the visitor to the ultimate message of the wall. Finally, images of artwork inspired by event allow observers to mourn the loss of the lives lived and acknowledge the broader community connection. These artistic expressions dot the mural, acknowledging that beyond this mural there are other sites of expression and pointing to the lasting effects of the event expanding beyond this one site into the broader city, region, and world. Moving outside of Orlando creates a global web of affinity, suspending the temporal and spatial limitations of the wall to muddle the specificity of this event and emphasizing that beyond this commemorative space there are other lives that must be addressed. And beyond the bullet-riddled building and the names on the wall are other stories that have been left untold yet form part of this mosaic. In creating a heteronormative narrative, Latinx lives are obfuscated, revealing the third meaning where queer Puerto Rican experiences are left out.

The collected images on the physical wall offer an idealized under-standing of the LGBTQI+ community in which everyone is accepted into the heteronormativity of the surrounding community. Institutional actors, activities, and a variety of racialized subjects appear to all be coming together, unified against the amorphous, vague term "hate." This commemoration creates a sanitized understanding of the community, one that is continuously impacted by the legacy of oppression. The images create an imaginary that disguises the real material and existential subjugations that occlude queer Latinx lives. Katie Acosta notes that not just Latinidad was erased but also other subjectivities that are central to the Latinx experience. She states, "They were immigrants and migrants, undocumented, English-as-a-second-language learners, family members committed to maintaining transnational ties with their children, parents and grandparents. All of these aspects of their iden-tities shaped their need and desire to attend the gay bar on Latinx night" (108). Acosta goes on to discuss the nuanced complexities of queer Latinx lives that are defined by love and rejection both with the Latinx commu-nity and in the broader hegemonic discourses, and notes the importance of celebrating the totality of these peoples as a beacon of resilience (109). The absence of these varied identities further emphasizes the flattening of the Puerto Rican experience, in which only singular subjective identity constructs are conceivable.

While the variety of images on the wall creates an interconnected cacophony of subjectivities, it obfuscates Puerto Ricans' and Latinxs' place in the US cultural fabric, further underscoring how they are at once present and invisible. The shrouding of Latinxs within the broader queer community is nothing new. The AIDS epidemic quickly erased people of color in media representations to bring attention to the emerging health crisis (Sturken 159). Scholars have commented on the centering of white gayness in broader theorizations of queer studies (La Fountain-Stokes; J. Muñoz; Cantú). The national media scrutiny that surrounded the event also erased Latinx people from the tragedy, focusing on a plethora of issues from gun violence to Islamic terrorism as reporters and pundits tried to come up with a narrative that complied with fixed narratives regarding the queer community. Ultimately erased were the intersecting realities of the lives that were lost and the importance of "Latin night" for queer Latinx peoples in the Central Florida region. This erasure was not lost on people in the local area, and a 2017 study conducted by Ramirez et al. shows the complexities within the mourning and erasure process that some Latinxs experienced. While many felt frustration about the erasures, other participants could not necessarily connect with the Latinx component of the tragedy since they did not see themselves in the mostly Puerto Rican victims. The Latinx tragedy sits as a specter within the overall wall, pointing toward the reality that the victims were overwhelmingly of color. This specter is seen through the secondary way Latinx representation is manifested on the commemorative wall. These almost ghostly occurrences sit in a present-yet-not-present state that challenges one-dimensional narratives and points toward the liminality of these intersecting lives. Traces of the Puerto Rican, Mexican, and other flags of Latin American countries can be found along the wall if you search closely enough. These minor indicia of Latinidad serve as small reminders of presence, asserting their existence in a covert manner.

The photographs on the wall are not the only way that Latinidad and queerness are in tension; this tension is also present in the physical location of the nightclub. There is a type of poetic malaise indicated by some of the mourners' plastic flowers, teddy bears, and photographs that sit alongside the wall. These objects point to the constantly unfolding nature of the wall, where trinkets and mementos reveal its vitality while simultaneously showing its decomposition. The slow decay is reminiscent of the way the tragedy has slowly faded from the minds of many outside the Central Florida community, the Latinx community, and the broader queer community, where the tragedy remains very much in a constant present.

The various objects along the wall form an inadequate "queerscape"—that is, a public place where queer peoples can assert their presence (Ingram 97). Outdoor spaces have long been locations where LGBTQI+ communities have gone to make connections—sexual or communitarian—and are inherently polymorphous places that constitute "a matrix of desire and power" (109). Through the limited Latinx representations, the wall contests the inclusive nature of this queerscape, and hegemonic actors' centering of certain queer lives over others weakens the power of the site.

The construction of space and its relationship to bodies is formed in tandem as one defines the other. Objects and bodies are oriented toward each other, which leads to the definition of the body and of the space the object and the body are in (Ahmed, *Queer Phenomenology*, 7–8). Not only does the orientation of the body give meaning—it also points to future understandings of what it means to be queer. The way queer lives inhabit a space is fraught with multiple layers of denials, and that is very much true for queer Latinx lives and this commemorative wall. The site contests space for queer Latinx lives, revealing both the possibility of the future and the materially decayed reality of the present, which coexist unsettled. The structure is part of the broader Orlando cityscape and sits outdoors in the sweltering heat. Situated on Orange Avenue, a major roadway that cuts through downtown Orlando, the wall occupies a space between the tourist-minded city that sees millions of visitors a year and the local population that surrounds it. Commercial buildings such as Wendy's across the street, Einstein Bros. Bagels, and Dunkin' Donuts cut through the contemplative nature of the site of memory, haunting its mourning power.

The intersecting tensions between queerscapes and Latinx barrios are further contested in this commemoration by placing the city of Orlando front and center. Images of the commemorations and vigils from around the city—Lake Eola, the Dr. Phillips Performing Arts Center, Disney World—mask the reality that not all lives are welcomed in the city. And some lives are obfuscated completely, such as those of the queer Latinx people from the Pulse massacre. This memorial site is in constant tension, forced to straddle a line between recognition by hegemonic cultural readers and adequate representation of the lives it seeks to honor. The site provides representational stability-in-tension for minoritized groups by allowing them visibility within a cultural construct that continually negates their existence. It allows for the cohesion of a subaltern group, providing the possibility of cultural, material, and political advancement. The memorial also asserts a self-definition rather than being limited to narratives that oppress and stig-

Figure 2.5. Image of flowers and stuffed animals placed by mourners. *Source:* Photo by the author.

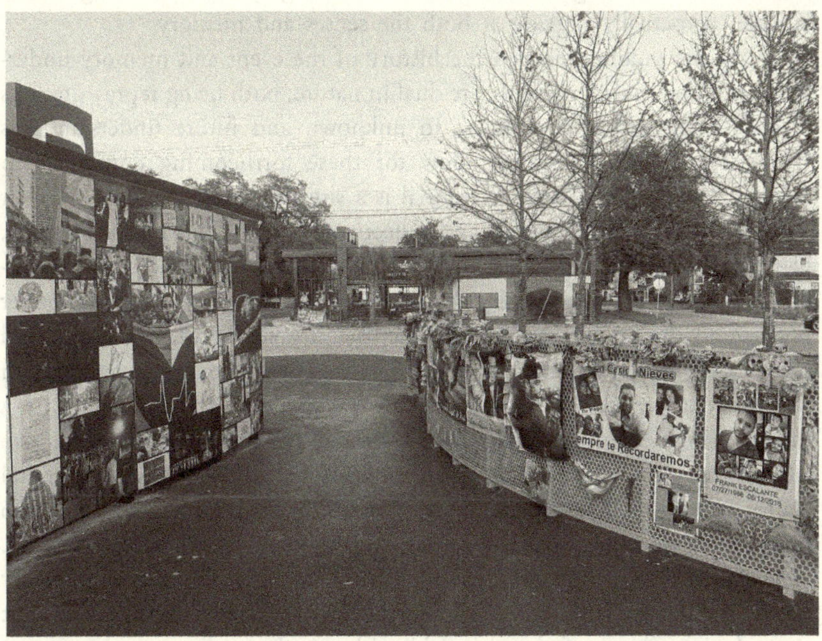

matize these groups. This commemoration is what Pierre Nora calls a *lieu de mémoire*, or site of memory, which inhabits an epistemological zone that contests the division between memory and history. This site both memorializes a tragic event for the LGBTQI+ community and creates a historical dialogue with past events. Nora points to the historicization of memory through memorial sites created by historians for national commemoration. Sites of memory exist in order to remember, according to Nora, and "because of their capacity for metamorphosis, an endless recycling of their meaning and an unpredictable proliferation of their ramifications" (19). These sites are in constant tension, being both "simple and ambiguous, natural and artificial, at once immediately available in concrete sensual experience and susceptible to the most abstract elaboration" (18). At the site these tensions are seen in the wall that snakes about two-thirds of the way around the bullet-riddled building before abruptly stopping. The images attempt, but fail, to obstruct the view of the gray nightclub that lurks behind it, baking in the Florida sun. A glass pane allows spectators to view the names of the victims and the remnants of what once was a happy place, a safe place for queer lives. The commemorative gestures and the material legacy of the building sit side by side, perpetually tugging at both the senses and memory.

Yet the pulling between the history of the event and memory underscores the way sites of memory are dual in nature, both being representations of themselves and also pointing to unknown and future understandings (Nora 24). Public memories allow for these forthcoming empathies to emerge. The National Pulse Memorial is a site of public memory, one that is mediated through individual and collective memory.[9] This public memory, like many other constructions of memory in general, is inherently malleable, constantly shifting depending on the time. Memory serves to better understand the present, yet this public memory sits between the past and the present. Edward Casey notes that public monuments have a "Janusian trait" where they are "both attached to the past . . . and act to ensure a future of further remembering of that same event" (17). The narrative created by the onePULSE Foundation underscores this in-between temporal reality, attempting to center the forty-nine lost lives of the tragedy while also maintaining a white hegemonic depiction prioritized by the society at large. New organizations have been founded that center the experience of queer Latinx groups and their specific struggles in the Central Florida area, but many Latinxs do not feel comfortable either in Latinx community centers or in queer support networks (Schneider). While the onePULSE Foundation celebrates the idealized concepts of love and hope, and their slogan asserts "We will never let hate win," the wall obfuscates the limited support in the Orlando area for queer Latinx lives. This tension replicates past injustices by decentering the Latinx-specific subjectivity at the core of the tragedy.

Digital Reconstructions and Queer Temporalities

While the physical space provides a snapshot of commemorative intentions through the examination of location and time, digital commemorations—in this case, the digital replica of the wall and the artistic archive—open up new avenues of participation and representation. By examining these two digital sites, I show how they are more inclusive of intersectional subjectivities, yet still impacted by hegemonic representations, so as to not flatten the Latinx and Puerto Rican experience. Similar to the way the street art murals in Chicago and Philadelphia recuperate erased peoples from history, digital commemorations recenter Latinx and queer lives in a way that acknowledges and celebrates the various subjective identities. Through the artistic rendering of the lives lost, one sees a humanity unfold that is in tandem with the physical wall's focus on the city of Orlando and collective mourning. In addition to the art, I will examine the fixed temporal representation of the digital wall replica, where queer temporalities are suspended, showcasing the idealization of a queer past but also the inclusion of a mourners from around the world. In each case, the digital space, much like the physical wall, is at once inclusive of and counter to hegemonic narratives. Thus, by examining these second digital commemorations, a broader archipelago of memory is formed that is inherently contradictory and yet inclusive of varied identities and experiences.

Digital commemorations allow for the expansion of what artifacts can be included, expanding the narratives that can be formed for and by the subjects being commemorated (Boehm). They also allow for an inclusion of subjectivities that moves beyond a stagnant articulation of the histories being told. Digital commemorative sites move away from official discourses and attempt to engage with nonhegemonic understandings of the events they are trying to tribute (Recuber 537). This gesture allows not just for the creation of the site but also a therapeutic result by incorporating the loved ones and family members to have a say in the process of commemorating (536–37). The digital commemorations and artistic productions post-Pulse force a reexamination of the layers of subjectivities and the power to disrupt fixed narratives. The digital sphere delinks minoritized subjectivities from the strict parameters of heteronormative discourses that seek to exclude—or annihilate—minoritized subjectivities of all stripes. This in itself is a revolutionary way to reexamine ethnic identities that move beyond replication of heteropatriarchal white discourses and center intersections of identity. Commemorations need not be singular narratives that celebrate one marginalized identity but can acknowledge the inherent mixture and fluidity of these subjectivities. These digital commemorative sites are formed by a plethora of identities so as not to lock in any single one, thus destabilizing and liberating the discourses.

Housed in and maintained by the Orange County Regional History Museum, the digital artistic archive echoes the physicality of the Pulse nightclub wall while rupturing and opening up new modes of representation. Containing over ten thousand artifacts, the One Orlando Collection stores a plethora of images, photos, trinkets, and other pieces of memory that members of the community have placed at commemorative sites around the city. Immediately following the shooting, staff members of the Orange County

Regional History Museum worked to collect and archive artwork and other artifacts. The staff's efforts became much more than a simple preservation project as the task was transformed into a memorialization of the event that gave community members a sense of relief away from the media (Schwartz et al. 112). The artwork serves both as an archive of the lives lost and as commemorative objects that assist the mourners in processing the event. The artwork and artifacts create organic and individual representations of memory, allowing for a global meditation that creates an addendum to the commemorative wall. It becomes, to use the words of González Espitia, the "dark side of the archive" (26). Similar to how González Espitia understands archives as the single receiver for housing knowledge, these artistic works provide a more holistic commemoration, in conjunction with the wall, that sits alongside the hegemonic narratives. By placing both official and counternarratives together, as this digital archive does, a less zero-sum commemoration unfolds. The "dark side" of this commemorative art evolves in tandem with hegemonic narratives, allowing for new, complicated—and at times contradictory—representations of queer Latinx life.

In line with this malleability, the archived artwork provides for a sort of create-your-own-adventure where participants can view the commemorative site(s) on their own terms—not negating the commemorative wall but allowing for spaces where hegemonic and subaltern forms of representation coexist. Thus, digital archives provide a space of education about LGBTQI+ lives within communities (VanHaitsma). Sarah Bay-Cheng reminds us that digital archiving tools break up the hegemonic stories within history and allow for a simultaneous creation, observation, and performance of history that "enable a conception of historiography that exists in multiple places at once, incorporates many voices (some contradictory), and is distributed, sometimes bodily, among many unique perspectives" (512). Compared to the commemorative wall, the artistic archive centers the victims in less essentialist terms, focusing on the lives they lived and their sociopolitical subjectivities. The digital archive sits on a plane between official commemorative narrative and user-led experience that underscores the complexities of archipelagoes of longing.

The user experience is present immediately on the website landing page, where the One Orlando Collection gallery informs users of the collaborative effort between the Orange County government and the Orange County Regional History Center to "document the impact and legacy of the Pulse tragedy" (One Orlando Collection, *Keep the Pulse*). Yet like the commemorative wall, it asks users to contribute to the story by sending photos.

Figure 2.6. Image of the One Orlando Collection Gallery landing page. *Source:* Photo by the author.

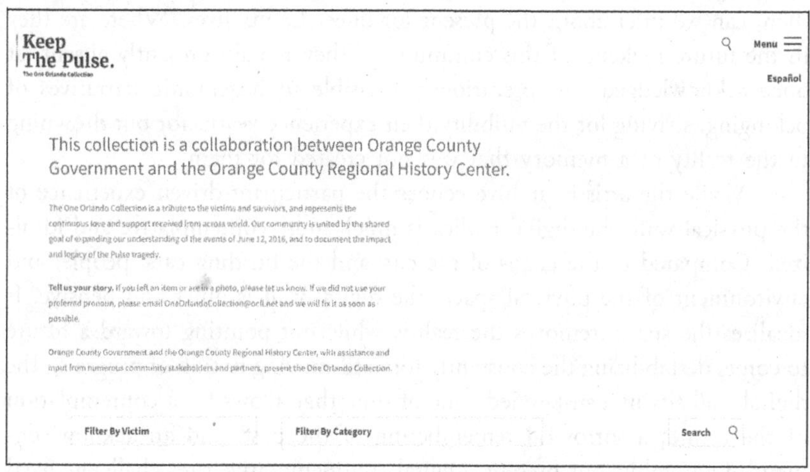

The performance of commemoration becomes a key feature of this archive. The tensions are laid bare: Hegemonic actors and mourning participants sit together. Users are requested, "Tell us your story. If you left an item or are in a photo, please let us now. If we did not use your preferred pronoun, please email OneOrlandoCollection@ocfl.net and we will fix it as soon as possible." This declaration mirrors the user kiosks at the physical site that ask visitors to send photos and participate in the act of commemoration. The digital space and the physical space become fraternal twin versions of each other, echoing the interactive nature yet providing for distinct contemplations to occur. While the wall presents a slowly decaying articulation of a commemoration's commemoration, the digital space and artifacts allow for a moving polyvocality to exist. The mosaic artistic archive allows for multiple contemplations that offer a sometimes-contested representation of queer Latinx lives. While not a wholesale solution, the simultaneous visibility and invisibility of Latinx peoples begins to offer open-ended, less sanitized contemplation of lives that are often overlooked in normative narratives. Speaking of queer temporalities, Alexis Lothian notes, "What looks normative and oppressive through one lens may appear differently through another, and we will better understand the complexities of queer political possibility in the present if we angle our analysis through multiplex frames" (10). The inclusive mosaic allows for a rupturing of normative understanding and replication of heteronormative patriarchal standards of memory by examining it through "multiplex frames" of gender, sexuality, race, and nation. What, then, can we infer about the present for queer Latinx lives? Where are they in the future makeup of this community? They remain presently absent, at once acknowledged and precariously invisible to hegemonic narratives of belonging, striving for the visibility their experience yearns for but drowning in the reality of a memory that was not created for them.

While the artistic archive echoes the participant-driven experience of the physical wall, the digital replica is much more contemplative and idealized. Compared to the chaos of the city and the bustling cars, people, and environment of the physical space, the digital wall is quiet and pensive. It idealizes the space, removes the reality, while not pointing toward a future to come, destabilizing the constantly forward-moving notion of progress. The digital wall sits in a suspended zone of time that allows for a contemplation of the future, a sorrowful remembering of the past, and an acknowledgment of an ambiguous present. Digital commemorative sites challenge fixed constructs of space and time by providing infinite and global access to the sites being commemorated, not limiting the spectators to members of the community (Widrich). The wall's temporal effect echoes what Lothian calls "old futures" that allow it to critically relay the way time and place affects queer lives. Rather than understanding queer futurity in idealized terms, one must contemplate the past, recognizing the present and trying to think through an equitable future (Lothian 2). In examining the past, present, and future, one can begin to fall into the idealized trap of that future, which negates the sociopolitical struggle of the present and carries said struggle forward and reproducing them (3). The replica does just that.

Initially the digital replica sits in a black void of the internet, lit by spotlight illumination. The spectator can then focus into the space. Once "inside," the viewer maneuvers around the digital replica by clicking on the images or on circles on the virtual floor. Viewers can zoom in on the images or through the circle to have a broader view of the images. Zooming in does not always provide a clearer view, but some images become grainier, erasing the individuality of each, while others remain the same as at the physical site. The spectator can take a 360-degree turn through the digital space, as if transported to the actual location. Initially the sky is twilit, with purple, pink, orange, and yellow hues lending an atmospheric feel to the wall. This dusk gestures to the lack of delineated problems that this site challenges, never clear whether it is day or night, light or dark, queer or Latinx. The cacophony of images, where smiling faces, grieving mourners, and a community in solidarity are pinned on an unchanging "serpentine billboard," honoring the lives lost in a timeless-scape, with a perfect sunset and cars blurred in the background as if time has stood still. As the spectator moves to the left using the dots on the ground, the sky begins to darken, eventually leading to the rear of the wall, where it is night and a rainbow light illuminates part of the wall itself. The digital wall is exclusive of the material realities of the real world, stuck in a place where perfect sunsets and social harmony rule the day. In this world the clouds never darken, the teddy bears never fade, and progress is never made either. A false sense of stability takes hold.

This archipelago of interests, mourners, faces, and feelings is a confluence of subjectivities in tension, not least because the events of June 12 put forth the place of queer lives on local, national, and international stories, but also because of the structures themselves. The digital wall remains an in-between commemoration, waiting for time to begin again, ever unresolved. Much the same way that we will see a looping of time in chapter 4 and a standstill of time in chapter 3, here there is a type of "liquid time," to use Marianne Hirsch and Leo Spitzer's term. The metaphor evokes the

Figure 2.7. Collection of painted tiles depicting Pulse victims on the One Orlando Collection Gallery landing page. *Source:* Photo by the author.

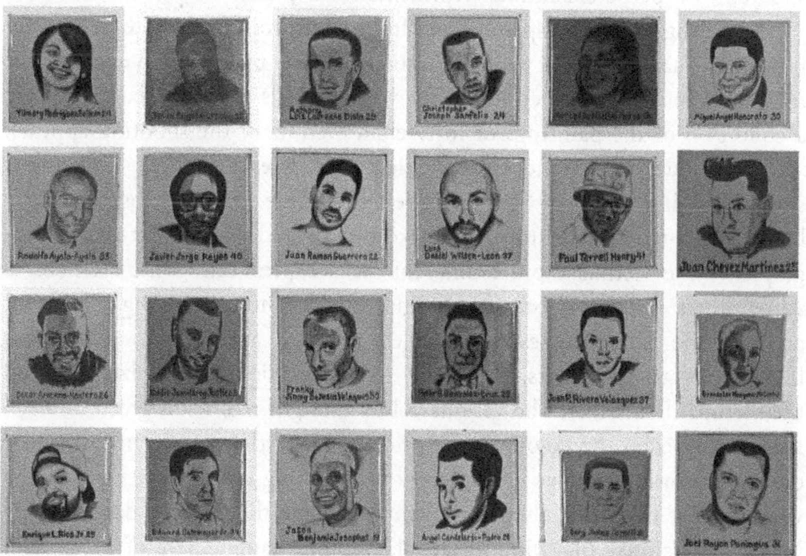

liquid chemicals used to develop film, where resubmerging the film in the liquid continues to change the development of the image and allows new interpretations to manifest (110). The digital space makes it possible for this liquid time to exist, having spectators come back to the images as they change, reinterpreting and reimagining potentialities that never were. Much like the place of Puerto Ricans in the US psyche, at once "belonging to" but not fully part of the United States, a type of stagnant change emerges. Similar to their political status on the island, which remains in a perpetual colonial limbo, the place of this commemorative site gestures toward the tense relationship. These unsettled details ultimately destabilize the fixity of memorial articulations often found in the narratives of traumatic events. While memory is often understood as inherently malleable and stemming from different points of interaction, vestiges of this idealized past and future are still found in this mosaic. The digital commemorative wall's mosaic holds together the many different aspects of the memory formations, which are contradictory at times, and idealized in other moments. Rather than presenting a future that simply replicates past pain, it sheds light on the present circumstance and subjectivity of this memory, one that is complex. This is a less seductive endeavor than the essentialist assertions of the past or the idealized, awe-inspiring thoughts for the future that often replicate the very power dynamics they attempt to break. This digital replica, with its incongruencies, sheds light on the way queer Puerto Rican bodies are situated in a perpetual liminal representational plane.

The digital wall suspends time in an anachronistic nod to a peaceful mourning that never was while the artistic archive pushes forth an inclusive representation. On the website, as the visitor scrolls down the landing page, a collection of tile paintings of forty-eight victims of the shooting appears. The individual tiles center, albeit briefly, the lives lost, each featuring a small black-ink image of a victim, their full name, and their age against a brightly colored monochromatic backdrop. In addition to the art, photographs of the victims capture different facial expressions; some are pensive while others smile, and others stare into the distance, providing a different angle of the archipelagoes of this memory. This approach to memory is less wedded to the events, to society, to the location, emphasizing instead the victims themselves. The various colors—bright red, neon green, orange, navy blue—echo the colors of the pride flag, yet they are in no particular order, celebrating a queer subjectivity but centering the victims' lives. When viewers click on a tile, they are taken to a page that simply describes the image as "Painted tile with image of [victim's name], part of a series of depictions of the Pulse Nightclub shooting" (One Orlando Collection, "Javier Jorge Reyes"). The only other information provided is the name of the victim and the artwork's size. Absent is any external information that would sideline the victim. This initial page recognizes the victims as people, not only their socially constructed subjectivity as to break up the shrouding that occurs in the physical site.

Within the landing page, participants are able to filter commemorative acts by victim or by category and are also allowed to search. When participants click on the phrase "Filter by Victim," all forty-nine names appear, compared to the forty-eight that are present on the commemorative wall. A plethora of Hispanic surnames emerges, underscoring the Latinx nature of the event and overtaking the non-Hispanic names. Seeing the list of names collected in this fashion further illuminates the impact on the Latinx community. Upon clicking on one of names, participants are presented with an archipelago of images that have been marked with the victims' names as keywords. Generic images, the same ones found on the commemorative wall, are mixed with more person-specific photos that heighten the humanity of the victims. These images move away from whitewashed depictions of mourners in state-backed forums, and rather portray individuals spending time with friends, asserting their sexuality, loving life. Take, for instance,

Figure 2.8. Page of the painted tile of Javier Jorge Reyes. *Source:* Photo by the author.

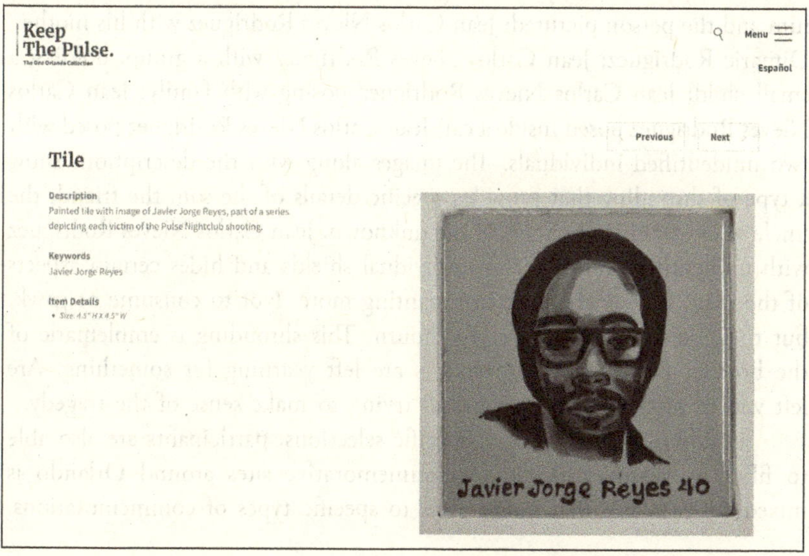

the page of Javier Jorge Reyes, age forty, who is represented spending time with friends, playing in nature, and posing for a selfie (One Orlando Collection, "Javier Jorge Reyes"). Other images include a Puerto Rican flag with his name on it. Many of the victims have their name on the flag of a Latin American country, pointing toward their country of origin. Almost all have US flags, confirming to viewers that these people were both US and of Latinx descent and asserting that they too are part of the national fabric, thereby connecting this tragedy to a broader national narrative where hegemonic discourses sit together with subjective identities. More personal notes, such as a handwritten message on a blue notecard that reads "We will never forget you" with orange stickers, recognizes a nameless friend who on the reverse says, "Javier Jorge Reyes / there's no tears in heaven / peace my friend (heart)." These artifacts weave a sparse narrative that is missing details that would be necessary to fully understand these lives but offers just enough to understand the humanity that was lost. Rather than essentializing the victims as solely queer Puerto Rican, Dominican, or Cuban, among other nationalities, we see a much more complex subjectivity that repeats certain hegemonic tropes while also celebrating their Latinidad.

What is often striking behind the victim-specific sections are pictures of their friends, family, relatives, nieces, and nephews. For instance, the section of Jean Carlos Nieves Rodriguez is flooded with images of a man living his life. Of the twenty-four images on the first page, nineteen are of him and his community. Clicking on the images reveals a description of him and the person pictured: Jean Carlos Nieves Rodriguez with his mother, Dimarie Rodriguez; Jean Carlos Nieves Rodriguez with a group, holding a small child; Jean Carlos Nieves Rodriguez posing with family; Jean Carlos Nieves Rodriguez posed inside a car; Jean Carlos Nieves Rodriguez posed with two unidentified individuals. The images along with the descriptions show a type of shrouding that provides specific details of the son, the friend, the uncle who was lost—but also of the unknown. Jean Carlos Nieves Rodriguez with unidentified child, friend, individual shields and hides certain aspects of the man, leaving the spectator wanting more. Not to consume or gawk, but to understand. To grieve. To mourn. This shrouding is emblematic of the broader mural, where spectators are left yearning for something. Are left with a plethora of emotions, all trying to make sense of the tragedy.

In addition to the victim-specific selections, participants are also able to filter by category. A list of commemorative sites around Orlando is mixed with themes that guide users to specific types of commemorations.

Figure 2.9. Screenshot for Jean Carlos Rodriguez's landing page. *Source:* Photo by the author.

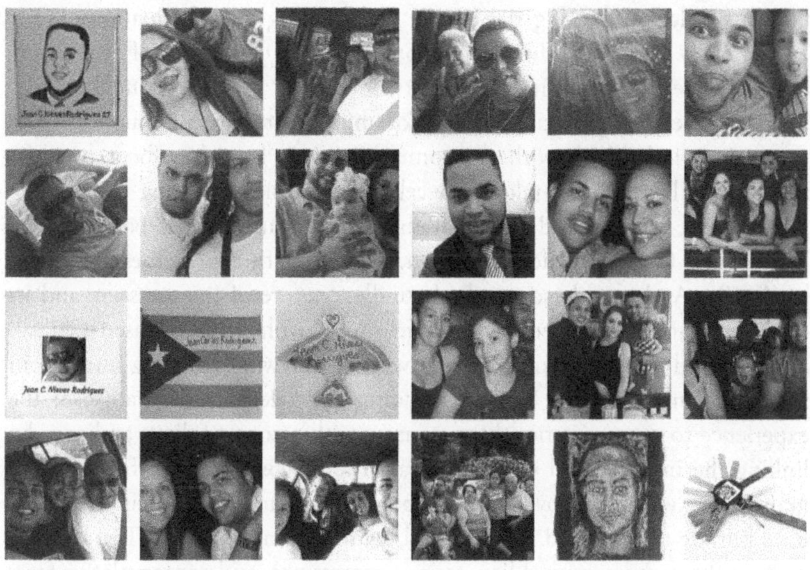

When visitors click on "Filter by Category," various topics such as locations, specific artworks, and a "General" category guide them through imposed narratives. The images are the same ones that are categorized under the victim-specific categories. Under "Events and Vigils," the pictures repeat the focus on commemoration around the Central Florida area. Groups of people praying, holding candles, and holding images of loved ones fill this category. It points to the commemorative wall by displaying pictures of mourners from the commemorative wall that establish a hegemonic narrative of whitewashed queer lives, reminding spectators of the power brokers involved. The "General" category shines the most, despite its unintriguing name. This section contains nothing but photos of the victims living their lives. It turns into a cacophony of proms, weddings, house parties, children's birthdays, dating app photos, and on and on. The victims are not, then, only serving as props in a national fundraising campaign but populate a collective album of memories for the world to see. These pictures become the world's pictures as it mourns locally, nationally, and internationally. People beyond Orlando can relate to at least one of the images. These categories work to move between the external world and the interior lives of these people. The artistic archives allow visitors to bounce around from topic to person to place, repeating the images and creating new destinations.

Finally, just like at the commemorative wall, a cacophony of experiences emerges here too, asserting the importance of the lives lived and lost. The images housed in the section titled "Community Artwork and Support" link the various individuals with the community writ large but focus on their humanity. These images take on a celebratory tone, depicting the smiling faces of the victims and using bright colors against black backgrounds. Within the One Orlando Collection, the series titled "Heroes for Love" by Aquiles Avalos underscores the boundless nature of the massacre and its commemoration. First seen on the website Movilh, the US-based Chilean artist created a type of kaleidoscope with the artwork, moving away from the sterile images of the wall yet echoing the kaleidoscopic nature of the experience to create a series that resonates with a cosmopolitan audience by linking the international with the local. The images are taken from photographs that were used by family members to memorialize their lost loved ones but are transformed into colorful commemorative pieces. Their smiles, gazes at the viewers, pursed lips, serious expressions, and contemplative faces once again challenge the unitary imaginary of queer Latinx lives. While the images have a connective color scheme and form, the artist balances the individual person with the collective experience to create a powerful kaleidoscope of queer (and allied) lives. Together these artworks and the digital space challenge existing narratives by creating an archipelago that is not settled but in constant contestation. It is not fixed or finished but opens up new contemplations regarding the tensions that Latinx subjects experience within the queer community and the US psyche broadly. The myriad commemorative photos do not fit into idealized narratives but instead into one that sits perpetually on a contemplative tension that reflects the unfinished nature of Latinx subjectivities.

The digital artistic space shows that by their nature commemorations are places filled with paradoxes that cannot be resolved. The act of commemorating is both social and political as it requires an understanding of both individual and group remembrances, and its "results may appear consensual when they are in fact the product of processes of intense contest, struggle, and in some instances annihilation" (Gillis 5). Queer groups have attempted to answer this "annihilation" by erecting their commemorations in what can be called queer monuments, "heritage sites" that specifically focus on the lives of the LGBTQI+ community that assist in moving away from stagnant hegemonic cultural representations (Orangias et al. 706). The artistic archives studied in this chapter decenter hegemonic discourses that concurrently exclude LGBTQI+ peoples and Latinx peoples by excavating queer Latinx victims at the center of the massacre. Queer monuments by their nature move away from stagnant ideas of commemoration to contest hegemonic cultural standards and allow the political intentions of the memorial sites to be read (Orangias et al. 706). While an engagement with the political intentions of the organizations responsible for these commemorative sites is not within the scope of this chapter, I want to emphasize the contradictory nature of this gallery. Hegemonic discourses and minoritized subjectivities sit together, providing for a more broadly encompassing commemorative wall. Through these artifacts, artworks, and the website, experiences and discourses are folded together. The delineation of each is muddled, acknowledging the simultaneous nature of archipelagoes of longing.

Conclusion

Memory always tries to conjure the past, changing and morphing to better understand the present. This elucidation is what allows for the structures and oppressions of the past to sit in the present and be carried on into the future. Memory creates a continuity in time and place that maintains power structures and narratives that are toxic to marginalized communities. In this commemorative wall and in the digital space, time is suspended in a way that contests the linear notion of progress. While the physical space experiences the visible vestiges of time going by, the digital space is set in a frozen (stagnant) zone that expands access and highlights the important traits of the wall. There is an inclusive-exclusion, what I label as shrouding, that defines queer Latinx subjectivities in the United States. The digital wall sits in tandem with the artistic archive that shows a plethora of lives, experiences, and identities that make up the queer Latinx community. Smiling faces, flags with names, notes to loved ones, and artistic renderings of the people lost come together to build out a second, inclusive commemoration that breaks fixed narratives around commemorative sites. Together, the physical wall, its digital replica, and the artistic archive show the incongruencies of commemorations and memory-making that must come together to understand the often uncomfortable realities of memory-making. Rather than give a singular understanding of the events of June 12, 2016, these collective sites show the diversity of life and experience that must be understood to represent justly.

Since the writing of this chapter, the permanent commemoration in Orlando has not manifested. Marred by issues of money and representation, in the spring of 2024 the City of Orlando bought the lot and has plans to build scaled-down version of the original plan. Meanwhile, the Osceola County, which has one of the largest communities of Puerto Ricans in the Central Florida area, has broken ground on a permanent memorial (Serrano 2024). Even San Juan, a city thousands of miles away, erected a commemorative site to honor the lives lost (Brydum 2016). Yet Orlando's site continues to languish, adding an additional representational blow to a community long in need of one. The power of commemorations sits in their ability to provide a physical, or digital, space where one can come with their thoughts and reflect, think, understand, and most importantly, feel. In the chaos of the Orlando site, Puerto Ricans have needed to find alternative ways to do so, and hundreds of murals and depictions have emerged across the city, demonstrating that one does not need hegemonic actors to have effective mechanisms for mourning and feeling. Orlando Ricans have found their own ways to engage in these acts, away from state actors, that show a bit of resistance. Much in the same way, these acts of mourning collectively will be the centerpiece of the next chapter.

These first two chapters have centered the representation of Latinx and Puerto Rican life in Chicago, Philadelphia, and Orlando, demonstrating that excluded peoples, national histories, and tragedy are complex, multifaceted sites where longing emerges. Archipelagoes of longing do the uneasy work of bringing in such disparate narratives into a singular fold. What follows are two chapters that center the experience of island-based Puerto Ricans and how colonialism warps longing. I move away from thinking with only neoliberal-racial constructs of representation and belonging to dissect how colonialism exacerbates existing systemic failure by administrative officials and the long history of mismanagement. The next chapter will focus on the way emerging affective consciousness creates a "Rican wake work" that explores longing in moments just after natural disaster strikes. Through the use of *testimonios*, the lines between a human disaster and natural catastrophe are blurred through affective charges. What unfolds is a contemplation of yet-to-be-finished longing that is a major element of the Puerto Rican experience.

Chapter 3

In Hurricane Maria's Wake

Mourning, Catastrophe, and Consciousness
in (Post-)Disaster Puerto Rico

> Y triste, el jibarito va pensando así
> Diciendo así, llorando así por el camino
> ¿Qué será de Borinquen mi Dios querido?
> ¿Qué será de mis hijos y de mi hogar?
>
> —"Lamento borincano," Rafael Hernández Marín

In the 1929 bolero "Lamento borincano," written by songwriter Rafael Hernández Marín,[1] the lyrics tell the story of a Puerto Rican *jíbaro* who migrates from the Puerto Rican countryside to the city to sell the crops he has cultivated. He leaves his home happy and hopeful, looking for better opportunities ahead, but when he finally arrives at the urban market, he ends up selling nothing. The *jíbaro* comes to learn that the city, too, is in need of economic resources, and his dream of material gain is quickly squashed. So, as the song goes, and as the epigraph notes, the jíbaro leaves saddened, asking, "¿Qué será de Borinquen mi Dios querido? ¿Qué será de mis hijos y de mi hogar?" (What will become of my dear Borinquen? What will become of my children and my home?). The song, written nearly a century ago, captures the early catastrophe that US economic policies were wreaking on Puerto Ricans in the initial days of the US occupation. Now, in the twenty-first century, it continues to have the same emotional resonance for Puerto Ricans lamenting their economic, political, and social reality. An unofficial national anthem, the song captures the emotional weight that colonialism has brought. As in the song, where Puerto Ricans lament—or mourn—an uncertain future, today Puerto Ricans continue to ponder what will become of their dear archipelago as climate change, economic policies, and colonial administration continue to ravage their home. The lamentation of today became much more acute after the passage of Hurricane Maria and an increased awareness of colonialism's aftereffects. While the *jíbaro* in Hernández Marín's song mourns his inability to feed his children and the uncertainty of his home, today Puerto Ricans lament natural disasters, colonial decay, and an uncertain future that will not improve. Lamentation becomes the central theme of this chapter.

So far, this book has concentrated on the ways visual representations attempt to recuperate excluded populations, histories, and stories from Puerto Ricans' past and national narratives. This chapter moves to a less concrete and more ephemeral aspect of longing that arises just after catastrophe strikes—or has always existed. The previous chapter explored the way that representation and longing after a massacre muddled the mourning process for the victims and families of the Pulse shooting. In that massacre Puerto Ricans mourned in the immediacy of loss after a violent act is carried out. In this chapter I shift the notion of mourning to a longer melancholia in the shadows of colonialism by examining selected *testimonios* from *Pa la posteridá: Antología sobre el paso del huracán María por Puerto Rico* (2018), edited by Lucía Orsanic and Jorge Fusaro Martínez, and *Voces desde Puerto Rico pos-huracán María*, edited by Iris Morales (2019).[2] These texts bring together a variety of artists, community activists, academics, and leaders to relay the destructive impact of Hurricane Maria on various aspects of Puerto Rican politics, society, and culture. Ranging in style, genre, and tone, the various works bring about a collective consciousness by detailing the material and political devastation that ensued. Rather than pointing the blame to a single person, cause, or event, the texts show the broad impact of colonial administration and how Maria has revealed this reality. Through these *testimonios* I show how emotions are an important and powerful tool in longing's emergence when things are not quite finished but new engagements with colonial structures force a material and existential desire to escape. The works analyzed reflect the constant toggling between material, emotional, structural devastations that are woven together by affective charges.

It is through testimonios inherent malleability that I demonstrate the multivalent nature of longing much in the way Christina Sharpe's *In the Wake: On Blackness and Being* paints a clear picture of the material and existential suffering along with consciousness-making that living in the wake of slavery forces. Sharpe constructs the idea of "living in the wake" for Black peoples in the Americas as a way to understand the legacy of slavery both materially and epistemologically (15). To Sharpe, living in the wake constitutes the realm of nonbeing within social and state constructs and the material decay that has continued since emancipation (5). Yet Black peoples in the Americas are not one-dimensional beings, and they too resist, eking out an existence in the face of colossal obstacles for a mere survival. Sharpe moves away from academic structures that reproduce the same corrosive forms that lead to premature Black death and thinks through what she calls "wake work," or "plotting, mapping, and collecting the archives of the everyday of Black immanent and imminent death, and . . . tracking the ways we resist, rupture, and disrupt that immanence and imminence aesthetically and materially" (13). The wake becomes both a praxis and an analytic for examining Black life. Sharpe divides her theorization of "living in the wake" into three main frames: wake as a type of mourning, wake as the material vestige of a ship passing in the water, and wake as a form of consciousness (21). As I explained in the introductory chapter, where Puerto Ricans are colonial-racialized peoples on the island and a second-classed racialized group once on the mainland, the same structural oppressions that Sharpe declares in her work—legacies of slavery, racism, capitalism—are at play in the Puerto Rican contexts. While Sharpe is speaking from a specific African American racial context, many of the all-encompassing aspects of slavery's aftermaths, including its racial and capitalist oppressions, have the similar impacts as colonialism's stifling present in Puerto Rico. Given this framing, *testimonios* provide a praxis and lens to better understand "living in the wake" for Puerto Ricans—ergo what I call a "Rican wake work." In thinking with Sharpe, I show the complexities of archipelagoes of longing that are not yet complete, continued, and continuing. The testimonials weave various moods, (im)materialities, and realizations that form part of the Puerto Rican experience. The testimonials expose the often incoherence of a Rican longing that stems from colonial exhaustions. A longing to go back to an imperfect past, a longing for a stable future that does not reproduce previous mistakes, and a longing for a sovereignty that has no clear end. Rather than engage with the aftermath of Hurricane Maria in fixed and concrete terms, I show how archipelagoes of longing excavate the yet-to-be resolved nature of Puerto Rican collective longing through an affective charge. Or, within a "Rican wake work," which is expressed through literary form and a way to understand Hurricane Maria and the events since 1898—if not more—that cause Puerto Ricans to live as an afterthought to the United States.

Furthermore, a "Rican wake work" has an affective core. Emotions, as Sara Ahmed reminds us, are relational, allowing us to move toward or away different objects and may stick or not to certain objects (8). Emotions need not have political ends to have an impact on the way people engage with the world around them. Thus, feelings and emotions open up new pathways to understand social relations. In reading these *testimonios*, I employ the lens of Raymond Williams's "structure of feeling," the social understandings that are lived and felt but that have not yet been concretized into formalized institutions (24). Manifesting in art and literature, these structures of feeling provide a framework for articulating emergent and pre-emergent ideas that move away from thinking of social forms in fixed terms. To Williams this is not an either-or dichotomy between fixed and unfixed, but a relationship between the two that is still developing. He uses the word "feeling" precisely because it does not delineate a "worldview" or "ideology" but rather underscores the in-process nature that occurs with affect (23–24). I use "structures of feeling" because this framework starts to put the contours of articulation to a consciousness that is being understood through affective moments. Puerto Ricans have long struggled materially under colonial rule, and the *testimonios* build out the various layers and nodes of consciousness that are linked to Maria but not solely because of Maria. The *testimonios* show a yet-to-be-defined process of affective manifestations that calls into question to what, by whom, and when emotions happen. The feelings brought about because of Maria are part of the fluid nature of archipelagoes of longing, the seas and oceans that connect the islands, which are not fixed but moving and constantly emerging. These undefined longing articulations add an affective layer that is important in consciousness-making.

Testimonios have long been a powerful tool in post-dictatorship Latin America for exposing the wrongs of previous regimes and providing a type of catharsis to a people reeling from the autocracies of past leaders. Straddling biography, fiction, and a political act, the genre resists a singular definition while dismantling hegemonic narratives in an attempt to make its own hegemonic story (Achugar). *Testimonios* in this chapter are akin to John Beverley's oft-cited definition of "a novel or novella-length narrative in book or pamphlet . . . form, told by a narrator who is also the real protagonist or witness of the events he or she recounts, and whose unit of narration is usually a 'life' or a significant life experience" (13). While *testimonio* writers often speak for a community (16), the writers in this chapter at once speak in a collective voice and for the community while also engaging with their own individual struggles post–Hurricane Maria. The devastations of the hurricane shape the fragmentary nature of the accounts that follow. *Testimonio* lends itself to this type of catastrophe writing because it opens up multiple pathways of expression that one single genre might not be able to accomplish. The two Maria-related collections include over sixty individual yet interrelated vignettes that range in scope of genre, style, and purpose. I have selected these pieces to provide a large breadth of style while also maintaining a cohesive thread of the work of the wake in this examination.

The dividing line between *testimonio* as an individual writing act and as a collective articulation of traumatic events and systems is blurry. The *testimonios* become a corrective to official government discourses that obfuscated actual death tolls (Robles et al.), a refutation of US government rhetoric about Puerto Rican mismanagement (Landler), and a denunciation of how Puerto Ricans received less aid compared to the victims of hurricanes in Texas and Florida (Johnson). In thinking of these indignities, this chapter examines the various ways the authors engage in their testimonials and push against hegemonic actors' accounts of the events and emotions of the hurricane. In the end, what makes these texts *testimonios* is their ability to write (and speak) against the hegemonic actors in Puerto Rico that have stifled narratives, changed them, or created false ones in an effort to perpetuate the colonial reality that the archipelago lives under. I read these texts a type of testimonio because they provide a plethora of genres that articulate Maria's aftermath and colonialism's continuation through various methods. Together these different genres build out a collective understanding that tackles various affective and material realities. Through form itself these authors convey various messages after Maria's wake. Thus, these *testimonios* become a vehicle for a "Rican wake work" in which Puerto Rican collective mourning, material aftermaths, and colonial consciousness are exposed and "attend to the direness of the multiple and overlapping presents that we face" (Sharpe 22). These *testimonios* are not only a documentation of this reality but also a therapeutic collective act that assists in providing alternative discourses regarding colonialism in the wake of Maria.

In what follows I toggle between texts from each collection to demonstrate three key points: the material and immaterial effects of colonialism, the power of affect, and future possibilities of colonial understanding. Longing straddles various nodes—past and present, material and affective, hope and despair—that underscore longing's contradictions. I begin with a contextualization of Hurricane Maria's material aftermath and provide a contemplation on how colonialism led to the catastrophic consequences of the event. I follow this explanation with an examination of electricity as a symbol whose material lack poses affective responses to the hurricane. Not solely a crisis of the hurricane, electricity becomes a powerful stand-in for colonialism writ large on the island. I move on to the power of mourning, not just of the lives lost but also with the realization that things were not better before the storm and likely will never improve. How do you mourn what never was and never will be? While this question is never fully answered, I show how these writers sit with this profound question in the midst of catastrophe. I end the section with the power of colonial consciousness. Here, I excavate how realizing that you are a colony is a powerful tool in building a way forward materially and existentially. In the various sections you will see how material affects, emotional responses, and political consciousness interweave to fill in the gaps of archipelagoes of longing.

Maria Was Just the Catalyst

The 2017 Category 5 storm left behind over four thousand people dead, millions of dollars in devastation, and the revelation for many Puerto Ricans that they are, in fact, colonial subjects. Much the same way living in the wake for Black lives constitutes mourning, a material vestige, and a consciousness, for Puerto Ricans in the archipelago, living in the wake of Hurricane Maria means mourning their colonial present and the real material destruction. A collective consciousness emerges. Natural disasters are apocalyptic in that they are revelatory; take, for example, the 2010 earthquake that revealed Haiti to the world. The earthquake, which killed hundreds and ravaged the island nation, laid bare the centuries of racist and colonial policies that never allowed the first Black republic in the Americas to flourish (Díaz). Likewise, Hurricane Maria and its wake revealed Puerto Rico to the world. And to itself. Puerto Ricans have long thought of their relationship to the United States as being defined by "the best of both worlds," where they are able to maintain their cultural autonomy while also holding US passports, deciding their own internal affairs, and being safeguarded on the world stage by US imperial endeavors (Bonilla, *La Brega*). Yet, the devastation of natural disasters and political turmoil have put a giant asterisk on these benefits and have started to make Puerto Ricans question the true nature of their relationship with the United States. Hurricane Maria is not the sole event that forced these doubts, but it is the final straw in a long list of instances where Puerto Ricans have been shown, told, and experienced their colonial status.

Hurricane Maria was neither the first crisis nor the last to hit the island, but its impact on Puerto Rican national consciousness cannot be overstated. For Puerto Ricans in the diaspora, the sense of despair knowing they could not help loved ones during the storm was only heightened by the gross mismanagement that followed. For Puerto Ricans on the island, the catastrophe that ensued was both mindboggling and all too predictable. The impact of the hurricane cannot be disconnected from the economic decline the island has experienced for the last several decades, nor from the colonial administration that had enacted failed policies, leading to an ineffective power grid, political system, and economic recovery. In this section I want to briefly contextualize the economic crisis that exacerbated Maria's devastation on the island and the colonial policies that limited, delayed, or even prevented aid to the island's 3.25 million people. It is important to note that prior to its passage on September 20, 2017, Puerto Rico had been recovering from the aftermath of Hurricane Irma, which struck ten days prior and wreaked havoc on the island, making it the second-costliest natural disaster only after Hurricane Maria (FEMA, 1–7). Hurricane Irma forced 70% of the island into darkness (Ferré-Sadurní). The return of electrical power was at best inconsistent throughout the island after Irma, where urban and wealthier areas saw the return earlier and faster (Talbot et al. 2022). Moreover, the blackouts after these two hurricanes accelerated the privatization of the public energy company by the American-Canadian company LUMA Energy (Roque Antonetty 67–68). While the purchase of the company initially spurred hopes of a revitalization of renewable sources of energy, the company has not be able to manage the problems that were facing the power system, which has led to public discontent (68)—just another example of the "aftershocks" where a series of catastrophes constantly impact the island, as discussed by Bonilla and LeBrón. Simultaneously, certain policies, such as the cabotage law that manages shipment policy for the United States, greatly hindered access to critical food, medical, and other lifesaving support the island urgently needed. The natural disasters of Hurricane Irma and Maria along with the colonial policies created a confluence of events that explain the various points of interest in this chapter. While in the introductory chapter I delineated the broad colonial relationship between the United States and Puerto Rico since the 1952 constitution, this section will focus on the economic policy of the second half of the twentieth century, leading up to the enactment of the fiscal oversight board.

Since the 1970s Puerto Rico has endured a series of economic policies handed down by the US Congress. Standing on the brink of an economic recession after the collapse of oil importation revenue in the early 1970s, in 1976 Congress modified part of the US tax code to allow tax exemptions on earnings made in Puerto Rico (Meléndez and Venator-Santiago 2). With the new provisions working as intended, by the 1990s Puerto Rico was a hub for pharmaceutical companies manufacturing medicine for the US market. With its combination of low wages and highly skilled workers, Puerto Rico had a robust economic output. Puerto Rico's colonial relationship provided certain economic benefits while maintaining the long-standing second-class affiliation with the United States' neoliberal policies that extract while extending a semblance of equality. But all good things must come to an end, and seeing that large corporations were making billions in tax-exempt profit, President Clinton and the US Congress enacted legislation that would begin to phase out the tax benefit by 2005. While Section 936 underscores the disconnect between economic policies and a people's political will, it also highlights how Puerto Ricans became a pawn in the broader political system of the United States. Puerto Ricans and their elected leaders had no say in this decision that affected the backbone of its economy.

Certainly, Washington's actions had an outsized impact on Puerto Rico's economic security, yet Washington is not the only villain in the story. Local elected leaders, too, added to the economic chaos. Shortly after the removal of Section 936, the government of then-Governor Pedro Rosselló began large infrastructure projects that needed financing through government debt. Projects such as the *tren urbano*, a convention center, and road improvements, among others, created a huge debt load for the island (Meléndez and Venator-Santiago 3). Alongside this debt load, local politics prevented leaders from implementing fiscal and developmental policy that would wean Puerto Rico's economy off its reliance on US tax monies and invest in local businesses and industries (Meléndez 47). This increasing debt, low economic output, and the economic crash of 2008 that lasted longer and deeper in Puerto Rico compared to the rest of the mainland US culminated with the economic crisis of 2014. Then-Governor García Padilla declared Puerto Rico's debt unpayable, unleashing a scramble by Puerto Rico and US officials to come up with a plan to stabilize the Puerto Rican economy (44). PROMESA, or the Puerto Rico Oversight, Management, and Economic Stability Act, gave Puerto Rico a mechanism to restructure its debt and begin the long process to achieve fiscal viability. While heavily criticized at the time, according to Edwin Meléndez it was the only legally viable path for the island's economy, leading to the prioritization of Wall Street hedge funds over the daily needs of Puerto Ricans (44–45). Here is where the sinister reality of neoliberal colonial relations come to the fore. PROMESA enacted a litany of economic policies such as the gutting of schools, pensions, infrastructure—including emergency management—and local investment; all were limited or eliminated to repay Puerto Rico's debt. These policies were not one-offs, but a collection of decisions made outside of Puerto Rico that negatively impacted Puerto Rican lives. Hurricane Maria just exploded it all. As you will see in the text analysis, many of the writers' comment on problems beyond Maria that created a national sense of despair.

Economic policies are one piece of the broader puzzle, and government maleficence also impacted the needs of Puerto Ricans. For starters, immediately after the hurricane the local and federal response was wholly inadequate. Vital resources were not allowed to dock in Puerto Rican ports because of the 1920 Jones Act's cabotage provision, which was intended to protect US maritime interests and mandates that goods coming into Puerto Rico must land in a US-based port first (Meléndez and Venator-Santiago 8). Due to this law, goods and aid piled up just outside the Port of San Juan, to the frustration of millions of Puerto Ricans (Gillespie et al.). This, combined with local officials' inability to distribute the aid, further exacerbated problems (Healy et al.). Trump's delay in approving a ten-day waiver was seen by many as too little too late (Meléndez and Venator-Santiago 8). To make matters worse, the electrical grid had essentially been wiped out. The grid, which for decades had problems with reliability and output, was an archaic system that relied heavily on oil. The main power generators were in the southern part of the island, where the hurricane hit, wiping out access across the whole island. It is important to underscore how political interests and a lack of "planning vision" hampered, and often even blocked, efforts to update the grid (O'Neill-Carrillo and Rivera-Quiñones 151). For decades, oil, rather than renewable sources, was privileged for the benefit of external stakeholders such as the pharmaceutical industry, negatively impacting local infrastructures and environmental practices (Roque Antonetty 65). I bring up these two main points—the government's immediate response and long-term issues—to demonstrate the ways these forces feed off each other in nonlinear and incoherent ways. It is important to contextualize how although Maria was a major hurricane, even a historic one, the real tragedy was born of colonial failures: political leaders unable to enact policies, colonial rulers indifferent to people's living standards where economic interests were valued over human lives. This context helps to see how Puerto Rican longing is at times fractured because it is often hard to point to a singular culprit in its devastation. Structural, historical, and manmade failures shape Puerto Rican's longing to past, present, and future justice. In what follows the authors in Morales's volume and Orsanic and Fusaro's collection explore Maria as a material, emotional, and consciousness-creating catalyst after the inadequate response in the hurricane's wake.

Electricity as Symbol and as Resistance

The economic decline and impact of governmental mismanagement of electricity informs the collective longing throughout the two texts. Electricity is presented, both explicitly and implicitly, as a symbol of the precarity of everyday life in Puerto Rico; in addition, the idea of electricity as possible liberation holds out hope for a future free of US colonial chains. In these texts, electricity points both to concrete colonial realities and also to an affective despair that cannot quite be pinned to a singular cause. Puerto Ricans long for the concrete material gain of electricity while also for the liberation having electricity represents. Electricity is linked to other structural problems while also serving as a symbolic stand-in for the perils prior to Maria. While the texts will show how electricity can be a powerful way to decolonize Puerto Rico, the reader is left skeptical of the practicalities of the way forward when as recently as 2024, the power company, LUMA Energy, raised rates even as residents continued to suffer through increased power outages (Murphy-Marcos). Electricity in Puerto Rico becomes energy both as a product and as a relationship to power that highlights the material realities of colonial governing structures (De Onís 12). Within this duality, Puerto Ricans are stuck in an inability to progress even as they know the solutions.

In Maite Ramos Ortiz's poem "Pos-Huracán María," she details the daily slog of not having electricity. The lack of electricity turns her life into an almost Groundhog Day–like recurrence seen through repetition of the phrase "Todas las mañanas" [Every morning] followed by descriptions of quotidian actions. These actions span her daily routine, acquiring ice and breakfast, cooling water, and sitting on her terrace hoping for the electricity to return. Longing for an electrified past that was also in perpetual disarray. Buying ice and cooling the water for little moments of luxury become gargantuan tasks during those early days after the hurricane. These efforts also underscore the lack of US comforts in Puerto Ricans' everyday lives. The poem as form provides the reader with the same rhythmic and exhaustive flow of the day, reading both as a list of emotionless tasks and also as the affective drain of living without electricity. The idea of cooling as a legacy of colonialism shows not only the excesses of America but also how normative ideas of engaging with the tropics persist into the present (Hobart 8). Additionally, it is also a need for survival as the climate continues to heat; cooling and staying cool are existential requirements, heightening both the devastation and the despair after the hurricane. Ramos Ortiz states, "Todas las mañanas salgo a comprar hielo y el desayuno también con el miedo de perder la vida en alguna intersección" [Every morning I go out to buy ice and breakfast with the fear of losing my life at some intersection] (136); the ice as a comfort comes face to face with the flows of traffic that rely on electricity, and daily tasks become treacherous endeavors. Electricity needed for cooling by creating ice, electricity as maintaining order by powering traffic lights at intersections, and lack of electricity as expanding frustration are folded into one. The material and the affective are fused.

Beyond cooling, the lack of electricity creates robotic-like behaviors as Ramos Ortiz participates in daily tasks with a monotony devoid of any care. Ramos Ortiz dries herself, brushes her teeth, combs her hair, and gets dressed all "en completa oscuridad" [in complete darkness]. After acquiring ice she returns home to cool her water and simply "me como el desayuno" [eat breakfast]. This is followed by making tea on a gas stove, whereupon she needs to heat water again. With each task Ramos Ortiz details the dullness, showing how the lack of electricity makes the task more tedious. She is almost haunted by this lack, forced to be aware of every minute aspect of basic parts of her day. After finishing her morning routine, acquiring ice, cooling water, and making tea, the poetic voice is finally able to consume the tea she just prepared and says, "Y me siento a esperar, si ese día, por fin, regresa la electricidad" [And I sit and wait if that day, finally, the electricity returns] (137). A repetition occurs where everyday tasks without electricity are followed by sitting and thinking about the return of electricity. Electrical energy becomes a haunting, all-consuming desire—always present but at the same time never fully there. It forces her, and many Puerto Ricans like her, into a liminal space of waiting for a future that has no certainty. Electricity is a stand-in for not only the colonial reality but also the existential state of Puerto Ricans.

While electricity as infrastructure directly impacts the narrative voice in Ramos Ortiz's poem, the aftermaths of the lack of electricity take on a different meaning in the short story style of Carlos García Zambrana's "La fila de hielo" and Laura García Urrutia's "Empty," where queues for ice and gasoline, respectively, lead to unfulfilled desires for coolness. Like Ramos Ortiz's text, in which she too joins a queue, "La fila de hielo" and "Empty" dissect the emotional wait of the numerous long lines in Puerto Rico to obtain basic services. Like electricity, these queues become a symbol of a deeper material collapse. There is a temporal quality to the endless waiting in lines. Similar to the looping of time that will be explored in more depth in the next chapter, the people in these *testimonios* experience a slowness of time that limits their progress forward. The emotional defeat in García Zambrana's narrative and the short spurts of movement in Urrutia's story underscore the limiting progress and perpetual wait. What are Puerto Ricans waiting for, exactly? Besides the immediate answer of gasoline or ice, they're longing for the precarious past that, while unstable, is known, serving as a type of delusional discomfort. They long for a semblance of stability and comfort they know will likely never arrive.

In "La fila de hielo" García Zambrana paints a panorama of a typical queue for ice, merging local vernacular and depictions of tropes of Puerto Rican society with his own impatience regarding waiting for the ice. Throughout the text, the emotional weight of the moment rapidly grows, starting from initial annoyance at having to wait for ice and peaking with the discovery that the ice has run out, whereupon he declares he will never come back. García Zambrana uses various words and idiomatic expressions to detail both the event and its affective charge. His temporal backlog is seen in this moment. Like other aspects of Puerto Rican life explored in this book—colonialism, migration, governance—Puerto Ricans are stuck in a perpetual cycle they cannot escape, always repeating the same structural inadequacies but in new iterations. While humor is used here through the litany of phrases and words, one cannot help looking away, overwhelmed by the relentlessness of having no ice. Individual and collective struggle become merged in this fast-paced text that details a growing desperation. García Zambrana starts with "Ayer fui la fila del hielo. ¡Ay, santo! ¡Ay, bendito! ¡Ay, deja eso!" [Yesterday I went to the line for ice. Oh lord! Oh Jesus! Oh, let it be!] (67), capturing the exasperation of waiting in line and using local exclamations to describe this annoyance. He describes the rationale behind waiting for ice and the deep longing for something cool in the face of the never-ending heat. The faces he describes exhibit various levels of defeat; the words he uses[3]—*eñemao* (tired), *enfuchao* (angry), *encaprichao* (angry because they will not give you something you want), *estotorlao* (fucked up), *estrasijao* (very tired), and *envenenao* (to be irate)—set the tone for the way people are engaging not just with the wait but also with the broader circumstances.

Desire, anger, and fatigue set in all together and capture not just the moment of the queue but the general melancholy people are experiencing.

Globally, melancholia exists because of the perpetual discourses around utopias that are never met (Traverso 18). Revolutionary ideas and various social movements have thought through a utopia that is informed by the hazards of the past and propels the world forward to a place that is never arrived at (3–5). To Puerto Ricans, longing for basic necessities is very much front and center in a system that never actually achieved normalcy. Puerto Ricans are not speaking from a place that seeks a utopian future but rather from one that seeks just a semblance of normalcy, a striving for equality. The chatty woman standing next to García Zambrana, the useless police officer, and the suspicious person make cameos in this Rolodex of characters who make up the queue. He contemplates the reality he is facing and the irony of it all: surviving Maria only to possibly die waiting for ice. The story ends with the crescendo of the ice maker declaring, "¡Se acabó el hielo! . . . ¡Mal rayo me parta! Por un pelo!" [The ice is out! May lightning strike me now! By a hair's breadth!] The narrator uses a common phrase in Puerto Rican Spanish that calls for a lightning bolt to cut the speaker in half because of the circumstances. The narrator has waited four hours, only to end in the same ice-less state in which he started. At this point, defeat starts to set in. Using a series of idiomatic expressions that suggest it's better to have nothing than to want for something, the author tries to move past what he has just experienced. Each expression shifts the affect from anger to the self-soothing needed to overcome this perpetual adversity: "Lo que falta es sarna pa rascarse.[4] Lo que no va en lágrimas, va en suspiros, pero el mal de mucho es consuelo de todos.[5] No le demos largas al asunto, que no es más rico el que más tiene sino el que menos necesita.[6] Ya sé del calvario de las hormigas cuando le pasa la podadora al hormiguero" (68).[7] The phrases convey a general sense of "get over it" that binds the group together, acknowledging the frustration that no individual stands alone, that the whole island is under the same pressure. The quotidian nature of these phrases is juxtaposed with the real material weight of the situation. The irony here is not lost; using everyday platitudes for the magnitude of the problems that face Puerto Rico underscores the sense of ridiculousness regarding the residents' lack of electricity and ice, which are really proxies for stability and equity. But what is almost universally understood is the stark reality: The thing he came for never materialized.

García Zambrana's text captures the high-octane, kaleidoscopic nature of waiting for ice, where cooling and anger throw reality into high relief.

Urrutia's "Empty" depicts a different queue, one of people waiting for gasoline. Here the impatience builds not through the collection of locally specific words that capture the moment, but through the various people waiting in the line alongside the main narrative voice. Futilely seeking to find peace while waiting for gasoline, the protagonist finds that various factors and actors prevent her from finishing her sudoku puzzle. With the puzzle still uncompleted and the gasoline acquisition thwarted, Urrutia's story culminates in collective defeat. The story begins with the narrative voice, positioned behind the wheel at the tail end of the queue, acknowledging the long road ahead to obtain the precious resource. Gasoline, used not just for driving but to run generators to create electricity in homes and hospitals, was a basic necessity in those early days post-Maria. The short story–like testimonio allows the author to build out a complex connection with the reader, connecting the reader to everyday tasks of waiting in line while also detailing environmental and sensorial aspects of the gasoline line. Throughout the text, the informal second-person *tú* is used, bringing the reader into the story and building out the collective emotion of waiting in a gasoline line that will never produce gas. In this way, Urrutia indicts the reader, making them part of the same slog she is enduring, moving the reader out of their own comfort and into the narrative voice's discomfort. The narrative voice is fourteen blocks away from the gas station and notes, "Son las seis de la mañana así que sacas el libro de sudoku y sonríes. Eres la última en la fila" [It is six in the morning and you take out your sudoku book and smile. You are the last one in the line] (69). Sudoku, a Japanese puzzle that requires players to set the numerals 1 through 9 correctly in a box and in columns and rows with no repetition, becomes a parallel to the struggle she is about to face that day. It helps keep her entertained in the car as she creeps toward the gas station but also is a challenge to complete because of the multiple distractions she encounters. A double-edged sword of sorts. The narrative voice describes her surroundings: the man in front of her with his three kids, the fallen trees on the sidewalk, the brightly colored skies. She is hyperaware of her surroundings, accentuating the lack of electricity and her inability to be on her cell phone while she waits, which is why she is working on a sudoku instead. She recalls, "Antes, hubiese esperado en la fila explorando tu teléfono pero ahora prefieres el sudoku y dejas el celular apagado para usarlo cuando sea necesario" [Before, you would have waited in the line exploring your phone but now you prefer the sudoku puzzle and leave the phone turned off to use it when necessary] (69–70). From here the tension builds with the sentence "Prendes el motor, avanzas en la fila, frenas, estacionas, y apagas el motor" [You turn on the motor, you move forward in the line, you break, you park, and you turn off the motor] (70), where the various people in the story perform the same actions as they advance toward the gasoline. The narrative voice becomes increasingly agitated—first by the children in the car in front of her, and then by the truck driver behind her. The children play, scream, and disobey their father, who is, in turn, becoming increasingly agitated, yelling at his kids to get in the car as he, too, slowly advances. The truck driver, on the other hand, does not turn off his car to save energy and, in contrast to the narrative voice, uses his cell phone. An almost claustrophobic sense sets in through the heat, the rowdy kids, the truck behind her, the car in front of her, and the fits and starts of the line. A feeling of being stuck overtakes the text, and the narrative voice yells at the father to get a handle on the kids while the truck driver blares his horn for her to move forward. She goes back to the solace of her sudoku, only to realize that she has made a mistake. In a fury, she tears up the book, and the text continues: "Bocina, los monos brincan al carro del frente, más bocina, prende el motor, Avanza, frena, Avanza, frena, bocina, y apaga" [Blare your horn, the monkeys jump in the car in front of you, more honking, turn on the motor, you move forward, you break, you move forward, you break, you blare the horn, and turn off the motor] (72). This rhythmic flow shows the emotional ups and downs all within a day of waiting for gas. Hours later, she has finally made it to second in line when the gas station owner tells her, "Baby, se acabó la gasolina, Vete para tu casa" [Baby, the gasoline ran out, go home] (72). As for García Zambrana, the event ends in defeat, with no signs of progress, suffering the whole time in the oppressive heat, and realizing there is no way forward. Time is suspended during these occasions where people are unable to move. A loop of disappointment is created, a colonial pause that has no apparent end.

Ramos Ortiz and García Zambrana show the endless nature of life without electricity, characterized by an increasing sense of living on a treadmill, constantly having to start over in the same disappointing place where one began. In "Lecciones lúmicas de liberación," Yasmín Hernández's essay, she flips the idea of light on its head, contemplating light not as electricity but as a connection to ancestors that gives strength. Consciousness as resistance starts to take form, changing the view of electricity and light from things to be consumed, as the colonial discourse would have it, to possible forms of resistance—epistemological resistance that does not replicate the age-old toxic colonial relations. Rather than offering anecdotes about the events post-hurricane, Hernández provides an autobiographical and essay-style contemplation about the legacy of light and electricity on the island and the ways they can be seen as resistance, abundance, and shifting perspective. In doing so, Hernández mixes the affective moments of the time without electricity and a more intellectual challenging of what electricity really stands for on the island. The essay style challenges the reader to build consciousness, a point I will delve into later on in this chapter. This testimony adds to the archipelagoes of longing by unveiling another desire rooted in Indigenous cosmologies and awareness instead of lack and disappointment.

Hernández begins her text with a New Year's celebration. While sitting on her porch, she observes the fireworks in the valley where she lives, calling them "un testimonio declarando en luz: otra familia presente; otra familia que había aguantado la tormenta; otra familia que no se había ido; otra familia más, manifestándose en luz a través de la oscuridad" [a testimony declaring in light; another family present; another family that withstood the storm; another family that had not left; one more family, manifesting in light through the darkness] (144). She is aware that the fireworks' light is a form of resistance in the darkness, which stands as a metaphor for the darkness that is colonialism on the island. But she then shifts, declaring that the valley was never dark in reality and that the light used to illuminate the island was a farce, having given the people of Puerto Rico a sense of superiority over the neighboring islands only for Hurricane Maria to wipe it out. What was revealed in the five months of darkness, as she says, is the connection to practices of the ancestors: washing clothes by hand, for instance. But Puerto Ricans were also forced to look at natural ways of manifesting light, such as the planets in the heavens and the bioluminescent bays that produce light on their own. To her, these naturally occurring lights are a form of resistance to the manmade light that was brought in by the colonizers. These organic light sources connect to the ancestors and resist replicating colonial relations. The fireworks and the planets, though more inconsistent, are natural to the people. Real light, to her, comes from natural sources, not from imported electrical grids.

It is this idea of the imported light as oppression that shows Puerto Ricans how to rethink energy. References to Yemaya, Oyá, and Guabancex delve into the power of the ancestors to relay the story of how, through darkness, the island can achieve power and freedom. Hernández critiques the idea of the hurricane as destruction, casting it instead as a reminder of how to live in harmony with nature, explaining that the Indigenous peoples believed hurricanes were sent by the gods and noting that Oyá and Guabancex remind us "que ya somos libres" [we are already free] (147). Colonial labor forces are contrasted to the liberatory quality of darkness and learning to be free again. Bioluminescent bays, the stars, and glowworms are evidence of the existing light on the island. She reminds readers that "estas tierras nunca fueron oscuras" [these lands were never dark] (148) several times throughout the piece, building to the decolonizing work and potential that is needed when Puerto Ricans seek out the ancestors for light. She asks at the end of the essay, "¿Cómo podemos nosotros tomar acceso energético al lenguaje de la luz, esa luz trascendente añejada por la oscuridad, donde yace la sabiduría ancestral?" [How can we give energetic access to the language of light, that light that transcends aging in darkness, where the ancestral wisdom is forged?] (149). Her answer is that Puerto Ricans must seek knowledge from the land to become better shamans, the shapeshifters or wise men who are beings of light and freedom. Hernandez provides a reframing for how to think about light and electricity beyond the traditional binary of having and not having, pointing instead to already-have-had. In this reframing, energy becomes a way forward ideologically, forcing Puerto Ricans to rethink their relationship to electricity and, by extension, their unfreedom. She reveals energy/light as a form of decolonizing relationships to light and moving away from oppressive mentalities.

Just as electricity as a form of oppression is evident throughout the texts, so too is electricity as a form of resistance. The fluidity of energy's nodes (13), to use De Onís's words, comes into view in Arturo Massol-Deyá's essay "Nuestra insurrección enérgica." His essay posits a "solarity" in which solar power can be used to move away from fossil fuels and bring forth a more democratic and just world. Solarity offers a way to think through social structures and their relation to energy that does not replicate the power structures of the past, but develops solar energy as a liberatory mechanism for a way forward (Szeman and Barney 4). While a utopian understanding of this energy transition is not inherent in solarity, being mindful of the potential pitfalls is what "makes solarity both political and not just a technical way to conceive of the future" (6). Massol-Deyá's essay takes on a slightly different purpose, as it is used to raise awareness rather than detailing a series of events from the past. Here, Massol-Deyá constructs a plan of action using Puerto Rican–produced electricity and clean energy for the island. The essay form provides an intellectual hope for the future. A solutions-based understanding of what the island can achieve. Rather than long for a past that is in disarray, Massol-Deyá shows how Puerto Ricans should long for a viable future of an energy-independent island. Similar to the work mutual aid organizations do in liberating people through coming together, Massol-Deyá shows the liberatory potential for Puerto Rico.

Massol-Deyá, president of Casa Pueblo,[8] examines how self-sustaining electrical energy can be used not only to produce power for Puerto Rico but also as a form of collective action against the colonial power structure. Furthermore, he calls for a comprehensive reexamination of the electrical grid to center community-based organizations and clean energy that can withstand any future catastrophe, natural or otherwise. Massol-Deyá uses his essay as a wake-up call to the Puerto Rican people. The hurricane, as he sees it, is a sort of revelation regarding the need for energy independence. Thus, solar energy becomes an existential independence from the fractured and unreliable energy grid that dominates Puerto Rico today. Energy as resistance takes hold. Massol-Deyá opens his essay by laying bare what is at stake for Puerto Rico and its future, blaming the colonial government for the energy grid's inadequacies and underscoring the broader social debate in Puerto Rico regarding its energy future. He points the finger at the energy companies in charge of producing energy for Puerto Rico and their prioritization of profits at the expense of Puerto Ricans (216). Establishing that the Puerto Rican people have become keenly aware of their colonial status, he centers the main questions blatantly, stating:

> El dilema es claro: o producimos nuestra propia energía en el lugar donde hace falta, de forma limpia y renovable, o seguiremos dependiendo de importar combustibles fósiles que, aparte de desangrar nuestra capacidad económica, contaminan y requieren de un sistema de distribución confiable para llevar la energía hasta su casa. (217)

> [The dilemma is clear: either we produce our own electricity in places that it is needed, in a clean and renewable way, or we will continue to depend on the importation of combustible fuels that, apart from draining our economic capacity, contaminate and require a reliable distribution system to give electricity to each house]

Massol-Deyá cites energy independence, environmental sustainability, and political autonomy in his enumeration of the benefits of solar energy on the island. To him, perpetuating energy dependence means perpetuating Puerto Rico's colonial status (217). He critiques government efforts that claim to promote clean, renewable energy only to use fossil fuels and benefit the oil and gas industry, admonishing the government's rhetoric for being deliberately misleading (218). Rather than relay an emotional account, Massol-Deyá uses facts and statistics to make his claim and reassure his reader of a potential future. Energy independence means resisting not just the colonial administration of the United States but also the greedy moneyed interests that exist on the island.

Thus, placing solar panels on people's roofs solves many of the existing energy problems, moving away from a centralized grid and focusing on clean sources that protect the island's natural beauty. Both structurally and politically, the solar panels offer relief from the previous instability. Massol-Deyá declares that this is the only viable way ahead that does not replicate the errors of the past and allows a freer, cleaner country moving forward (220). Social, political, and energy policies are wrapped into one, and Massol-Deyá understands the connections among the three. Like solarity, which understands energy as also the "destitution and constitution of social and political forms" (Szeman and Barney 7), Massol-Deyá understands the transformative power of solar energy for the island. In connecting these various tentacles, Massol-Deyá builds out the possibility of collective resistance in the energy policy already happening on the island. As will be explored in chapter 4, on the power of collective action and mobilization, Massol-Deyá demonstrates the existing work and possibilities that energy provides. He offers less a document of facts than a call to action for a people tired of constant blackouts, government corruption, and colonial decay. *Testimonio*'s power here is to resist and look forward, to breathe a sigh of relief that there is a way out, to counter the official government's discourse on the impossibility of improving the power grid. These testimonios understand longing for changes in the here and now and the then and there. Electricity—as a way out and a way forward that does not replicate colonial epistemologies or material relations—gives hope to a people ravaged by Maria and colonialism.

On Mourning and Colonial Consciousness

Electricity and the lack of it serve both as a symbol of the colonial present and as resistance to future colonial structures. The notions of having, not having, gaining and then losing, and reimagining are instrumental in thinking through the way archipelagoes of longing are formed in these testimonials, where contradictory ideas of electricity emerge. Losing something or never having it are key factors in the mourning process of many of the testimonials. In Sharpe's wake work, mourning is not in opposition to the Black being but rather needs to be rethought, and she asks, "[H]ow does one mourn the interminable event?" (19). Mourning assumes that the event has ended, that one has been given the space to examine, process, and come to terms with the event. However, mourning needs to be thought in the Puerto Rican context with what Yarimar Bonilla and Marisol LeBrón call "aftershocks of disaster," where traumas such as Hurricane Maria are another event in the long line of colonialism's catastrophe in Puerto Rico (2–3).[9] Given these aftershocks, Puerto Ricans are left asking, just like Sharpe, "[H]ow does one mourn the every day? How does one, in the words so often used by intuitions, 'come to terms with' (which usually means move past) ongoing quotidian atrocity?" (20). A "Rican wake work" opens up this examination, allowing these testimonials to process the event(s) and mourn the everyday. These testimonials mourn the lives lost, mourn the material lack, and mourn their colonial realization. Mourning in these texts comes about through various emotions—anger, apathy, resignation, and defeat—that do not end. Maria becomes an "interminable event" protracted through affective struggle.

Like the way electricity and energy are stand-ins for broader structural precarity in Puerto Rico, material loss is a stand-in for the lack of agency within the colonial power structure. Alejandra Rosa's "Grietas" (or "Cracks") paints a picture of the emotional and material fractures that the hurricane exposed. Between a short story and an essay, the text follows Rosa as she tries to decide whether to leave her zinc-roofed home during and after the hurricane and the various economic, emotional, and structural breaks she experienced before, during, and after the hurricane. The narrative style allows Rosa to go back further, weaving previous frustrations with local issues with the immediacy of the current moment. Characters, such as her landlord and child, are described in deeper details that show the complexity of the human experience during and after the hurricane. Her narration spans the night of the storm and her own emotional processing after the storm. Past affective responses become present. A young mother with a three-year-old child, Rosa recognizes the inadequate housing she lives in, leading her to seek shelter in her landlord's house because "las paredes de su apartamento se le habían deshecho con ella adentro" [the walls of her apartment had been undone with her inside] (29). The mother toggles between comforting her child and being frustrated with the failed assurances from Don Julio, her landlord, that the roof will hold. She admits she did not believe him when he first told her but explains, "pero no le peleo ni le reclamo, ya para qué?" [but I don't push back, why bother?] (30). Her despair makes one think: Is it just Don Julio whom she does not want to fight? Resignation and exasperation dominate where the lack of adequate housing is a common problem not easily resolved. Wooden structures with tin roofs are common in Puerto Rico because of the low cost of the materials, leaving people living in housing not suitable for hurricane-strength winds. Like Rosa, people are aware of this inadequacy but must make do with the housing available to them.

Once Maria passes, Rosa's emotional cracks become more salient as material cracks appear in the streets. As local residents begin to clean the area in Trujillo Alto, where the narrative takes place, large cracks begin to splinter the roads. She is amazed to watch the small fissures grow into large cracks and sees them as a metaphor for the broader hurricane response, where seemingly trivial examples of inadequate government mismanagement have created a colossal nightmare for residents. Rosa states, "Desde la incertidumbre uno siempre piensa en lo peor. He escuchado la palabra sobrevivir muchas veces pero solo ahora, que escucho el llanto de mi niño bajo un techo que podría aplastarnos en cualquier momento, siento su verdadero horror" (31) [From the unknown one always thinks of the worst. I have heard the word "survival" many times, but only now, that I hear the cries of my child and a roof that could crush us at any moment, I feel the true horror]. This housing precarity puts a real focus on exposing the existential dread many residents face and elucidates other frustrations. As the cracks in the streets and in her building begin to grow, so does the frustration she feels about her housing situation, a frustration paralleled by her child's growing fear. Looking back on the night of the storm, she explains that she should not have listened to her landlord when debating whether to flee on the night of the hurricane. Now, she is faced with a dilemma: escape the crumbling building or face the wind outside as her child fears the chaos. She states, "[A]rriba no hay grietas pero el viento no se marcha. No se marcha. Y el nene no es que lo sepa, es que lo siente" [above there are no cracks but the wind doe not end. It does not end. And it is not that my little boy knows it, it is that he feels it] (32). The child's fear and anxiety are palpable to the reader. But what holds it all together is the mother. She holds her landlord's shame, her child's fears, and the community's worries. She explains that this is what mothers do, stating, "Eso también son las madres, techos que aunque a veces se agrietan tantas veces más lo sobreviven todo" [That too is what mothers are, roofs that even with so many cracks survive it all] (33). Rather than mourning the circumstances, the narrative voice is resigned to reality as a mother. Tragedies lead to a collective mourning (Williams 148), and in Puerto Rico, tragedy—and this natural disaster in particular—leads to a mass Puerto Rican resignation to the failed policies of the colonial regime. While many resisted, and still do as will be explored in the following chapter, one can almost hear the collective sigh in the story.

While Rosa's melancholic realization understands both the inescapable reality of the present colonial regime and the structural impossibility of moving forward, Francisco García-Moreno Barco's "Cuerpos en sal" takes a more creative approach that nevertheless captures how cheaply life is valued. In this short story, García-Moreno Barco takes a fictional turn, rather than the essay and documentary style I have analyzed thus far, to critique the disregard for life amid the hurricane's chaos. The more fiction-like narrative allows García-Moreno Barco to capture the guilt many Puerto Ricans felt and still feel after the hurricane. It almost haunts them, not allowing them to completely move on and long for a personal peace after the insurmountable human loss. The story follows two men who have been tasked with taking bodies to a warehouse in Maricao, Puerto Rico, from an undisclosed location. The story begins with the men arriving at a blocked road and finding themselves unable to reach their final destination. As night begins to encroach on their journey, they scramble to think what to do given that it is getting late and they want to return home. Because of the unplanned stop, the men start to question what is in the boxes they are transporting, contemplating the tension between their high pay and the morally questionable task they have been hired to complete: "¿Qué había dentro de la caja? Ni lo sabían ni les importaba un cará—recordó a su madre diciéndose que un cará es menos carajo que un carajo" [What was inside the box? If they knew they wouldn't care one bit—he remembered his mother saying that a shit is less of an asshole than a big shit] (74). The real material need that Puerto Rico faces post-hurricane has forced many into questionable tasks. But the question of what to do with these metal boxes is still front and center, regardless of their contents. Reality must be faced: "No había luz, no había agua ni hielo ni gasolina; no había nada, cará, excepto militares por todos lados, y 200 pesos era un dinero" [There was no electricity, no water nor ice nor gas; there was nothing, damnit, except soldiers everywhere and $200 was a lot of money] (74). As in many of the other texts in this collection, the lack of basic resources for living in the twenty-first century has always been central to many Puerto Ricans. But ignoring the contents of the boxes becomes impossible as a strange smell begins to issue from them. One of the men remarks, "Huele como raro, ¿no?" [It smells strange, no?], setting off the impending realization of what the boxes contain—or, rather, forcing the men to come to terms with what they already knew.

The two men begin to contemplate whether tossing the boxes into the road would make more sense, since people would not find them for weeks. One asks what will happen if the authorities find the boxes, but the driver replies, "¿Qué van a encontrar? Además, ¿no han estado tirando sacos de perros y gatos por los puentes hasta hace poco? ¡Y estaban vivos! Estos, al menos, están muertos y estamos en estado de emergencia, puñeta!" [What are they going to find? Still, haven't they been throwing dogs and cats over bridges up until recently? And they were alive! These, at least, are dead and we are in state of emergency, goddammit!] The connection between animals and humans brings to mind the questions of what constitutes a "grievable" life, to use Judith Butler's term. For Butler, what constitutes a grievable life is conditioned upon recognizing which lives are vulnerable at all, forcing questions of political recognition (25–26). In using the term "muertos," a term they had eschewed for much of the story, the men are forced to contemplate their collusion with the government as bodies piled up, making excuses for their actions because no one would be the wiser. The men are now faced with the reality that these bodies are their Puerto Rican brethren, that in tossing these bodies off a bridge like sacks of animals, they are devaluing their own lives. Yet, when they start to act on discarding the bodies the driver believes the boxes are moving, making them wonder who is in the boxes: a diabetic who did not receive his insulin on time, or an old man who could not bear that the hurricane took his home and his life, or a small boy carried off by a rush of water in the river (García-Moreno Barco 76). These bodies become of a type of zombie or living dead that according to Jossiana Arroyo "reflect sites of melancholia where social action—be it individual or collective—is required" (338). In the midst of these musings, the second man goes off to urinate, and when he returns the driver is nowhere to be found. Panic sets in. The man feels the dead looking at him—"Querrián vengarse de él ahora que estaba solo" [They wanted to have vengeance now that he was alone] (77)—and guilt over his treasonous thoughts starts to set in. Collective responsibility and collective mourning become present in the story, forcing questions of moral fortitude when faced with the reality of whose lives are grievable. It is through mourning that a collective solidarity can be formed, according to Butler, and Barco forces the reader to consider these issues. How can we as a people move forward without taking our dead? How can we move on when thousands of people died at the hands of government negligence? Where can the blame lie? These questions are not answered in the story but capture a generalized grief and melancholia in Puerto Rico with the passing of the hurricane.

Collective guilt and processing are central to Torres Ramos's piece, highlighting the tension between surviving the hurricane and living in deplorable economic conditions. This tension shifts toward pure anger in Ana Portnoy Brimmer's poem "A Julia Keleher, secretaria de educación de Puerto Rico, quien se encontraba en el mismo vuelo de American Airlines que yo, cuatro meses después de María" [To Julia Keleher, secretary of education for Puerto Rico, who I found on the same American Airlines flight four months after Maria]. The title directly points to what is about to be read, notes on encountering the former secretary of education, who serves as a stand-in for the broader corruption on the island. The poem allows for an irony to unfold, detailing the ridiculousness of Keleher's impact on the island, and forces the reader to sigh in disbelief along with the author. Similar to other texts, Portnoy Brimmer brings the reader in to her own emotional struggle. Sentenced to twelve months in federal prison for corruption stemming from charges that she took kickbacks for federally funded construction projects (Mazzei), Keleher epitomizes the destruction that the colonial hurricane has brought to Puerto Rico. The text, part poem and part journal entry, speaks directly to the former education secretary, critiquing her cluelessness about the effects of her decisions. Opening with the disconnect between Keleher and her acts as education secretary, the text reads, "Probablemente crees que 199 no es una cifra muy alta / pagaste más de cinco veces eso por tu asiento 'Priority' / y recibes 1,330 veces eso en salario anual / y no son más que escuelas hay otras . . . siete pueblos arrasados más allá" (159) [You probably think that 199 is not that high of a statistic / you paid more than five times that for your "Priority" seat / and you make 1,330 times that in annual salary / and they are only schools . . . seven towns leveled over there]. Portnoy Brimmer points to the lives devastated by Keleher's actions, having observed the closures of hundreds of schools that destroyed communities. Partly because of the fiscal oversight board and partly because of development plans from the Rosselló administration, Keleher supervised and implemented these closures, which further atrophied the already ailing public education system in Puerto Rico. The optics of a white American woman taking the helm of the education department and causing pain in these communities led to a public relations catastrophe. Keleher is a proxy for the colonial relation that exacerbates the suffering in people's lives. Portnoy Brimmer uses the staggering statistics—25,000 school-aged children unable to attend the 188 schools still closed months after the hurricane—to put numbers to the lives impacted. Yet the poet exposes the irony of numbers, saying,

"[P]ero yo no me dedico a las estadísticas / las cifras siguen cambiando se me corta la respiración y no quiero hablar de números" [But I no longer deal with statistics / the numbers keep changing and I lose my breath and I don't want to talk about numbers]. Here, the poet is frustrated with the use of numbers to make a point when the government also uses numbers to destroy lives or hide the destruction of life. Whether in lies about the official death toll or justifications of school closures with statistics, we see the erasure of lives through numbers.

Portnoy Brimmer also points to the obliviousness of Keleher, accusing her of failing to notice the ruptured dams across the island and claiming she is fine because "tienes tu botellita de agua y whiskey incluidos así que no tienes por qué preocuparte" [you have the little bottles of water and whiskey included so you don't need to worry]. Her privileged status that leaves her unaffected by her own actions feeds the increasing anger. The poet moves on to depicting the airplane as an animal that is digesting the people on board, or "las mihajas de rehenes que llevas detrás" [the many hostages that you leave behind] (160). They are all on a plane, but the plane for Keleher is different from the plane for the Puerto Ricans who are seated in coach, held hostage by disastrous policies and serving merely as fodder for the capitalist system embodied by American Airlines. The flight is not for freedom—it is a hostage taking. As the plane takes off, Portnoy Brimmer muses on the changing view of the island as she looks down at the "residuos de las escuelas" [residues of the school] in "un paraíso de tu creación" [a paradise of your creation] (169) continuing with depictions of FEMA tarps and military trucks and the destruction of the island. The poet ends by describing Keleher "haciéndole pucheras a [su] piña colada desde la mesita de patio en la terraza techada (mire qué suerte) de su casa" [mixing around your piña colada from the table of your roofed terrace (gee what luck) of your house]—a reference to a luxury apartment Keleher was given as part of the kickbacks. This indifference is even more difficult to swallow as thousands of Puerto Ricans remain without homes several months after the hurricane. Portnoy Brimmer interweaves the immediate effects of the hurricane with Keleher's actions. She toggles between anger and defeat in response to the government mismanagement made worse by the hurricane. Or did the hurricane make the mismanagement worse? The answer to this question proves difficult to tease out and adds to the persistent emotional effect of the text.

Consciousness, or awareness, of the colonial condition is seen through the anthology's various essays, short stories, poems, and interviews. To Sharpe, consciousness is ever-present while in the wake, always aware of the "continuous and changing present of slavery's as yet unresolved unfolding" (14). Being aware allows one to process, to grieve, but it also allows one to resist the ever-encompassing presence of these afterlives. Consciousness allows for the breaking up of these silences that are enhanced by "black social and physical death" (22). Much in the same way, being aware of the colonial reality, and not using euphemistic terms such as "territory" and "commonwealth," allows for the beginning of a new path forward. What precisely is the path forward is not defined, but the affective focus of the collective leads the way. These writings are not necessarily leading to the next revolution, but acknowledging and putting a name to a condition begins the process of maybe not moving past but at least not continuing the same old structures that drag out Puerto Ricans' precarious colonialized life. It is a mere kernel of change that begins to move the discourse away from repeated mistakes. Poetry and essays are used depict the various tentacles of the colonial apparatus that affects Puerto Ricans. The texts indict the island's colonial status, delineate its absurdity, and provide a burgeoning plan of action to move forward. This section echoes some of the ways that a "hopeful pessimism" builds a way forward, through protests that will be discussed in chapter 4. Puerto Ricans have now realized that even before the hurricane hit, social and political conditions were bad; calling for an end to the colonial state just might make things better because the current course of action is no longer tenable.

In "Grito a la Patria," Mariela Cruz goes beyond asserting the colonial situation and points to a much more existential global threat: the lack of freedom for the Puerto Rican people. Framing it as a David-and-Goliath-type battle, she calls her fellow Ricans to arms, to "grita[r] fuerte reclamando, libertad" [yell strongly demanding, freedom] (203). The poem begins by declaring the tyranny of an unnamed oppressor that uses both material and immaterial methods to keep a people down. She shifts from pointing the finger at the oppressor to calling for the people to unite. As I have described in the previous chapters, colonial structures spread their insidious tentacles, warping power relations. In Cruz's poem, the will of the individual and that of the collective are warped into one. As Sara Ahmed informs us, feelings have a social presence that muddles the distinction between the "I" and the "we" in a such a way that defines the boundaries between an individual and a collective. Or, alternatively, the boundaries of the two are shaped "by the contact with others" (10). In Cruz's text we see the molding of the collective and individual together, where the suffering of one is interpolated to the collective action of the whole. In not declaring concretely whom or what the people should attack, she relies on emotional response rather than a specific political agenda. Cruz echoes José Martí's famous 1891 essay "Nuestra América," in which he uses powerful imagery and poetics to rally Latin America against the Spanish. Martí never mentions the United States or Latin America by name but captures a certain political revolutionary moment of the time.[10] Cruz's consciousness has always been "congruente la verdad, mi bandera y estandarte" [congruous to the truth, my flag and standard] (202), connecting her desire for freedom and political affinity for the flag. Resisting efforts to beat her down, Cruz declares that they, an amorphous enemy that can be understood to represent colonialism and its perpetrators, "intenta[n] destruir," "golpea[n]," and "ataca[n]" [they try to destroy, hit, and attack] the consciousness of the people. The use of the present tense indicates that these actions continue even today—not in the past but in the here and now. Still, she remains strong, stony in the face of the oppressor's impatience to oppress. She continues delineating her grievances against the oppressor, declaring that "el hambre y la ignorancia" [hunger and ignorance]—a reference to the poverty on the island and the lack of funding devoted to educational services—"son cadenas" [are chains]. She expresses outrage at the "scraps" that are provided, interpreting them as insults she refuses to accept. Ultimately, Cruz captures the general anger and frustration of the people while attempting to channel those emotions into collective action. She leaves no man behind in these efforts.

From here the voice shifts from blaming to declaring battle, stating, "Dispuesta a la lucha estoy de pie" [Ready for battle I am standing]. The phrase is a dual reference not just to the will to stand against the constant onslaught of subjugation but also to standing up for a fight. She goes on by saying she does not fear the giant. In framing the conflict as one of a giant against a small person, the stakes become bigger than simply material; they become a matter of pride. The asymmetry of the battle gestures to its futility. She asserts the use of writing and words as her weapons and declares herself "la voz de aquel que nunca habla" [the voice of those who never speak] collectivizing the country as a whole and not leaving anyone behind. Connecting herself to the land, she repeats the word "soy"; she is the wall against the gravely injured, the machete, and the rock in your guts. The machete is a reference both to the revolutionary group Los Macheteros and to the use of the machete in the fields. She is the *ceiba*, a large tree indigenous to the Caribbean that offers shelter to people, and she is the *jaiba*, a small crab that outsmarts its prey. With this weapon, tree, and animal she alludes to the local resistance already happening, saying that she is culture, she is language, and she is land. She then shifts to the people, saying, "Somos uno cuando tocan nuestro orgullo, ya queremos alcanzar nuestra Victoria" [We are one when they touch our pride, we want to reach our victory] (203). Declaring again that words are her weapons, she calls on the people to raise their voices for those who cannot speak. Using the plural *somos*, or "we are," she says that we are a race, we are soul, we are a mind, and we are a people that stands out for being brave. She ends by saying that "we" should all shout so the world sees the naked reality and urges the people to demand freedom. Through pride, the collective and the individual are shaped by each other; they become one.

Cruz uses poetry to call attention to the various oppressions facing Puerto Rico, but Roberto Ramos-Perea delineates what the colonial state looks like on the island through essay. In "Una nueva dictadura se ha instaurado en Puerto Rico" [A New Dictatorship Has Been Established in Puerto Rico], Ramos-Perea describes the interwoven duality of colonial governance of local leaders, US colonizers, and financial interests. Declaring the fiscal oversight board a dictatorship, Ramos-Perea forcefully declares that the New Progressive Party (PNP) has helped this "dictatorship" to take hold. He lambastes the party, saying, "Es una dictadura de impunidad, corrup-ción policiaca y explotación económica del pueblo puertorriqueño" [It is a dictatorship of impunity, police corruption and economic exploitation of the Puerto Rican people] (167). The vulture-like relationship is then explained in detail. Ramos-Perea has no kind words for the pro-commonwealth party, the Popular Democratic Party, which according to him also assisted in gutting the public sector and hastening the atrophying of the economy. As a result, Puerto Rico is unable to pay its own bills, depleting its basic government functions in favor of repaying corrupt creditors. He bluntly states, "El gobierno de Puerto Rico y la Junta de Supervisión Fiscal son dos garras de una misma fiera" [The Government of Puerto Rico and the Fiscal Oversight Board are two claws of the same beast]. Two claws of the same beast—this language reflects the disdain Puerto Ricans have for fed-eral officials but also the growing realization that their own elected leaders are the problem. It is one thing to point the finger at the United States, but coming to terms with the fact that the Puerto Rican elite serves and is part of the beast is another frustration. He underscores how this fiscal structure has led to the current state of the catastrophe, which has left tens of hundreds of Puerto Ricans without electricity and covered with tarps. The Puerto Rican government takes the disaster one step further by selling the island's main energy company, closing more than three hundred schools, and slowly destroying the University of Puerto Rico, filling government posts with North American bureaucrats. Ramos-Perea declares, "Eliminan de raíz todos los presupuestos culturales, porque la cultura puertorriqueña es resistente de la asimilación a Estados Unidos" [They eliminate from the roots all of the cultural budgets, because the Puerto Rican culture is resistant to United States assimilation] (168). He moves from the economic to the existential. What will become of a country that has no educational foundation? How does a colony continue to grow when its people are ignorant of imperial injustices? The government itself is the culprit, allowing government services to go away while corporations benefit. This is the dictatorship that has taken hold in Puerto Rico: a neoliberal economic dictatorship that actively seeks the destabilization of lives for profit.

But given this awful state, Ramos-Perea calls for an international reckoning because "Estados Unidos no asume ninguna responsabilidad tras haber invadido militarmente y bombardeado nuestras playas en 1898" [The United States does not take any responsibility for having invaded militarily or bombarded our beaches since 1898]. At fault is not just the economics but the physical harm that the United States has caused to people on the island. The United States, he says, has no interest in making the island-nation part of "their Union" but rather aims to chop the island into pieces and sell it to big corporations (169). Acknowledging the real limitations facing Puerto Rico, he says, "Necesitamos el apoyo internacional" [We need internation support] because the world must know about this "genocide," not just for Puerto Ricans' sake but for that of the power balance in the world. By making a direct link between colonial government officials, economic interests, and US colonial devastations, he paints a grim picture of the "new" dictatorship—not just new in the sense of the next phase of Puerto Rican governance, but a new structure that causes the same harms of the past. What one sees here is the evolution of a global capitalist system at its extremes, where the United States and the entire world sit back and watch as a people suffers and justify these acts for profits.

With the new regime in mind, the essay "Un chiste de mal gusto" [A joke in poor taste] by Enrique Figueroa Cabrero examines the indignity of being a colonized subject during a disaster. Moving past the material—though those issues remain central to his point—Figueroa Cabrero shows the way Donald Trump took away the dignity of the Puerto Rican people after his visit. Speaking for the collective, the narrative details the almost shell-shocked response to the president's visit. Through the use of the essay form, Cabrero fluctuates between mocking, disdain, and shock to demonstrates the indignity that Puerto Ricans suffer as a colonized people. Calling him the president of the "empire," Cabrero opens by both insulting and critiquing the colonial state, saying that Trump "atravesó valientemente a very big ocean para visitor su colonia isleña de ciudadanos legales de segunda clase, arrasada por el huracán y el endeudamento" [he crossed a very big ocean to visit his island colony of legal second-class citizens, hit by a hurricane and debt] (87). Cabrero directly asserts the colonial relationship and the second-class nature of Puerto Rico's legal entanglement with the United States. He mocks Trump for saying he crossed "a very big ocean" and also notes the second catastrophe, the island's crippling debt. As in other narratives, one catastrophe is linked to the other. He continues criticizing the US president's comments, saying that as any leader would, he tried to lift the people's spirits by "record[ándo]les que deberían estar orgulloso porque su sufrimiento/hambre/destrucción/número de muertos no constituía a real catastrophe y que los esfuerzos para ayudarlos thrown our budget a little out of whack" [reminding them that they should be proud because their suffering/hunger/destruction/number of dead do not constitute a real catastrophe and their efforts to help them have thrown our budget a little out of whack]. Trump's flippant disregard for the suffering of a people deepens the rift between the United States and its colonial subjects. Not only do they not get the same material support, but they do not receive the same empathetic response from its legal leader.

Cabrero then takes aim at the colonial government officials present, noting that though they were stoic in their response, "era obvio que se estaban riendo. Tal vez se reían por dentro. O tal vez reían para no llorar" [it was obvious they were laughing. Maybe they laughed on the inside. Or maybe they laughed so they wouldn't cry]. This observation notes not just the absurdity of the president's comments but the complicity of the local government officials in the ineffective response on the island. It is like needing to do a double take at your officials; you do not want to believe that they would just endure the humiliation as their country suffered, as their homes too were destroyed. But they sit and take it. Take it for the people. To add to this indignity, the president thanks them "for not playing politics." Labeling Ricardo Rosselló "el gobernador colonial" [the colonial governor], Cabrero notes both the passivity in his response and the praise he gave the president for his aid efforts. But Puerto Rico remained dumbfounded as "la colonia intentaba reconciliar los comentarios de su líder, legal y no electo, con lo que ellos mismos habían presenciado y vivido" [the colony tried to reconcile their leaders comments, legal and not elected, with which they had experienced and lived] (88). In this attempt to reconcile the events, a litany of thoughts plagues the country. Collective reckoning for what has occurred. While previous Puerto Ricans had placed these frustrations in books, speeches, art, and poems, the people are resigned to the reality that "pero eso era antes" [but that was before], as if the past held some type of answer that the present cannot resolve. But the collective asks: How did we get here? While the past was not perfect by any means, Cabrero points out, they ask themselves how a desire for a better life could have led to "monstruos de corrupción, hipocresía, desprecio, intolerancia, desigualdad e indiferencia" [corruption monsters, hypocrisy, slights, intolerance, inequality and indifference]. Yes, the author continues, over time some good things did emerge, such as the preservation and enrichment of culture, but these positives do not sweep aside the lingering question of whether the president's visit was done only as "un chiste de mal gusto," or a joke in poor taste. The colonial consciousness and the excuses people have made for decades are beginning to crack. Even if, for some, the colonial relationship may have provided certain material benefits long ago, the question now is, Does this relationship still serve us? The president's visit is not just a realization of their second-class status but also a malaise to said realization of fact. Cabrero moves between these emotional responses, leaving the contemplation as a joke in poor taste hanging in the air, like the colonial status that continues to plague the island.

Conclusion

In this chapter I have shown how "Rican wake work" can be used to think through those still undefined versions of longing that toggle between the material and the affective. Rather than consider longing as a fixed collective construction, we see how longing for Puerto Ricans, particularly after disaster, is marked by continuities from the past into the present that remain unsettled. Electricity becomes a symbol of colonial decay, ongoing frustration, and possible future escape. Despair, anger, and hope are merged together, inseparable from longing. Similarly, what is being processed is also muddled, with colonialism and the disaster response one and the same. These writers articulate a sense of longing for a past that never really existed but that was more knowable than the current precarity. The longing for the lives they once had is muddled. This affect leads to the political consciousness. The anger, the frustration, the despair of knowing you are and were always a colony. Emotions, here, serve as a continuous malleability of the archipelago that at once connects and flows but also is distinct from the specific islands that make up an island chain. Fixity and unfixity come together.

Whereas this chapter has centered the way emotions and consciousness form part of archipelagoes of longing, the following chapter examines the way repetition, protest, and mutual aid begin to construct a way forward and a longing. Using the documentaries of Juan C. Dávila, I will examine how this unfinished longing starts to take the form of consciousness of the now and of political action for the future. Similar to the way that longing emerges in this chapter after Hurricane Maria, Dávila's documentaries concretize that consciousness and show how Puerto Ricans have already done the work necessary to combat the colonial malaise. Interweaving Yarimar Bonilla's "hopeful pessimism" with the documentaries, I show how archipelagoes of longing as a framework can be used to think through a real way forward that combines lessons and emotions from the past to construct new understandings of colonial relations that begin to move the country forward. In ending the book with these documentaries, I show how archipelagoes of longing can be a tool to combine an uncomfortable present with its potential future.

Chapter 4

Political Resistance, Collective Action, and Hopeful Pessimism in Puerto Rican Documentary Film

> Mucho de lo que habíamos querdio decir y hacer lo habíamos dicho y hecho en el proceso, en el intento inacabado.
>
> —Xavier Valcárcel, *Aterrizar no es regreso*

In the summer of 2019, as thousands of protesters began to demand the resignation of then-Governor Ricardo Roselló, *el perreo combativo*, or combative *perreo*,[1] emerged as a form of protest. The demonstrations began after leaked salacious text messages between Roselló and his top aides revealed misogynist, racist, homophobic, and classist opinions of their fellow Puerto Ricans during the recovery from Hurricane Maria in the archipelago. It was out of this anger, and a focus on groups minoritized in terms of sexuality, gender, and race, that Perra Mística and Kaya Té organized the *perreo combativo* on the steps of Old San Juan's Catholic cathedral, where reggaeton music blared and people engaged in sensual dancing, laughing, and other pleasurable behaviors alongside protest signs that clamored for the removal of the governor and the *junta*, a local term for the fiscal oversight board. The *perreo* dance is closely associated with the musical genre reggaeton and involves the sensual movement and grinding of the hips along with close contact with a dance partner. The dance has been associated with crudeness and the source of controversy in Puerto Rico. Using the *perreo* dance, often seen as being in poor taste, as a form of resistance challenged not only

129

the material and colonial decay facing the archipelago but also notions of respectability and class. This act of protest not only centered the female and queer lives that were at the heart of the governor's controversy but also created a space "where oppressed populations can live and experience joy" (LeBrón, *Against Muerto Rico* 45). Through this joy a queer hope emerges that reorients these bodies and gestures toward a more just future. This hope centers what Sara Ahmed calls a queer pleasure that is defined by the endurance of life in the face of constantly being in "the not" (165). In this hope, the *perreo combativo* created solidarity and unity at a time when Puerto Ricans were constantly being asked to be resilient in the face of persistent economic precarity. Hope and protest are intricately linked where protest provides a unique juncture of not just the intersection of past oppressions but also the possibility of a future—albeit a "hopefully pessimistic" one, to use Yarimar Bonilla's term—that begins to build a more equitable existence for Puerto Ricans through communal mobilization.

Resistance, collective action, and hope are among the many ways that Puerto Ricans in the documentaries of Juan C. Dávila vent their frustrations about a consistently inept government and colonial relations. The previous chapter focused on the affective power of longing through *testimonios*, where colonialism and disaster created mixed emotions regarding longing. In this chapter I engage the continued subjugation and simultaneous resistances of longing in Juan C. Dávila's documentary films *Vieques: Una batalla inconclusa* (2016) and *Simulacros de liberación* (2021). These two films reveal how archipelagoes of longing are manifested in the collective mobilization of Puerto Ricans as they grapple with the contemporary colonial reality, its material consequences, and potential future escapes. The documentary form provides a polyvocal way to depict a constantly evolving, and as yet unfinished, collective longing because of its ability to narrativize disparate, often incongruous, yet interconnected colonial aftermaths in a cohesive frame. With these two documentaries as the basis of analysis, this chapter shows how Dávila's films create a Bonilla-esque "hopeful pessimism" that allows for a realistic "out" of the current situation, an escape that challenges the failures of idealizing the past and the overly optimistic future projects. In Bonilla's articulation, a "hopeful pessimism" allows for the archipelago to "open our eyes to the hard tasks required to transform the here and now" (*Postdisaster Futures* 157). This better serves the purposes of the people of Puerto Rico, not replicating overly optimistic, ill-conceived ideas of the past to create a more just future, but rather envisioning a reality-based future and assessing what can be done, what is being done, and how Puerto Ricans can move forward collectively. Rather than being defeated by the current atrocities, hopeful pessimism opens up possibilities in realistic terms in order to better accept and change the present. The longing in these documentaries is seen through the collective will for change. A longing for a future that does not replicate the past or present. A longing that understands the reality of what is being faced. A longing for a future that might just be a little better. Never isolated to a singular cause or problem, and exhibiting many moments of resistance and collective action, Dávila's documentaries demonstrate the layered oppressions and resistances that Puerto Ricans face and enact, which form part of the tensions inherent in a hopefully pessimistic archipelago of longing.

Vieques: Una batalla inconclusa (2016) focuses on the decade following the 2003 withdrawal of the US Navy from the eponymous island municipality. Divided into seven sections, the documentary contextualizes the historical invasion of US imperialism on the island, explaining the military exercises that began in the 1940s via commentary by local leaders and activists that explore the political, social, environmental, and economic impacts. It then takes the viewer through the protests, the transfer of control from the navy to the US Fish and Wildlife Service, the environmental investigations, and the final movement to clean up the military contamination on the island. The film highlights the tensions between the mainland and Vieques and the political opportunism that extended the United States' destruction of the island. Images of protests and their impact on the navy's expulsion play a starring role, with local activists praising the power of political protest for effecting change. Even so, the reality of the US Fish and Wildlife Service that took over the administration of the land becomes a point of criticism. The documentary explains the environmental and political continuity of the bombings, emphasizing the "navy's poison" on the island's people and environment. The documentary ends with the defeatist reality that no one will be held accountable for the devastation. By weaving various stories and stakes together, Dávila reveals the pessimism that undergirds many contemporary issues in Puerto Rico.

Simulacros de liberación (2021) echoes many of the same issues that appear in *Vieques* but starts to think through possible alternative futures. Focusing on political actions beginning in 2016 and extending to the protests that led to Ricardo Roselló's resignation in 2019, the film demonstrates the ways political action can serve as an alternative to colonial government's failed administration. In tandem with the indictment of the archipelago's governance, Dávila critiques the federal government's—at best—indifference to the people in the archipelago and the continued colonial relationship between island and mainland. The film begins with the 2016 passage of the Puerto Rico Oversight, Management, and Economic Stability Act (PROMESA), which set up the current fiscal oversight review board. Dávila explains the supposed need for the board and follows the protests that erupted around its first meeting in San Juan in 2016 and the inherent corruption of the members that make up the board. The film follows protesters from the organization Se Acabaron las Promesas, which is seeking the disbanding of the board and reparations for colonial mismanagement on the archipelago. Dávila then weaves in the various disasters, particularly Hurricane Maria, and the impact the colonial government has had on the people. Throughout the film he follows a variety of protesters and activists on the archipelago, from student unions to mutual aid groups, all of them resisting the defeatist colonial legacy that has often infiltrated the Puerto Rican national psyche. Mutual aid, in Spanish *auto-gestion* or *autogestionarse*, literally translates to "self-management" or "self-reliance" but can also mean self-gestate or incubate (Bonilla, "The Coloniality of Disaster" 28). It is through these works that something new is forged that does not reproduce the same racio-capitalist colonial system that produced the devastation in the first place but something local, autonomous, Puerto Rican. Thus, it is through these local activists that Dávila points to a way forward as a society, where mutual aid networks are doing the work of the government, and unpacks how institutional leaders are failing to provide for the people of Puerto Rico. In this film, more than in his others, he inserts his personal subjectivity alongside the narrative to highlight what is at stake both for him and for the broader nation. Dávila lifts up a mirror to the Puerto Rican people as if to say, "Yes, we can do this without the United States"; the title, *Simulacros de liberación*, or simulacra of liberation, points to the ongoing and unfinished nature of the efforts on the island where a longing for a future based on present resistances takes hold. A future not wedded to colonialism's oppressions. Dávila does not give a concrete answer to the island's current political and existential woes but points to a way forward.

I examine these documentaries in tandem to show the repeating and cyclical nature of longing for Puerto Ricans that opens up future possibilities. Dávila uses firsthand accounts, archival footage, voiceover, and sound work together to challenge the Puerto Rican people in critically thinking through the perils of their colonial status. In doing so, the documentaries challenge idealized images of a past that never existed and a future that might provide a semblance of stability through present machinations. Like the *perreo combativo*, which redefines and reinvigorates fights against oppressive systems, analyzed together these documentaries demonstrate the reimagining of contemporary Puerto Rican conditions that are neither wholly fatalistic nor optimistic. Dávila's films fall within a broader trajectory in Latin American documentary filmmaking that disrupts official discourses in an effort to raise consciousness for the masses, providing the simultaneous continuity and discontinuity that defines the archipelagoes of longing for Puerto Ricans. Archipelagoes of longing are instrumental in understanding Dávila's films as he diligently crafts the multifaceted nature of colonial, environmental, and economic precarity that are linked (and repeated) in Puerto Rico. With these two documentaries, one can see Puerto Rico's continual contradictions within a colonial relationship; though they do not always make sense to outside viewers, they are the lived experience of the people of the archipelago. Dávila uses longing in the films to enact the actions of the present toward a continued future. It elongates longing, acknowledging the actions of here and now to take to the *then* and *there*, à la Esteban Muñoz, of a possible future. This longing merges political, material, and existential desires all into one unknown, yet slightly familiar, future, ultimately creating new understandings of liberation.

Documentary as Form, the Puerto Rican Film Industry, and Dávila

Documentary films in Latin America have long proposed a political inquiry—such as criticisms of dictators, the problems of US imperialism, and the importance of collective rights, to name a few—that merges the moving image with civic questions. Used to interrogate official state narratives, the documentary form is an instrumental tool to create a national consciousness that challenges ineffective accounts. Both *Vieques* and *Simulacros* take up these questions and actively challenge hegemonic narratives around colonial debt, military action, and material precarity while also celebrating the Puerto Rican people's will to be not merely passive actors but active in their island's governance. While the documentary style has existed since the introduction of cinema in the early part of the twentieth century, the form in Latin America took on a particularly important resonance in the 1960s and 1970s as a type of political speech. After decades of dictatorships across the region that saw the silencing of the popular will, Latin American directors, inspired by European-style realist filmmaking, took up the documentary form to contest the disinformation and silencing that occurred under autocratic regimes. By focusing on realistic depictions in films and rejecting profit-driven works, directors in the region not only refused the political forces within their country but also challenged neocolonial experiences that impacted specific events.

These realities created what Julianne Burton calls a "social documentary" that focuses on social woes and puts a mirror up to the political decay that the region has endured. As Burton notes, documentary filmmaking in Latin America goes hand in hand with political transformation (25). The 1960s, 1970s, and 1980s saw the proliferation of documentaries that underscored the political turmoil in many parts of Latin America. Disavowing Hollywood-style aesthetics, these directors centered realism to represent the ills facing their countries (Tomkins 17). Puerto Rico followed many of these same trajectories in the 1970s, with the creation of both the documentary form within cinema and documentaries dedicated to the establishment of a political consciousness (Castillo).[2] Attempts were made in the 1980s to strengthen the film industry on the island and focus on "Puerto Rican" themes that celebrated the archipelago's history, literature, and people, but by the late 1990s the industry saw interest in Puerto Rican–made productions and screenings decline on the island (Castillo). Across Latin America, the industry in the late 1990s and at the beginning of the new millennium experienced a shift in the documentary style with the increased political stabilization and transitions to democracy taking place in many countries. This led to a much more reflective, director-centered documentary style that evaluated both the director's own subjectivity within the country and the limits of the democratization efforts (Arenillas and Lazzara 5). Yet, as in many aspects of Puerto Rico's colonial economy, the film industry looks to Hollywood to make and produce large blockbusters on the island, funded by tax incentives that governments over the past twenty years have used to lure the industry to the island. As with almost every other industry on the island, these subsidies use Puerto Rican resources, both technically and intellectually, and extract them for the benefit of outsiders (Espada).

It is with this context that Dávila produces his films. Directors, according to Arenillas and Lazzara, use documentary's reflective method to "question conventional truths and to challenge objectivity both formally and politically" (6). Dávila's films challenge the colonial structures that plague Puerto Rico and assist viewers in thinking through new, collective ways to move forward. Dávila falls into what Fernando Solanas and Octavio Getino call a *tercer cine* that challenges imperial, colonial, and capitalist structures, not just through the narrative but also through the mechanisms of filmmaking. To them, this third cinema attempts to decolonize collectively through the cinematic form (88). Speaking about Island-based documentaries, Frances Negrón Muntaner notes that directors tend to focus on the causes of colonialism and how specific issues are rooted to its Puerto Rico's colonial history. Dávila challenges the conventional colonial mentality that Puerto Ricans and Puerto Rico cannot fend for themselves or have not done what it takes to be a free sovereign nation. Dávila's films are didactic in nature, trying both to have local Puerto Ricans see the reality they face and to encourage non-state-sponsored modes of resistance. Even how Dávila disseminated *Simulacros* was a crowdsourced method called "cine combativo" or combative cinema, which sought to hold screenings of the film away from main movie theaters after its initial screening and was sponsored by local activists (Dávila, "Hoy es la última"). I myself first saw the film for the first time through a screening held by the Partido Independentista de Puerto Rico in 2021 in Utuado, Puerto Rico. Dávila believes that the documentary style provides many avenues and possibilities in the face of a Puerto Rican film industry increasingly focused not only on Hollywood-backed films but also on films that do not relate to people's daily quest to survive. He states, "El género tiene mucho que ofrecer, tantas distintas posibilidades. . . .Creo que es un género que puede ser muy amplio" (Interview with Veronica Fonseca) [It's a genre that has a lot to offer and many possibilities. . . .I think the genre can encompass a lot of different things]. These many possibilities are seen in the way the films take on a plethora of interlocking causes that make up an archipelago of longing. These films show how Puerto Ricans can begin to build out alternative worlds, even if in minuscule ways.

Of interest here is not just what the genre provides but also for whom the films are intended. Speaking on *Simulacros de liberación*, Dávila states that he wants US-based elites to recognize their own involvement in the systems that create the conditions in Puerto Rico but also wants to provide a documentary that is accessible (Interview with Nelie Diverlus). But he's also conscious that documentaries need to "ir más allá" (go beyond) the elite, white, intellectual groups that gravitate toward these types of films, instead meeting broader populations where they can. This social commitment gives a bottom-up framework to his documentaries, collectivizing the voice and decentering him as a director. Dávila's work sits at the nexus of challenging US-based film industry influences in the archipelago and the socially conscious tradition from which Latin American documentaries have emerged. Dávila's work focuses on environmental issues and collective action, focusing on the way ordinary people challenge state and colonial apparatuses to effect local change. *Compañeros en lucha* (2012) and *Farmers of the Sea* (2024) explore not just environmental problems but the interconnected nature of colonial policies, federal administration, and economic interest. Beyond these films, his other projects examine the ways social issues, economic conditions, political interests, and the colonial reality constantly impact the different peoples in Puerto Rico today. *La generación del estanbai* (2016) and *Aftershocks of Disaster* (2020), a film made in conjunction with Yarimar Bonilla and Marisol LeBrón's book by the same name, move beyond this environmental focus to engage with wider social issues facing the island. As one watches the films, one sees Dávila's commitment to the social causes while also highlighting the precarious situation and acts of resistance people on the archipelago have done and continue to do in the face of insurmountable hegemonic forces. His documentaries are what is labeled "compromiso social," or a commitment to effecting social change. The documentary form fosters a focus on topics that are often overlooked but that impact large portions of minoritized people. Latin American documentaries come out of this tradition, and Dávila situates his work with this ethical aim in mind. Moving beyond the affective processing of the previous chapter, this social commitment takes archipelagoes out of a merely visual register and into action that encompasses a broad swath of Puerto Rican society. Hs films ultimately show concrete ends, both present and future, of the longings from throughout the book. Longing takes a slight step into reality.

Images on Repeat

Simulacros and *Vieques* reveal the archipelagoes of longing by repeating and reconstituting the collective representations of Puerto Rican colonialism. These events and structural subjugations fold into each other, creating new iterations that are still linked to historical moments and contemporary intersectional subjectivities. This section will focus on the narrative, filmic, and collectivizing techniques used in these documentaries to reveal an additional facet of US–Puerto Rican relations. The previous chapter examined how a temporal looping emerges post-disaster; in this section I excavate the seemingly endless temporal elongation that takes place. By depicting a time of stagnation and a time of great change, Dávila exposes colonial temporality that is circular in nature and breaks the bounds of traditional progress. Each documentary's differences and similarities toggle the various stagnations that are in constant play, defining Puerto Rican power struggles. The repeating images, sounds, and interviews weave together a dizzying documentation that has no definitive start or end. Each documentary depicts a longing to leave this time.

Photos, newsreels, stock footage, and raw footage are key elements in both *Vieques: Una batalla inconclusa* and *Simulacros de liberación* as a collage that creates a broader didactic impetus. In *Vieques: Una batalla inconclusa*, Dávila offers, as the title of the documentary indicates, an inconclusive ending to the larger narrative. Through visual aids he demonstrates the continuous loop of events that lead to no resolution except ongoing violences that play out in debates, political exclusions, and pyrrhic victories where colonial violence never ends. The visuals in *Simulacros de liberación* are used to assert a cohesive narrative that highlights the ways various groups' interests are exasperated by capitalist-colonial practices. The images delicately thread together a collective resistance, underscoring the excesses of colonial violence. In doing so, both films point to a way forward where people are already engaging in the community-building efforts and mutual aid networks that provide material assistance in the face of a crumbling infrastructure and political system. It is through these acts that a semblance of liberation is born, where the people's protests, mutual aid, and acts of resistance demonstrate, in the now, a sovereign future that could come. Longing's future projections, wedded in present actions, take root. The films showcase the incongruencies and continuities that build an archipelagoes of longing. In both films the pieces and parcels of resistance, subjugation, protest, and their repetitions show a longing that changes and comes anew.

Vieques: Una batalla inconclusa moves in chronological order, detailing the marines' arrival, use of the island, and eventual removal by presidential executive order. The military is often understood as a central pillar of US cultural pride, where existential strength is linked to its military might. Yet, in this film the US military is portrayed in a much more paradoxical way: as a source of oppression woven with memories of Puerto Rican participation in the armed forces. The film opens with credit-style words explaining how Vieques's nightmare began in 1941 with the US Congress's passage of Law 247, granting the marines access to the island municipality. Dávila demarcates a specific moment in time as a start date for his narrative, one that goes further back than the protests of the 1970s and deeper than the average Puerto Rican is aware. The colonial roots run deep.[3] Dávila's minimal historical explanation serves to move away from official discourses around the bombings and center local protesters and activists. Dávila opens the film with footage of military prowess, depicting fighter planes flying overhead, naval ships in the ocean approaching a mass of land, and navy personnel preparing a ship for battle. No direct reference to the island is made initially, so it remains obscured, unknowable. The footage creates a feeling of immanent invasion for the island, mirroring the affective charge of past US military incursions. It differs here in making a more generic depiction, one less factually linked to the island but more emotive in its construction. The fast-paced, animated speaking of the narrator is matched with clips of Air Force jets, ships approaching the island, and bombs being detonated. Only through a passing comment from the narrator does the audience realize that the island of Vieques is the site of these moving images, which hint at the problematic nature of the US exploitation of the island. The planes, ships, bombs, and amphibious vehicles point toward the all-encompassing nature of the military exercises and subtly foretell the environmental devastation to come. The footage is used to convey the colonial invasion that Vieques experiences, and the distinction between military experimentation and military exercises on foreign land is not clear.

The moving images create a narrative, a parallel of the real, but the footage used evokes for the audience the US military's conquests, tying it directly to the US military devastation of the present. The director forges a narrative with this footage that parallels the material, existential, and environmental loss experienced by the people of Vieques. It is not separate from the real but rather a collection of the various issues at play that are often lost in the official discourse of these events. It becomes an inclusive corrective of the real. As Elizabeth Cowie notes, documentaries are "both referential and in excess of the referential it invokes, both a sign and as the real" (135). This footage is in excess of the material impact that it points to, creating a broader arc of understanding. The footage echoes familiar footage of US military incursions in places such as Europe and Asia during the Second World War, making it immediately knowable, evocative of all the discourses about the military of years past. In doing so, an understanding emerges: the United States invaded Vieques just as it has done other faraway lands. But in this case, the faraway land is an island off the coast of Puerto Rico inhabited by fewer than ten thousand US citizens whose lives have been sacrificed to the military's benefit. Colonial relations and US imperial desires abroad become one and the same. Colonial excess is repeated.

As the film unspools the story of Vieques's plight, the military intervention evolves from acts of invasion carried out by marines to the arrival of federal agencies that police the island through the early 2000s. Photos and footage of military past and present where viewers see the changing of administrative hands from military to civilian, and Puerto Ricans and military personnel are fused, maintain this asymmetrical colonial relationship. These depictions morph into one another throughout the documentaries, providing continuity in time and despite the rotating cast of federal agencies involved in the administration of the land. After the US military is forced out through mass protest, the wildlands of the island are then administered by the US Fish and Wildlife Service. The Federal Bureau of Investigation plays a key role in removing protesters and merges into the broader monolith of federal agency policing. These various agencies become one, repeating power differential that Viequenses have combated for the better part of the last three decades. As Marisol LeBrón explains, policing and colonialisms are intricately linked on the island, stemming from policies in the 1990s that tried to elide the ruptures of colonial capitalism at the cost of imposing abusive policing practices on the island (11). A military branch is exchanged for civilian administration. In other words, same story with a different department.

Whereas depictions of the military invading the island in *Vieques* show a resistance to power, in *Simulacros* the police become a military-like defender of the capitalist system that sustains the flagrant abuses on the archipelago. Dávila to a certain extent flips the script, making the police the military and showing two sides of the same colonial coin. In *Simulacros* the police appear only at protests and serve as a much more direct representation of territorial governance than in *Vieques*, though the effect remains the same. In *Simulacros*, viewers see a much starker counter positioning between state actors and participants in the 2018 protests against junta-imposed austerity measures in San Juan's Milla de Oro, the main business district. Over the course of eight minutes, Dávila builds the tension around the protests, which saw thirteen people arrested and fifteen police officers injured (Mazzei "Protests in Puerto Rico"). Footage of protesters slowly amassing, as the song "La liberación reclama" plays, is juxtaposed with clips of police in full SWAT and riot gear, preparing for what seems to be battle. Police in Puerto Rico have long used violence and intimidation to prop up the existing political order during moments of crisis (LeBrón 51). Close-up shots of police officers standing idle culminate in an image of a wall of these armed men waiting for protesters to arrive. As for the demonstrators, Dávila chooses footage of slow marches coming together from different parts of San Juan through aerial shots, on-the-ground long views, and close-ups of protesters, climaxing with a line of demonstrators holding homemade wooden shields emblazoned with the Puerto Rican flag rendered in black and white. In this juxtaposition, Dávila establishes the tensions at play: police officers protecting the economic interests of the elite (Puerto Rican or not) while ignoring the needs of everyday Puerto Ricans. Protests challenge set notions of what constitutes a people that are often marginalized and at the limits of state-sanctioned personhood (Butler, *Notes Towards* 5). Those who live in perpetual precarity and come into the streets to challenge these material obstacles form "nascent and provisional forms of popular sovereignty" that force a new understanding of democratic will (16), much the same way that Puerto Rican protest does the work of thinking beyond the colonial structures and asserts the citizens' right to material improvement by placing their bodies on the streets.

However, much like in *Vieques*, loyalties become muddled, colonial policing practices are intensified, and the line between victims and perpetrators is blurred. The police officers become what Michael Rothberg calls "implicated subjects," they themselves being people who suffer under the very colonial reality they are forced to protect (2019). Defense forces inhabit a paradox in which they defend the people through violence, creating a situation where precarious bodies are placed in additional danger by those who have been set to protect them (Butler, *Notes Towards* 17). In protest, as people place their bodies on the streets, they challenge the political order simply

Figure 4.1. Protesters from *Simulacros de liberación*. *Source:* Screen capture from *Simulacros de liberación*.

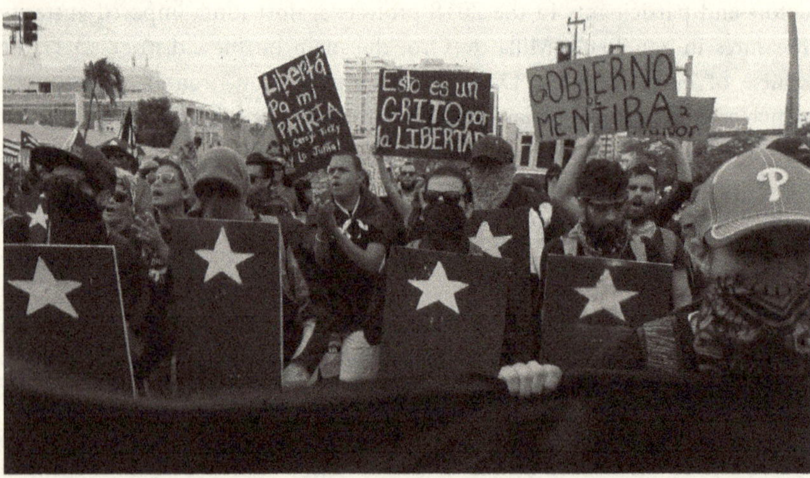

Figure 4.2. Line of police officers from *Simulacros de liberación*. *Source:* Screen capture from *Simulacros de liberación*.

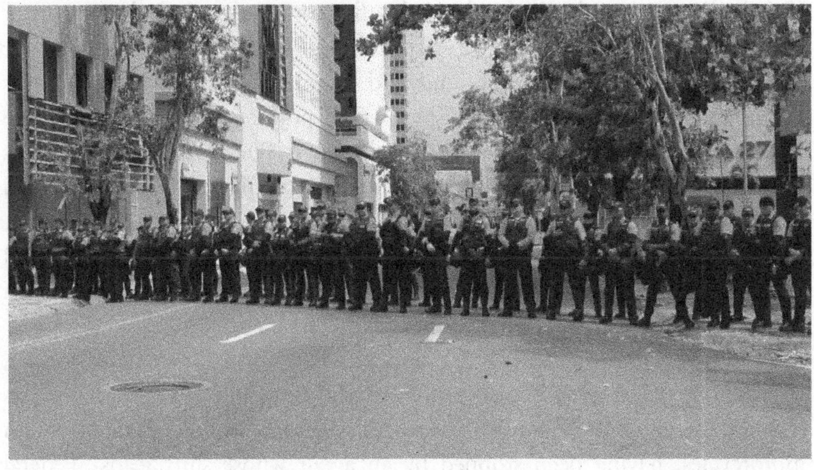

by demanding the right to assemble (18). Two versions of the people come to the fore; Dávila puts protesters and officers in tension with each other but recognizes the near absurdity of the tension and forces the question, Whose side are they on? In this jumbling together of the two sides, Dávila challenges the directional nature of memorial representation and questions the victim-perpetrator dichotomy, which falls apart in Puerto Rico. Who is to blame when Puerto Ricans themselves are recruited into the efforts to maintain the colonial project?

Whereas the use of footage in *Simulacros* builds the complicated tensions between the state and its people, in *Vieques: Una batalla inconclusa* Dávila uses photographs to link together the continuum that leads from the military to the police to government agencies. Photography is used to provide concrete evidence of events and their aftermath. It is a more memorable medium than the moving image because it captures a discrete slice of time rather than a flow (Sontag 18). These still images take on a life of their own, allowing for messages and interpretations to connect together. They become the grout connecting the tiles; they fill in the blanks of memory (23). These photographs expose the interwoven nature of the power dynamics—military, personal, political, and civil—that protesters face. In one image, police officers dressed in army fatigues are arresting protesters who are unhappy with the transition from the military administration of the US Navy to civilian administration by the US Fish and Wildlife Service. Three police officers are holding plastic ties as the protesters look on calmly. One protester is standing with his hands raised over his head, his fingers interlaced. A fourth officer holds him gently as another officer speaks. The second protester, on the far right, stands with his hands bound and a stoic expression on his face as the police officer speaks to him. The merged power becomes salient in the image, where it is not clearly delineated who is Puerto Rican and who is not. The fatigues become not only a military camouflage for war but also a camouflage of their sociopolitical affiliation, stripping them of their identity. The camouflage allows them to go incognito as to their loyalties. Colonial control and the relationship to the United States are more important than individual autonomy and environmental preservation.

Whereas the officers' agency and national affiliation remain unclear, in other images Dávila clearly points to the Fish and Wildlife Service as the new perpetrator of control. In one, a group of young residents sit on motorcycles, having been stopped by an agent whose shirt reads "Federal Agent" in large bold letters and "Fish and Wildlife Service" underneath. The female federal agent is positioned like a police officer questioning the five local residents as she relays unknown information. The possible meanings of the photograph expand. Viewers do not know who approached whom, what information is being given or received, or even why the interaction is occurring at all. What is clear is the position of the Fish and Wildlife

Figure 4.3. Image of protesters being arrested from *Vieques: una batalla inconclusa*. *Source:* Screen capture from *Vieques: una batalla inconclusa*.

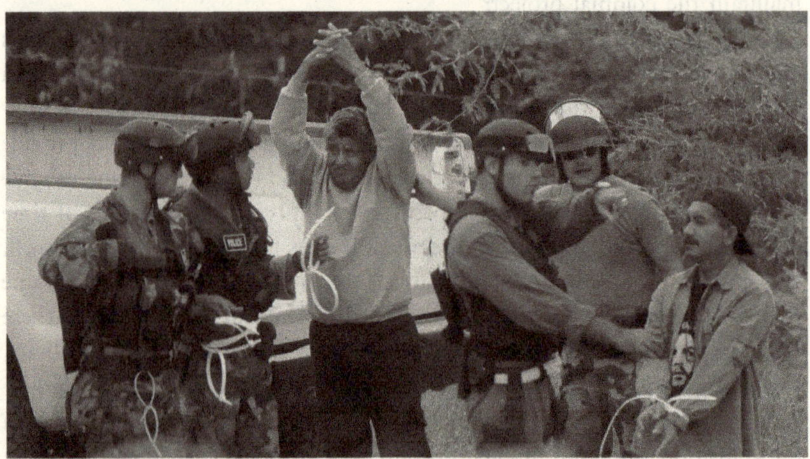

Service as an authority figure that polices the environmentally devastated area around the bombings. Dávila pairs this image with one of the same woman looking into a civilian's car as she speaks to the driver. The driver stares down at a sheet of paper as the woman, captured midsentence, explains undisclosed information. Standing outside the vehicle and framed by the car window, she is the outsider invading the man's space with information. His dangling Puerto Rican flag and tropical flowers convey that the space is Puerto Rican and she, the intruder, is violating that space. The images are worth a thousand words. Offering depictions of quotidian traffic stops and police checks, they draw direct links between the violence of the policing Puerto Ricans are accustomed to and the labeling of federal agencies with seemingly mundane titles. The message remains clear: The Fish and Wildlife Service is the new US Marines. While the link might seem incongruous, the same colonial power dynamics are enfolded within the agencies. The entity has changed, but the old colonial policing practices stay in place.

The military-police fusion in these documentaries makes repetition and change a signature piece of the archipelago of longing. The military power shifts and morphs but maintains its connections to the broader colonial trauma that Puerto Ricans and Viequenses endure. The palimpsestic folding together of these powers calls into question notions of progress and underscores Vieques's stagnant political reality. Rather than a singular struggle to push out the US Navy and other military forces, these images

Figure 4.4. Federal agent speaking with local residents. *Source:* Screen capture from *Vieques: una batalla inconclusa.*

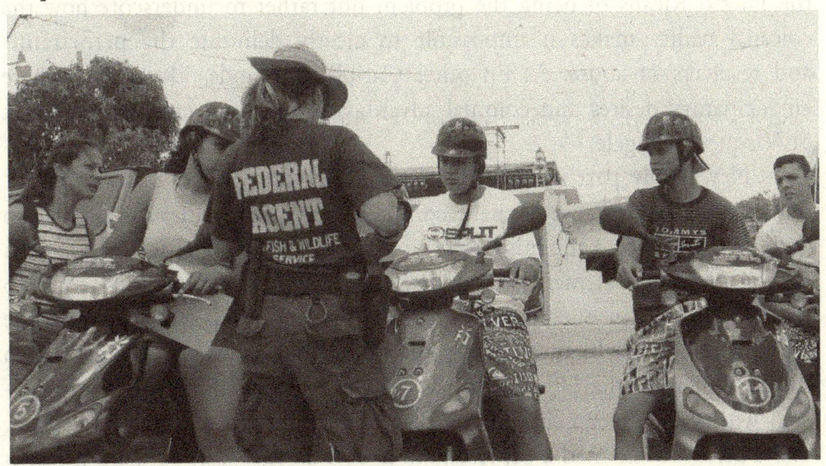

Figure 4.5. Federal agent speaking with local resident in vehicle. *Source:* Screen capture from *Vieques: una batalla inconclusa.*

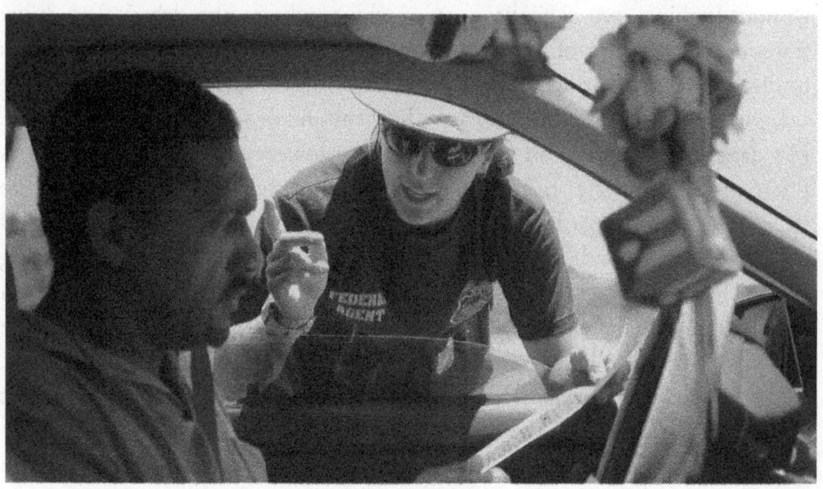

depict a complex variety of problems related to rights, land, colonial status, and military might, creating a refracted understanding of the colonial, militarily occupied, and second-class status that Puerto Ricans must endure. The tensions in these documentaries are further muddied by Puerto Rican participation in the armed forces. Puerto Rican military personnel are at once part of the problem and against it. My intention here is not to accuse the Puerto Ricans of being the problem but rather to underscore how the colonial reality makes it impossible to clearly delineate the perpetrators and receivers of abuse. As on other Caribbean islands, identifying where emancipatory desires and colonial advantages begin and end becomes part of Vieques's struggle.

Never fully part of the national fabric of the United States but constantly exploited because of the need for Puerto Rican bodies in war, Puerto Rico's relationship to the military is a troubled one. Puerto Ricans have been serving in the US Armed Forces since 1899, when the Battalion of Puerto Rican Volunteers was established as part of an effort to "Americanize" the island and its inhabitants (Franqui-Rivera). The representation of Puerto Rican soldiers in the US military has become intersectional in nature, layered with various segments of colonial, racial, and national contradictions. The Puerto Rican media representation of Puerto Rican soldiers presents a complex picture of mixed belonging and not belonging to the United

States nation. During the twentieth century, as Puerto Rican servicemen returned from the Korean War, the US military pathologized Puerto Rican national affiliation, blaming the soldiers' Puerto Ricanness for their higher rates of mental trauma rather than understanding the issue as one affecting all returning soldiers as they struggled to come to terms with the ravages of war (Avilés-Santiago 6–7). This impacted the representation of Puerto Rican soldiers in the Puerto Rican media, which often depicted them as troubled war veterans grappling with mental health issues stemming from the armed conflict (28). The relationship to Vieques in the 1990s changed this depiction from harmless veterans to aggressors against their own people sowed negative connotations of invaders, challenging Puerto Ricans' once neutral perception of the US military (8–9). The discontinuities in these documentaries unsettle the military-colonial divide that the island faces.

In the film, David Sanes Rodriguez is depicted as the catalyst for a major popular uprising in the 1990s; images of the young man saluting in military-like fatigues are intercut with photos of Sanes Rodriguez in his casket wearing the very same clothing. The voice of Pablo Connelly Pagán, a local activist, explains that Sanes Rodriguez's role as a security guard on the base and his subsequent death as a result of military negligence are exemplary of the economic need and political helplessness that Viequenses suffer. Sanes Rodriguez became a symbol for the movement writ large, the last straw for a people struggling under colonial rule. The depiction of Sanes Rodriguez in a military-adjacent job that led to his death further serves as a humanizing aesthetic in which his innocence is seen through the lens of military imagery, serving as a warning to non-Ricans: If they can do this to us, they will do this to you. The images provide a parallel story that, like the military footage, replicates incongruous tropes and repeats—and feebly contests—colonial-military relations. The military does offer certain material benefits, providing jobs and other economic opportunities, yet the reality is quite grim. The military presence is inherently toxic, pushing the people down even as it provides certain gains. A longing to be seen as equals but knowing the contradictions are exposed in these military depictions. The relationship is a self-sabotaging one in which the benefits to Puerto Rico of US involvement do not seem worth the cost.

Environmental Continuity

Much the same way that the military personnel fold into the various Puerto Rican and non–Puerto Rican actors, the military's environmental degradation continues the *longue durée* of colonial malaise. These colonial aftermaths become what Rob Nixon famously calls a "slow violence," or "a violence that occurs gradually and out of sight, a violence of delayed destruction that is dispersed across time and space, and attritional violence that is typically not viewed as violence at all" (2). Following Nixon, the environmental violence is so commonplace and entrenched in the Puerto Rican psyche that they are "not viewed as violence at all" but are instrumental in understanding longing for Boricuas as the violence continues in environmental contamination and health problems on Vieques. In *Vieques: Una batalla inconclusa*, this violence is further exposed through the juxtaposition of political narratives between local activists and governmental actors whose collective story reveals the disconnect between peoples' everyday ills and the need for cleanup efforts. By setting in parallel the two sides of a single story, the director takes a backseat, appearing subtly in the film and letting the stakeholders (i.e., policymakers, protesters, activists) speak for themselves. In these interviews a paradox emerges, where official narratives sit together with counter-discourses, demonstrating a plurality of voices in the collective longing. The film offers a concrete example of how the broader colonial continuities unfold, where small pyrrhic victories lead to one a single question: Will the colonial devastation ever end? The films forge a more complete picture, allowing space for different versions of longing to unfold.

The film toggles between two entrenched narratives that persist on the island: that nothing can be done to save Puerto Rico and that more could be done. Through interviews with expert witnesses, Dávila confirms that the cleanup efforts have been mismanaged to a degree that is bewildering and practically absurd. Jorge Fernández Porto, a biologist and adviser to the Puerto Rican Senate; Laura M. Vélez, an attorney and president of the Junta de Calidad Ambiental; Jorge L. Colón, a chemist and professor at UPR-Río Piedras; and Arturo Massol-Dayá, a microbiologist and professor at UPR-Mayaguez, trace out the long narrative arc of the cleanup effort. The explanation begins with Jorge Fernández Porto, who notes that, according to US law, any federal entity that causes environmental contamination is responsible for cleaning up the contamination. He further explains that the government entity—in this case, the US Navy—is supposed to set up advisory boards to explain to the community what cleanup effort is occurring. He makes it clear that the role of these boards is not to enforce laws but to inform the community on the efforts. Colón and Vélez then take up the story, emphasizing that from a legal and chemical point of view, the navy was responsible for chemical cleanup, but that said cleanup never occurred.

The viewer now understands the legal mechanism, but the film turns to biology professor Dr. Arturo Massol-Dayá, who explains that the cleanup effort is fundamentally a farce. For instance, in the western part of the island, almost two million pounds of waste such as oil, solvents, lead paint, and acid have been dumped in the mangroves and wetlands, joining the unexploded bombs that already peppered the area (McCaffrey and Baver 123). However, Massol-Dayá notes that in fact the land was being cleared of live munitions, not decontaminated. He goes on to explain that the company the navy hired claimed to have cleaned up 5 percent of the munitions and detonated 38,000 live bombs in the fields. The interview footage is interlaced with photographs of the removal, showing hundreds of piles of bombs. These images become a type of "memory mapping," to use Kaitlin Murphy's concept, where "memory and materiality can be deeply intertwined" (67). The images become anchors for the audience, where a particular object not only relays meaning but is also a physical vestige of the slow decay of the environment. They map the past's devastations, a slow violence into the present, reminding viewers of the injustice Viequenses have lived and continue to live. Part of the navy's exit from the island mandated policies to clean up the island by various government agencies, including territorial and federal groups (122). The cleanup is a hangover from the decades-long fight to remove the US military. Yes, the military's departure is a win, but Puerto Ricans are left reeling from the environmental toll. As these bombs at once puncture the consciousness of the viewer and merge into the landscape, the film further unfolds the environmental violence through expert interviews about the bombings. A violent past forges a violent present.

The film moves on to another witness who comments that the cleanup is in fact a further bombing of the island, and that the efforts are replicating the same destructive practices that occurred when the military was still in control. Footage of legal experts in suits and scientific experts in white coats being interviewed in laboratories and offices with diploma-filled walls add credibility to the explanations. The film lays out the facts in a rather dry, straightforward manner, allowing the experts to speak with authority and forcing viewers to feel the visceral exhaustion of the endless battle Vieques faces. Here, Dávila uses the scenes to connect the film to the real world, building a palpable tension. Building tension in a documentary that leads the viewer to some kind of action is more effective than offering merely a spectacle with an ambiguous and inconsistent end (Gutierrez-Alea 33). Collections of interviews are usually used to decenter the authorial voice and shift the credibility away from the director. In doing so, the director's view is mediated through a curated set of voices that create a single message (Chapman 104). Yet here, in moving in and out of the various opposing voices, a fatigue starts to set in. These experts, both those arguing for a military cleanup and those defending the government's actions, are juxtaposed, telling similar stories with radically different conclusions: on the one side, that state actors have done their best to remediate the contamination, and on the other, that state actors flat-out lied to the people about the decontamination effort. As with the marines and police officers, loyalties are warped, colonial power dynamics are reified, and Viequenses continue to suffer. In this exhaustion, we see how, as the title of the film attests, the battle is not over. Longing to escape this battle but knowing one must endure is depicted for viewers.

In the next section, "Peligros en aguas viequenses," the film continues discussing the cleanup effort by traveling to areas that have been blocked to human access. The film explores the case of the Laguna Anones, or Anones Lagoon, which was closed for many years and whose contaminants seeped into local waterways, further polluting the ocean and local residents. Once again, the film centers the experience of local activists and scientific experts, who have a detailed knowledge of the inconsistencies in Fish and Wildlife's official explanation. The film places "both sides" of the story together. For instance, the film presents Francheska Ruiz, a biologist for the agency, who states unequivocally that the lagoon is closed and that any indication otherwise is merely "gossip." Her assertion is then challenged by a local fisherman named Cacimar Zenón Encarnación, who says the lagoon is open and has documentation to prove it that is then shown to the audience. The film continues with Vieques's secretary of natural resources, Carmen Guerrero, to explain the methodology used to find further bombs around the island. The film moves back and forth, with a local fisherman, Ruiz, and the secretary detailing the same story from different angles. The archipelagoes of longing are formed when these various actors, often at odds with one another, all together create a collective detailing of the impact on the environment and fishing industry. The viewer is caught in a dizzying tug-of-war between reliable witnesses and expert testimony over the span of eight minutes in what becomes a polyphonic array of facts, arguments, and images to spark outrage over the authorities' inaction. The viewers witness the futility of working with powerbrokers and the real material devastation inflicted on local people who seem to not be a priority for anyone in charge. The mode of relaying the message becomes a vehicle for the emotional weight of the subjects being portrayed. An affective turn, if you will, that mirrors the frustration of locals on the island. This emotional weight makes the viewers feel the exhaustion that Viequenses feel to underscore the slow violence that drags on and on. Viewers are left asking: Who is at fault? When will the island be cleaned up? When will their lives go back to normal? Through the collection of interviews, one cannot help feeling defeated by the continued inability to bring about change.

Environmental contamination goes hand in hand with negative health effects for the people of Vieques. With one of the highest rates of cancer in the archipelago—and higher still compared to mainland US residents—the island's people have experienced the detrimental impacts of the lasting contamination from the military involvement (Pelet; Sanderson et al.; Rice Kerr). The lack of environmental cleanup itself can create further health problems, and the nonexistence of access to contaminated lands becomes a focal point in *Vieques*. The sixth section of the documentary focuses on "el veneno de la marina," or the navy's poison, and takes on the health ramifications directly. It opens, like the other parts of the film, with expert medical witnesses who explain the toll on human health of the decades of bombings. Dr. Carmen Ortiz Roque, an obstetrician and gynecologist, explains the physical toll that mercury contamination has caused for child-bearing and infant maladies. In one study, Ortiz Roque found that 27 percent of the Viequense women participating had high levels of mercury, compared to 6.6 percent in northeastern Puerto Rico and 7 percent on the US mainland. This high level of contaminants can cause intellectual delays, autism, and even death to the child. Ortiz Roque goes on to explain that in her study she tried to find other sources of contaminants and concluded, along with the EPA, that the US military is the only source of such leaks. Ortiz Roque puts the blame squarely on the US Navy and its bombings on the island's coast. Viewers cannot dispute her facts, thus homing in on the human toll of the military's contamination. Though the film begins by portraying the political upheaval of a colonized people fighting for their rights, it turns into a much more somber reality where solutions are few and the persistent legacy seems infinite.

The testimony by Ortiz Roque is only heightened when Dávila himself goes on a drive with Carlos Ventura, a biologist and fisherman who has given testimony previously in the film. The scene plays out with Ventura listing for nearly a minute all those who have died of cancer in recent memory or currently have cancer. It begins with a shot of Ventura and Dávila sitting in the car as Ventura points out the window, stating, "Una señora que vive ahí esta padeciendo de cáncer, el señora que vivió aquí murió de cáncer, esta señora murió de cáncer, Don Isaac murió de cáncer, Doña Anita murió de cáncer, Doña Marta murió de cáncer" [A woman who lives there is suffering from cancer, the man who lived there died of cancer, this woman here died of cancer, Mr. Isaac died of cancer, Ms. Anita died of cancer, Ms. Marta died of cancer]. With the names arrayed in a long list, one cannot help seeing in stark detail the death toll and bodily contamination that the people of Vieques suffer. Numerous academic studies (Jirau-Colón et al.; Sanderson et al.) show the elevated rates of chemical contaminants in Vieques, and other reports have drawn links between these contaminants and the elevated rates of cancer and other ailments on the island (Torres-Vélez, "Reification, Biomedicine, and Bombs"; Roman; Hay Brown). While cancer rates in any population are multicausal, Dávila directly frames the impact of the military's presence and cancer rates in Vieques. One need not see a scientific report to know the long-term health risk for a people. Medical problems, military decay, and coloniality become one long tragic continuum for Viequenses that does not stop. The various longings fold into each other. The longing for clean environment, a longing to bring back those hurt by the bombs, a longing for justice, and a longing for a better future all are in play. They all are exposed and their abundance reveals archipelagoes of longing that knows no bounds.

We Suffer, We Resist

In *Vieques* expert and witness interviews are used as voiceovers to create a cohesive narrative of the perils of colonialism in the archipelago. Environmental and physical contamination forge the sinister bond Viequenses share after the military's departure. Likewise, in *Simulacros de liberación*, the film combines various viewpoints, opinions, causes, and peoples to create a broad, kaleidoscopic collective imagination. In linking these causes, a cacophonic visual is presented of the same frustrating story seen through different lenses. In addition to this collective, the director also centers his own subjectivity in relation to the events of the film, guiding the viewers to the didactic conclusion that says "We can do better." He becomes another actor in the events that unfold, showing that he, too, is impacted by what happens, putting a human face to the bleak reality the archipelago must confront. In conjunction with the director's narration, activist testimonies show the challenges to official discourses regarding the colonial present. Even as the people change, the voices shift, and the cause warps, the same collective struggle and resistance emerges: Together we suffer, but together we can resist.

In *Simulacros*, firsthand narrations are used to counter the official narratives Puerto Ricans have become accustomed to that allow colonial blight to persist. Much like *Vieques*, *Simulacros* centers the voices of the protesters, here not through interviews but through monologues that showcase their collective resistance through mutual aid. Mutual aid is often understood as a collective organization to meet people's material needs when government stakeholders fail to provide (Spade 7). In doing so, they move people into action and raise awareness of shared plights (12), helping collectives build people "infrastructures" that center care and a way forward (20). The depictions of mutual aid offer hope for things to come, delinking them from past ills and sharing in what is being done. The film parallels the collective action of the various groups into a cohesive understanding that underscores the mutual aid efforts. The hope in "hopeful pessimism" comes alive where Puerto Ricans long for this version of peace is depicted. The film shows the quotidian nature of mutual aid organizations, depicting first a meeting of residents in San Juan's Río Piedras neighborhood uniting to clean up the city, and then a meeting of various organizations coordinating efforts to feed the hungry. They discuss logistics, goals, and purpose in the face of the governmental inaction. The scene feels almost like a city council meeting where local officials discuss ways to improve their area. In their place, however, we see local activists seeking to fill the void left by the government. These groups create a broader solidarity known as *la olla común*, or "the common pot," that feeds people with donated food items. The scenes show people cooking, cleaning, and organizing the space for the arrival of hungry residents exhausted in the aftermath of Hurricane Maria. The only voices we hear are of the students, organizers, and activists who explain their reasoning for coming together. One student, Marisel Robles Gutiérrez, explains that people coming together and providing what they can, even if only their time, is more valuable for the common good because "la precariedad ya está a un nivel extremo que lo único que nos queda es estar juntos" [precarity is already at an extreme level, and the only thing that we have left is to hang together]. She goes on to say that the only way forward is to construct everything themselves and not return to the way things were before. Togetherness is the resistance.

This same sentiment is seen in the transformation of a school into residential space in Lares and a water tank installation in Bucarabones; these projects are among the mutual aid efforts occurring around the island. The activists responsible for these efforts know full well the precarity community members face but act in order to move forward. Through this action, hope emerges, allowing people to take back control and provide for themselves. Each effort underscores a specific aspect of governmental and colonial failure on the archipelago. From crumbling infrastructure in the cisterns of Bucarabones to the failed school system and its conversion in Lares, the audience becomes witness to both the colonial decay and a people's resistance. The people here are, as Yarimar Bonilla has criticized, "resilient," where time and again Puerto Ricans suffer material devastation as a result of governmental ineptitude ("Why Must Puerto Ricans"). But to what end? These acts of mutual aid and solidarity become means of protest as well as means of challenging government institutions to do better, if only by getting out of the way for the common good. Here, we witness hopeful pessimism in full view, with the various people come together simulating some degree of liberation from state actors and government entities. The picture is not perfect, however, and colonial decay sits side by side with these moments of resistance, but the scenes force viewers, and Puerto Ricans generally, to acknowledge that the actions of liberation are being carried out in the here and now.

In portraying collective action by Puerto Ricans, the film shows the various actors at play in Puerto Rico's collective longing. Dávila straddles a line between centering his subjectivity as a filmmaker, centering his identity as a Puerto Rican, and centering the voices he is trying to highlight at different junctures in the film. His insertion of his personal experience creates an affective bond to the audience, putting a reflective spin on the events that moves away from seemingly objective interviews to his own emotional relationship to the film. Questions of truth and fiction are often at stake within documentary film, and audiences engage with films along a continuum of fact vis-à-vis fiction (Roscoe and Hight). These documentaries become less a detailing of events and more a labor of love pushing for audiences to understand the political, material, and existential stakes for Puerto Rico, where government officials change narratives to fit their colonial political agenda or, worse, lie about the human toll straight to the people's faces.[4] Who is allowed to tell a story, who listens to it, and what message is permitted beyond the immediate political agenda are all intertwined in these films.

Beyond the contextualization of specific events in the film, Dávila's personal opinions bookend the film in his opening and closing commentaries. He does not appear until five minutes in, after a montage that explains the politicking and US discourse leading up to the passage of PROMESA in 2016. Seated at his work station, Dávila provides a voiceover as images of him editing, filming, and contemplating the events appear on the screen. He asserts that after the legislation passed, he wanted to create a film on austerity measures on the archipelago and poignantly asks, "[P]ero cómo se realiza la austeridad en un lenguaje cinematográfico?" [But how do you represent austerity in the language of cinema?], claiming that it is this question that led him to the project. He goes on to explain that to understand this question, one must focus on sites of resistance that challenge power structures. Images of people protesting, being removed by police, and insulting the government fill this montage before it moves on to describe one specific organization, Se Acabaron las Promesas, a group that shows up several times throughout the film. Dávila provides an initial thesis for the film, guiding the audience into the project's original purpose.

The sympathetic depiction of protesters is set in contrast to the scornful depictions and criticism directed at members of the Financial Oversight and Management Board of Puerto Rico (FOMB) through cartoonish graphics. Here, again, Dávila uses his own voice to ground the narrative, giving the audience a compelling narrator and providing a face for the events. Throughout the documentary, the graphics are used to inform the viewer while also mocking the absurdity of the events taking place. The graphics are carnivalesque in nature, showcasing the inane reality of the FOMB and highlighting the various actors at play. Rather than understand the carnival as a jovial place for amusement, here the carnivalesque parallels the real in serio-comical fashion. Mikhail Bakhtin identifies three characteristics that define the carnivalesque in literature: It creates a new relationship to reality, moves away from legend, and uses various genres that contest uniformity (152). The carnivalesque is, by its nature, dualistic (170), linked to the prevailing power structures but also challenging them. The carnivalesque allows for a challenging of authority and creates a new world, or, better yet, a clearer understanding of the current world. The carnivalesque in *Simulacros* reveals the ludicrous effects on the everyday by pointing to the colonial relationship that defines the FOMB. Investor interests are in tension with Puerto Ricans' daily material needs.

Dávila mixes cartoonish graphics that resemble paper collage with real images of the various actors on the review board to show the carnivalesque nature of PROMESA. Fusing information with commentary, Dávila provides the viewers with critical data to construct his argument while poking fun at the stuffy capitalists who are preying on the suffering of Puerto Ricans on the

Figure 4.6. Cartoonish depiction of Arthur González from *Simulacros de liberación*. *Source:* Screen capture from *Simulacros de liberación*.

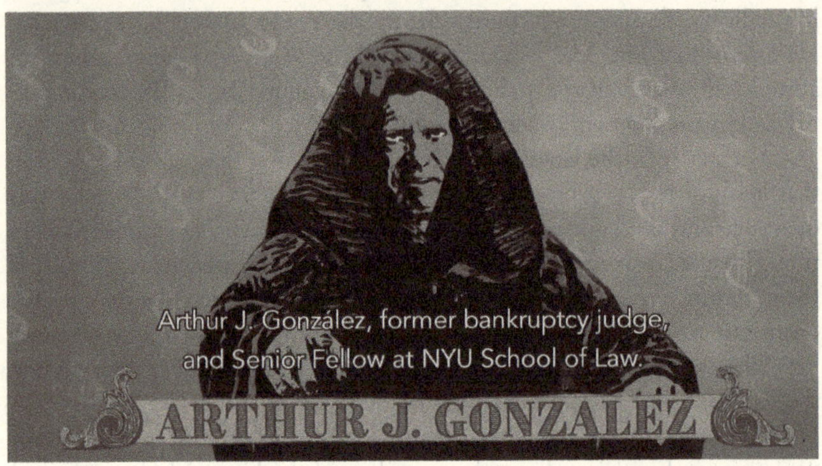

island. Dávila goes through each board member, explaining their relation to Puerto Rico and broader capitalist institutions at the heart of the problems the archipelago faces. Beginning with José B. Carrión III, the chairman of the board, Dávila presents video of him sitting at an official table before the first board meeting and then superimposes a cartoon sketch in black and white with a neoclassical frame around him identical to those on US currency. In the background, a red backdrop with dollar signs emphasizes Carrión's nefarious relationship to finances on the island, explaining that his firm Carrión, Lafette, and Casellas is a financial insurance company whose employees worked for the Puerto Rican Development Bank and were in charge of fraudulent bonds that accelerated the financial crisis on the island. Dávila provides the same treatment to Richard Carrión, president of the Banco Popular de Puerto Rico; Carlos García, also a banker; José G. González, another banker; Ana J. Matossantos, former finance secretary of California, whose family business would benefit from actions taken by the board; Andrew Biggs, a member of the American Enterprise Institute; David Skeel, an academic; and Arthur J. González, a bankruptcy judge. Interspersed throughout this montage, Dávila pokes fun at some of the members, describing Biggs as "this guy who is falling asleep" when he introduces him, commenting that Skeel practices "legal Christian studies," and noting Arthur González's resemblance to the Emperor Palpatine from the Star Wars franchise, further highlighting the sinister nature of the fiscal oversight board's decisions and its actions on the island. Dávila makes sure to underscore the capitalist interests of these people and, through the graphics, notes how they are in conflict with the FOMB's stated mission "to achieve fiscal responsibility and access to the capital markets" (*Public Law 114-187*, 5). What is revealed in these cartoons is a neoliberal colonial relationship that exploits the Puerto Rican people. The audience is forced to laugh at the cartoons because the reality is just so dire. These images along with Dávila's explanation further expose the absurd machinations of Puerto Rico's finances, but one can't help also feeling angry about these interwoven strands of corruption. The pessimism in hopeful pessimism comes to life, where the audience faces the grim reality of colonial exploitation.

However, all is not lost, and protests are a way to push back against Puerto Rico's colonial woes. The film opens with a full minute of footage of the summer 2019 protests in Old San Juan. In this opening sequence, peaceful demonstrators walking to the rhythm of pounding drums are interspersed with images of graffitied walls that demand "Ricky Renuncia," "Abajo el gobierno de los ricos," and "Muerte a la monarquía." The almost festive vibe of protesters waving Puerto Rican flags and celebrating the motorcyclists revving their engines is abruptly cut by an escalation of violence. The scene shifts as it captures the standoff between the nebulous authority and the people of Puerto Rico: shots of protesters lobbing back tear gas canisters, dumpster fires lit to block the passage of police vehicles, and peaceful protesters sitting on the ground being showered with pepper spray to disperse them. The screen goes black as a cacophony of people chanting "Ricky Renuncia y llévate a la junta" [Ricky, resign and take the junta with you] fills the streets. No commentary is made, no interview is given, no music is heard; the only sound is the chants of the people, the clamor of protest, and the firing of tear gas canisters. Dávila sets the tone for the film, not just one of contemplation but also one where he lays the stakes bare, creating an us (Puerto Ricans) versus them ("the system"). The scene closes with a graphic of the words "Three years earlier" that leads into a discussion of the legislation passed by the US Congress that led to the protests of 2019. The preamble combines the various threads into one broad collective, signaling to the viewer what is about to unfold in the film. The film centers the protests and protesters vis-à-vis the state to pique the viewers' interest. A similar technique is used with the protests on the Milla de Oro, the student protests, the teacher protest, and the protests that led to the governor's resignation; here, Dávila centers the protesters and their cause rather than his commentary on the events. In doing so a broader solidarity is created by putting seemingly disparate interests together into a whole, a group whose constituents are all affected by the colonial reality in different yet related ways. The archipelago comes to life as the various groups—teachers, students, workers—are linked by the same colonial inadequacies piece by piece, or island by island.

After laying out the solidarity and resistance movements by various social groups in Puerto Rico, Dávila loops back around at the end of the film to explain his inspiration for the project. He notes that he wanted to document austerity measures to create consciousness in the viewer before a terrible calamity occurred. Lamenting, he states, "Se me hizo tarde" [I was too late], and says that "en realidad todo empeora" [in reality everything is getting worse]. As he explains the situation in early 2020, when a series of earthquakes ravaged the island and were then followed by the COVID-19 pandemic, the audience sees that Puerto Rico is always having to respond to new crises, but he hopes that the strikes, protests, and mutual aid networks "hayan servido como simulacros que nos dispongan a una liberación de este sistema colonial dentro de este estado constantemente en crisis" [have worked to serve as a simulation of liberation against the colonial system in this constant state of crisis]. Explaining how he views simulacra, Dávila unmasks the true impetus of the film, creating a revelation for the viewer of the possibility that can grace the archipelago, a future that he hopes will come based on the reality of the present. In the end, the film's "hopeful pessimism" is revealed, emphasizing the fact that the work is already being done and that action moving forward has been put into practice already. The solutions are not panaceas but rather material alternatives to the colonial decay of administrations past and present. Simulacra that point toward liberation become key to show that the work has started, and Dávila leaves no room for error in this interpretation.

Conclusion

In an interview I conducted with Dávila in the summer of 2023, he stated that one of the major reasons he uses filmmaking is as documentation. Acknowledging the environmental and political destructions in Puerto Rico, he stated that some of his footage might be the only shot of a beach, a protest, or a building that will remain for future generations. The act of documenting is an active form of remembering, and Dávila's films allow for a longing to be expressed. When major news organizations and government officials lie or obfuscate to the nation, his films provide for a bottom-up perspective to take hold by emphasizing the interlocking nature of the events unfolding on the island. Rather than relying solely on hegemonic actors to convey information, Dávila adds marginalized voices and stakeholders that are often forgotten by the US and world media. Dávila's films are an expansion of official narratives, inserting into those narratives voices that have a real impact on Puerto Rico's material and existential present. In documenting, Dávila's films become one aspect of the broader archipelagoes of longing.

In this chapter I have shown how Dávila meticulously weaves various causes—education, infrastructure, political, coloniality, and mutual aid—to underscore the political stakes at play in Puerto Rico. Together the films show both the historical and the contemporary, subjugation and resistance, the errors of the past and a possible way forward that is already being enacted. *Vieques: Una batalla inconclusa* shows the environmental devastation and the continued struggle the people of Vieques face as they deal with the cleanup effort and the government mismanagement that followed. A longing to escape but to also enact the same resistances into other corners are shown. Dávila provides a cacophony of voices, decentering his own subjectivity and presenting those who were missed or lost in the broader power struggle between the US government, the Puerto Rican colonial government, and the municipality of Vieques. Similarly, *Simulacros de liberación* exposes the material and political decay Puerto Ricans face, revealing the interlocking nature of various social movements. Rather than centering one cause, Dávila exposes how failures in education, health care, and infrastructure can be combated through mutual aid, collective action, and political mobilization. The films show how Puerto Ricans long for a future unwedded to the chaos of the past, even in incremental ways. The films offer a demonstration of Yarimar Bonilla's hopeful pessimism in full view, where concrete measures are being enacted that do not replicate old hazards. By juxtaposing these documentaries, I reveal an archipelagoes of longing, where various pieces, policies, actors, and movements come together, linked by a broader colonial present. Various longings come to the fore. Dávila shows how the different groups in Puerto Rico are all linked through the colonial decay that ravages communities, devastates infrastructures, and divides a people. In doing so, the documentaries reveal a present colonial admonition that allows a longing of an unclear future to take shape.

Conclusion

Bad Bunny's Longing and Puerto Rico Today

> Esta es mi playa, este es mi sol
> Esta es mi tierra, esta soy yo
> Esta es mi playa, este es mi sol
> Esta es mi tierra, esta soy yo
>
> —Outro by Gabriela Berlingeri in *El apagón* by Bad Bunny

"Debí tirar más fotos de cuando te tuve," sings the chorus of Bad Bunny's 2025 song "DtMF" from his album *DeBí TiRAR MáS FOToS*. It continues, "Debí darte más beso' y abrazo' las veces que pude / Ey, ojalá que los mió' nunca se muden / Y si hoy emborracho, que me ayuden." Although the recipient of the kisses, hugs, and photos is never explicitly stated, it's clear the song is directed toward Puerto Rico. The song's first verse opens by describing another beautiful sunset in San Juan and enjoying all the things "those who leave" desire. Part love song and part ode to Puerto Rico, "DtMF" captures the mixed emotions, the regrets, the pride, that *Archipelagoes of Longing* has explored through murals, commemorations, testimonios, and documentaries. Much has been said and studied regarding Bad Bunny. Whether in the way he challenges masculinity (Rivera Figeroa 2020), his political activism (Chocano 2022), his global presence (Iasimone 2022), or his genre-bending musical talent, Bad Bunny shows the dynamism of contemporary Puerto Rican music. What has been less studied is the way Bad Bunny captures a certain Puerto Rican vibe—something less concrete and more affective—in his relationship with the island. Similar to the way this book has explored the mix of emotions, desires, frustrations, and hopes,

Bad Bunny has been able to weave the euphoria of being Puerto Rican with the material, political, and existential struggle that defines Puerto Rico today.

I end this book reflecting on Bad Bunny's music because his latest album parallels some of the same broad questions that started me on this project. Issues of sovereignty, pride, hope, and place permeate Bad Bunny's work in much the same way they flow throughout this project. *Archipelagoes of Longing* has allowed me, as a Puerto Rican who grew up in the Orlando diaspora, to bring together various emotions that come with being a Rican in the States. I often find myself struggling to make sense when I see a people that I love and care for uprooted, a culture that I hold dear constantly fight against erasure, and political systems inflict their absurdity as people try to find ingenious ways to feed themselves, house themselves, and celebrate life. I struggle to understand a place that is at once home and an enigma, and—even with everything I have studied, learned, reviewed, and personally experienced—still cannot fully comprehend how Puerto Rico and its people have ended up in this awful situation. *Archipelagoes of Longing* has allowed me to think through my own subjectivity and to understand what it means to experience disasters and dislocations while inhabiting in-between places, identities, and catastrophes. *Archipelagoes of Longing* has provided a way to think through various atrocities, both systemic and episodic, whole and incomplete, new and old, on the island and elsewhere, to better understand my own positionality within these incongruencies. Moreover, it has provided a way to help me explain to others how to best assess the Puerto Rican present both nationally and globally. Through the various chapters, I have shown how archipelagoes of longing allow us to understand colonized people's often fragmented sense of longing. In this way, it is both a tool for understanding and a framework that enmeshes longing in varied cultural products that reveal the interlocking ways structural oppressions continue to impact Puerto Ricans even while the longing is nascent, new, and contradictory.

At the core of the book is an emphasis on thinking through and examining the Puerto Rican experience that is inclusive of often little-studied areas in the diaspora and on the island. Much the same way that Bad Bunny opens *DeBí TiRAR MáS FOToS* by centering the US experience with the song "NUEVAYoL," this book begins by centering Puerto Ricans in Chicago, Philadelphia, and Orlando to underscore the connection between the diaspora and the island. The song, an homage to salsa music and its importance in Puerto Rican culture, riffs on the band El Gran Combo de Puerto Rico's classic "Un verano en Nueva York"; the fusion of genres echoes the way that the diaspora is part and parcel of the Puerto Rican experience, moving past Arcadio Díaz Quiñonez's 1993 critique that more needs to be done to include the diaspora and its history in the broader Puerto Rican fabric. Bad Bunny does just that, not making a distinction between the salsa of the past and the reggaeton of the present, but asserting both as part of the present and future and combining music from the diaspora and the island into a compelling whole.

Thus, in an effort to decenter the island-to-mainland focus within Puerto Rican studies, I opened this book with an examination of the way Puerto Rican artists in Chicago and Philadelphia use street art murals to retell a national history that too often excludes people of color, diminishes political movements that are uncomfortable, and rejects utopian tales of migration. Through the various street art murals, I excavate how neoliberal agendas and political goals can sit together to create a new understanding of the Puerto Rican experience in the United States that is more inclusive of the lived experience of those in the diaspora. The murals in these chapters have two main purposes: They recast historical narratives and they assert a sense of place for Puerto Ricans in Chicago and Philadelphia through racial and ethnic solidarities. Here we see how murals are both a form of examination and a mechanism for resisting failed representational initiatives. Where Puerto Ricans had been slowly pushed out along with other Latino communities, the murals assert a sense of place by reminding Puerto Ricans of their history, decolonizing racist constructions and creating a source of pride within a neoliberal system that actively seeks their exclusion. The murals engage with a range of political agendas, racial narratives, and historical markers that build out a reimagined longing for the past that recuperates histories of exclusions and omission, thus creating a radical nostalgia that looks to the past to rewrite the present. This retelling of the present is more inclusive of a diversity of stories and challenges both systemic and historical erasures, allowing the murals to display a longing to belong on one's own terms. The mural form also creates a sense of place, putting Rican stories front and center for passersby, not just for the people of Chicago but also, more important, for Puerto Ricans and Latinos in these communities. The murals reveal not just a Rican longing but also the political work of asserting Puerto Ricanness.

Thus, murals like Cristián Roldán's *Taínas* and John Vergara's *The 79th* remind Puerto Ricans of their cultural roots and their racial and ethnic heritage that come with them to Chicago, reimagining and recreating a definition of Puerto Rico that is inclusive of all erased histories. Likewise,

Edgardo Miranda Rodriguez's *La borinqueña* and Betsy Casañas and Ian Pierce's *Sanctuary City, Sanctuary Neighborhood* provide new understandings of Puerto Ricans' environmental and solidarity connections that make up often ignored yet equally important collective longing formations in the twenty-first century. These murals demonstrate various entry points when thinking through Puerto Rico's migration story and nation formation narratives that are inclusive of all Ricans, even as the island itself increasingly becomes an inhospitable place. For decades, Puerto Ricans in Chicago and Philadelphia—along with other hubs such as New York and Orlando—live with a constant desire to return that coexists with an understanding that going home is not the panacea it is often sold as. Moreover, we also know that life in the United States requires losing a part of ourselves, a history, a culture, a language, which makes us question whether the migration was truly worth it. In each of these desires, one does not have clear-cut, or soothing, answers and must live with the constant doubt, the what-if, the *quizás*. These contemplations are difficult to untangle but form part of the collective longing that Puerto Ricans in the diaspora constantly face.

In Chicago and Philadelphia, one sees the community come together, if imperfectly, to create a sense of place through art. In chapter 2, however, Orlando's Interim National Pulse Memorial tells a different tale. In the second-largest Puerto Rican community outside of the island, Orlando Ricans face unique challenges of belonging highlighted through the Interim National Pulse Memorial, digital replica, and artistic archive. In this chapter I unpack how commemorations, by their nature, are contested sites of memory, battling hegemonic narratives with grassroots memorialization desires. The Interim National Pulse Memorial is no exception, highlighting the tensions inherent in representing queer Puerto Rican lives. These intersectional identities challenge normative and singular narratives surrounding tragedy and force a new conception of the place of Puerto Ricans that does not flatten their existence into fixed memorialization. A longing to be represented, with all the subjectivities, takes hold. These commemorative sites show the tension in belonging of queer Ricans who battled for adequate representation in both the queer and Puerto Rican communities. These commemorations do not provide a panacea for the representations but allow the tensions to sit together. To acknowledge that representational solutions are messy, but in that mess we can begin to think through the complexities of identity. The shrouding of the queer Puerto Ricans in this chapter mirrors the obfuscation of all Puerto Ricans who must think through how to situate themselves in ways that do not flatten their experience.

Therefore, constantly striving to be seen and represented, Puerto Ricans—and Latinxs more broadly—are at once present and absent in the commemorations, revealing two main issues: the inability of the US media to cover intersectional identities, and the uncomfortable place of not knowing where Puerto Ricans sit in the broader national imagination. As I discussed in the chapter, both the media response and the commemoration's creators turned the tragedy into a "gay" tragedy, removing and obscuring the overwhelming majority of Puerto Rican and Latinx lives that were lost on the night of June 12, 2016. Occurring on a Latinx night, the bar attracted many Latinxs and people of color to celebrate their culture and sexuality simultaneously, centering an intersectional subjectivity that is rejected in both queer and Latinx spaces. But the memorial actively hides this fact by focusing on the collective mourning, gatherings, and celebrities who flew to Orlando to participate in a type of "trauma tourism" that sees monied, media, and tourist interests supersede collective commemorations. Yet, this inability to recognize Puerto Ricans and Latinxs is one example of the place Puerto Ricans find themselves relegated to in the United States. To leave the story there would not do the Puerto Rican experience justice, and as with the murals in Chicago and Philadelphia, Puerto Ricans have found ways to assert their presence through the digital archive. Through this mass collection of artifacts, one sees the Puerto Rican, Mexican, Guatemalan, and Honduran flags alongside smiling faces, laughing faces, and sexy faces that build out a broader humanity and complexity for the forty-nine lives lost. Centering these lives and moving away from generic commemorative images reveals an inclusive exclusion that forces Puerto Ricans to the sidelines but also a place to understand the fluidity and inclusive power of longing. The interim memorial is all-encompassing of the off-island experience of a community that is marginalized in both the United States and Puerto Rico, and it reflects the confluence of global and national policies that led to the tragedy. The Pulse memorials show the various layers, nodes, and subjectivities that make up a collective longing where queerness and Latinidad are seen not as mutually exclusive but rather as cohabiting identities that deserve their own commemorative moments. Rather than a single narrative, identity, or structural oppression, these memorials open inclusive contemplations that move toward, but never achieve, the fullness of collective longing for Puerto Ricans. Archipelagoes of longing here helps illuminate the photographic negative—the other side of the queer Rican experience—since commemorative sites are often inconclusive, demonstrating how longing is never a settled matter when it comes to remembering and honoring the victims who were lost.

Even prior to *DeBí TiRAR MáS FOToS*, Bad Bunny slowly came out of his political shell with songs like "El apagón" in which he critiques the current state of Puerto Rican electrical grid and the constant blackouts, or *apagones*, that plague the island. Bad Bunny and other artists such as Ricky Martin and Residente were among the many singers who went to Puerto Rico during the resulting protests to lend support and a morale boost to the cause. For Bad Bunny, this was almost a political awakening, inspiring an urge to be back in his homeland with his people for a cause he believed in and to voice a frustration that many on the island felt (Ortiz). Not only did Bad Bunny reflect the moment's push to collectivize and be together as Puerto Rican people, but he also spoke for all Puerto Ricans both on the island and in the diaspora. Just as the 1968 Chicago riots were galvanizing for the Puerto Rican community in Chicago, a point I explore in chapter 1, these protests served as a sort of awakening for the Puerto Rican people out of their colonial state, and Bad Bunny channeled the rage, the hurt, but also the hope and the desire to be together.

These ideas of collectivity, hope, and the frustrations of colonial realities are themes that are carried into the second half of the book. In chapter 3 I analyze how *testimonios* after Hurricane Maria show the affective struggle of colonized people trying to make sense of various interconnected tragedies. I show the more amorphous nature of memorial constructions that are less fixed and still emerging, or "embryonic," to use Raimond Williams's term. Whereas the first chapter focused on the rehabilitation of a national long-ing and the second engaged with the shrouding of queer communities in commemorative sites, this third chapter turned to the just-created nature of longing that is still forming. The emotional charge with which the various authors of the testimonials write their experiences shows both the material and the existential reality of being a colonized person with a catastrophic event in the background. Or is the catastrophe the colony and not the hur-ricane? This answer cannot be settled, as the two are intricately enmeshed in the same colonial structures. On the one hand, you have the colony as the problem, and on the other, you have the hurricane's devastation exac-erbated by the colonial power's lack of attention to people's suffering. All of this adds up to the present.

Material desires, historical corrections, and consciousness creating come together to build out these new forms of longing post–Hurricane Maria. Christina Sharpe's "living in the wake" and Williams's "structure of feeling" help understand the unfinished nature of longing and memories that are so new, yet impactful, that have not been concretized yet deepen the ways that archipelagoes of longing can be used to engage and incorporate the yet-to-be-defined parts of longing. Testimonios open up these contemplations, speaking for both the individual and the collective, for the material and the affective, and for the plethora of emotions that come with catastrophe. The testimonio as a form unfolds emergent contemplations, acknowledging that longing does not always need to be finished in order to be studied. To remember that the past is in the present, not in a symbolic sense, but in real material, systemic, and affective fragments, challenging the mind to think through solutions. Fragments that have not crystalized but point toward pasts and futures that need to be understood. Memories and desires, yet to be defined, are critical pieces of collective longing because they leave something undone and are not prey to the structural problems of hegemonic memories. In the end this emergent longing seen through affective representation is folded into archipelagoes of longing to broaden the way longing is constructed and expand not just representationally but affectively as well.

These embryonic memories are a preamble to a "hopefully pessimistic" representation that begins to think through a way forward that becomes the focus of the fourth and final chapter. This chapter engages with Yarimar Bonilla's "hopeful pessimism," in which she delineates how Puerto Rico's affective crisis, just as much as the material and political one, needs to be grappled with to move the country in an alternative direction, to explore the documentaries of Juan C. Dávila *Vieques: Una batalla inconclusa* and *Simulacros de liberación*. I use these films to analyze the ways that continued structures have led to a general malaise, but one that Puerto Ricans have resisted and continue to resist. Documentaries provide for a narrative of longing in the here and now but also the then and there. They depict how people challenge power structures and represent how longing need not be solely about the past but about the present and future through visual form. In creating these narratives, Dávila's films weave the various political stakes—education, housing, infrastructure, political will, food security, and environmental realities—that must be contemplated to obtain a complete picture, a complete reality of how colonized people struggle and resist at once. The documentary form connects and educates people, specifically Puerto Ricans, who live this reality, but when protest and action are placed together, the documentaries construct longing that is both current and recurrent.

Vieques shows one aspect of the collective longing where government officials may change but the same system of oppression remains, as does the ongoing devastation done to the environment and peoples, where colonial continuities are present. Even so, Puerto Ricans have found ways to push back. Massive protests and collective action forced the US military out of the island, and while vestiges of structures remain through environmental degradation and existing inequalities, one cannot fall prey to despair. In *Simulacros de liberación*, Dávila takes us in a new direction, having the audience examine the real work that is being done in the here and now in Puerto Rico through mutual aid and collective action. A simulacrum, or an unsatisfactory imitation or substitute, can not only be presented but also be used as a road map for a way forward, one that does not simply reproduce past harms, as Bonilla indicates, but is not unrealistic in its outcomes. Dávila's documentary illustrates the active engagement of Puerto Ricans in their efforts, demonstrating that progress is being made. It suggests that subsequent steps may be more attainable than previously perceived. These mutual aid networks are not calling for revolution per se, but they do pose a vital question: If we work together, move away from the current power structure, and develop a way forward in community, what good might come from it? The film is pessimistically hopeful in the sense that it recognizes the ills of the past but thinks through new ways forward. It is unsatisfactory, but it is a start. The concept of archipelagoes of longing facilitates the convergence of affective moments, enabling the exploration of nonlinear approaches that offer liberatory pathways forward.

Dávila's films in many ways provide an archiving of what has happened and a roadmap that parallels the woes of the US state of Hawaii, a place Bad Bunny reflects upon in "Lo que le pasó a Hawaii" from *DeBí TiRAR MáS FOToS*. The song's chorus states, "Quieren quitarme el río y también la playa, / Quieren el barrio mío y que abuelito se vaya, No, no sueltes la bandera ni olvides el lelolai, / Que no quiero que hagan contigo lo que le pasó a Hawaii." I end the book on this note because it captures an inflection point that Puerto Rico faces. As big business and investors are increasingly trying to take over the beaches of the island (McCaffrey, "Las Playas"), and more and more Puerto Ricans leave the commonwealth due to systemic governmental failures (Meléndez-Badillo), the song's warning that Puerto Rico must not be lost to capitalist interest grasps the seriousness of the island's problems. While there are movements to bolster autonomy and mutual aid organizations do important work, Puerto Rico remains at the mercy of a mercurial president ready to cut ties for racist reasons (Baker and Glasser 355–56). What this book has sought to do, and what Bad Bunny captures, is the affective response to the onslaught of issues facing Puerto Rico and its diaspora. With both hope and fear, pride and shame, desire and neglect, these mixed emotions capture the desire that inhabits Puerto Rico's present in a way that is complex and compelling without falling into platitudes and simple conclusions. Yet nothing captures this mix of emotions more fully than Bad Bunny simply saying, "Yo soy de p fuckin' r."

Notes

Introduction

1. For a more detailed accounting of the debt crisis and the impact on the island's political, economic, and cultural systems, see Ed Morales's *Fantasy Island: Colonialism, Exploitation, and the Betrayal of Puerto Rico* (2019); A. W. Maldonado's *Boom and Bust in Puerto Rico: How Politics Destroyed an Economic Miracle* (2021); and Naomi Klein's *The Battle for Paradise: Puerto Rico Takes on Disaster Capitalism* (2018).

2. The field of memory studies is an expansive one, and though recent scholarship has begun to engage with the multivalent nature of memory, the field still struggles to adequately encompass the lived experience of colonized peoples as they continue to engage with systemic forms of oppression. Approaches such as Michael Rothberg's "multidirectional memory," Kaitlin Murphy's "memory mapping," Stef Craps's "postcolonial witnessings," and Astrid Erll's "traveling memory" provide frameworks for understanding the various historical, spatial, subjective, and cultural nodes that comprise memory formations.

3. Other Caribbean thinkers have also reexamined the role of history and the articulation of memory in the Antilles. Yarimar Bonilla's "The Past Is Made by Walking: Labor Activism and Historical Production in Postcolonial Guadeloupe" (2011) shows how memory walks create new historical archives and memory constructions that are not wholly linked to hegemonic actors. Similarly, Rolph-Michel Trouillot's *Silencing the Past: Power and the Production of History* (1995) challenges the unitary nature of history formation in the West, which is used in memory formations.

4. Scholars have critiqued the notion of political independence within the broader Puerto Rican consciousness (Acosta Cruz) and the importance of the in-between status (Soto-Crespo). The use of the term "liberation" throughout the book is not just political but also thinks through the existential, material, and ideological freedoms that the cultural products speak toward. The longing for liberation is less political and more about being less oppressed within existing power structures.

5. I take this term from Mariposa Fernandez's 1993 poem "Ode to the Diasporican," where she celebrates the lived experience of Puerto Ricans who live outside the island.

6. I examine the works of Cristian Roldán, Sam Kirk, and John Vergara from Chicago and Danny Torres, Betsy Casañas, Ian Pierce, Mario Galan, Jose Bermudez, and Hector Rosario in Philadelphia.

Chapter 1

1. Las Puertas del Paseo Boricua is a community-based arts project that brought together sixteen artists to paint representations of their culture on Division Street doors, curated by Chicago-based artist Sam Kirk and assisted by Cristian Roldán Aponte.

2. Author translation.

3. Taíno petroglyphs can be found in many parts of the Caribbean and created over the course of nearly a thousand years. For an in-depth anthropological examination of the petroglyphs, their meaning, and their history, see Jose R. Oliver's *El centro ceremonial de Caguana, Puerto Rico: Simbolismo iconográfico, cosmovisión y el poderío caciquil Taíno de Borinquén* (1998). Throughout the Caribbean, petroglyphs are etched into rock formations holding both religious and mythological importance for the native Taíno people of Puerto Rico. Observations of the rock art can be found as early as 1793, though academic study of the formations has proliferated since the 1970s (Hayward et al. 116). They are disconnected from their original locations, the meaning the Taínos gave them, and their religious significance. Additionally, for further reading on the complexities of Indigenous people in Puerto Rico prior to European colonization, see Reniel Rodriguez Ramos's *Rethinking Puerto Rican Precolonial History* (2010), in which he unpacks the colonial history within Puerto Rican archaeology and provides new understandings of the place of Indigenous groups in Puerto Rico and the Antilles more broadly.

4. Street art murals and their meanings are in a perpetual state of tension. Questions of what constitutes street art, its purpose, who creates it, who sanctions it, and who views it complicate the more direct nature of museum-located art. Street art and public art are in a constant tug-of-war with their own definitions. Street art is commonly defined by its use of the street in an integral way, and that use impacts the meaning of the piece of art (Riggle 245–46). Street art also has a location-specific meaning and loses its significance when removed from the location (244). Street art is traditionally not sanctioned by the state, thus becoming an anti-establishment form of expression and also communicating with all members of the broader city (Waclawek 80). In more recent times, street art is being used by state actors as a way to bring investment to cities, taking an art form that "rages against the machine," so to speak, and incorporating it into official state business. Seen this

way, street art has become a part of what defines the "global city," used to mark a city's cosmopolitan credentials while eschewing the medium's antiestablishment ethos.

5. Nostalgia is often linked to right-wing mobilization and nation-building efforts that seek to reinvent the past for xenophobic or racist national narrativization (Bonnet; Kenny; Tinsley). Within these tropes, a cementation of hegemonic national narratives occurs in which the past is implemented in racializing discourses. This is what Svetlana Boym calls restorative nostalgia; it is different from reflective nostalgia, which aims to create a "total reconstruction" of the past that is monolithic in nature and usually linked to nationalistic understandings of origin (41). This type of nostalgia is one-dimensional, seeking to reestablish old tropes and exclude nonhegemonic members of an ever-changing society.

6. The artwork in this chapter is not graffiti, though the street art here shares many political similarities with graffiti. For further reading, please see Konstantinos Avramidis and Myrto Tsilimpounidi, editors, *Graffiti and Street Art: Reading, Writing and Representing the City* (2017); Armando Silva, *Atmósferas ciudadanas: Graffiti, arte, nichos estéticos* (2013); and Anna Waclawek, *Graffiti and Street Art* (2011).

7. For a full historical origin, significance, and description, see Teodoro Vidal's *El vejigante ponceño* (2003).

8. In her 2001 article "Coloa Subjectivities: PortoMex and MexiRican Perspectives on Language and Identity," Rúa theorizes the concept of making coffee (*colar*) as a method of examining racial and ethnic constructs in Mexican and Puerto Rican communities in Chicago. Using the many meanings of the word *colar*, from "passing through" to "emptying," Rúa sees it as a metaphor for the various ways MexiRicans and PortoMex peoples in Chicago navigate their identity in a way that is multifaceted and at once rejects and acknowledges the nuances in their identity.

9. Recent census work has challenged the dominance of US racial categories. Data from the 2020 census show a marked increase in Puerto Rican identification as mixed race, jumping by 3.3% from a decade earlier (Cordero Mercado). Additionally, Colectivo Ilé, an antiracist organization that works to foment and celebrate Afro-descendant culture in Puerto Rico, launched a campaign during the census to have Puerto Ricans have their racial identity adequately reflected on the census ("Resultados Censo 2020").

10. For more on urban-based racial categorizations in Puerto Rico, see *Locked In, Locked Out: Gated Communities in a Puerto Rican City* (2013) and *Policing Life and Death: Race, Violence, and Resistance in Puerto Rico* (2019) by Marisol LeBrón.

11. The Puerto Rican Cultural Center is a community-based organization that promotes cultural and social services for Chicago Ricans. Founded in 1973, the organization has been a pioneer in advocating for education, health, and housing as well as preserving Puerto Rican culture through art and digital media ("The Puerto Rican Cultural Center").

12. For further reading on the riots, see Lilia Fernández, *Brown in the Windy City: Mexicans and Puerto Ricans in Postwar Chicago* (2012).

13. Midcentury Chicago Ricans were already disgruntled about mistreatment and harassment by police and the lack of accountability for city officials. The 1966 killing of Arcelis Cruz and subsequent cover-up, coupled with long-held frustrations over the threat of gentrification and poor living conditions in the area, ignited the unrest. Ending on the night of June 15, the riot saw the ravaging of police stations and local businesses and led to the arrests of thirty-seven people.

Chapter 2

1. The use of the word "shrouding" is inspired by Zachary Blair's 2022 essay "Orlando's Rainbow Shroud," where he criticizes the economic interest and LGBTQ obfuscation in the 2022 "community rainbow run" in Orlando. While Blair only uses the term in his title, I find it an apt description for the presence of Latinxs and Puerto Ricans in the Interim Pulse National Memorial.

2. Twenty-three of the forty-nine lives lost were Puerto Rican and 90% were Latinxs (La Fountain-Stokes, "Los puertorriqueños queer").

3. Following the shooting there was much media attention on Mateen's sexual orientation and motivation behind the shooting. It is now believed he chose the location at random (Fitzsimons 2018), did not lead a secret gay life (Greenwald and Hussain 2017), and has no formal ties to organized terrorist organizations (Bergen 2016). However, the need to formalize these connections by the media demonstrates Puar's homonationalism in this case.

4. As of the writing of this chapter, the planned permanent memorial and museum have been canceled due to representational disagreements and economic uncertainty regarding the project (Kuo 2023).

5. One of the victims' names has been removed at the request of their family.

6. I explicitly use Clark's term "trauma tourism" rather than Bridgette Sion's "death tourism," as I believe the broader issues of trauma and memory in these commemorative sites engage various subjectivities and broader issues that cause trauma. While Sion's articulation is instructive—and certainly applicable to the Pulse National Memorial—I believe for this project Clark's definition better encompasses the issues of identity, erasure, commemorations, and global forces. For further reading, see Laurie Beth Clark's "Coming to Terms with Trauma Tourism" (2009) and Bridgitte Sion's *Death Tourism: Disaster Sites as Recreational Landscape* (2014).

7. I want to briefly recognize the focus on Latinx representation in this chapter at the expense of the many other identities in commemorative sites. Scholars in Latinx studies have long noted the one-dimensionality of Latinx peoples as presented in the media and the culture at large. Numerous subjectivities have been funneled into the US racial binary by privileging whiteness and erasing or downplaying other racial categories (Beltrán; Beltrán and Fojas). These representations also fuse subjectivities

such as race, class, and ethnicity in ways that essentialize Latinx identities into neoliberal ideas of multiculturalism (Urciuoli). Finally, the place of "other Latinos" such as new arrivals from Central and South America have challenged the perceived homogeneity of Latinx peoples in the United States (Falconi and Mazzotti). These representations both reimpose and challenge a neoliberal understanding of Latinx peoples in the United States that flattens their specific cultural, national, and immigration experiences. I want to acknowledge the various identities that were lost at the Pulse massacre that will not be discussed in this chapter, including immigrant, racial, and class status. These other intersectional identities deserve further exploration, but for reasons of scope and cohesion, I will not address them in this project. I implore other scholars to examine the depiction of such subjectivities in the commemorative sites to add depth and further criticism of this wall. My aim is to shed light on the varied nature of queer Latinx representation and to avoid repeating in this chapter the same type of shrouding that occurs in real life.

8. Barthes explains that images have three meanings. The first is the literal elements of the image such as people, objects, and places that directly relay certain facts. The second meaning elucidates the symbolic understanding of those people, objects, and places that give those things culturally relevant significance. Rather than understanding images as only the first (literal) or the second (symbolic) meaning, the third symbol moves beyond these two and points to other possibilities. This third meaning is much more difficult to read and interpret as it does not sit neatly in the framework of the image itself but "exceeds the copy of the referential motif" and "compels an interrogative reading" (319).

9. My understanding of collective memory is the personal-social construction of remembrance, where the collective and the individual cannot be de-linked and one informs the other. For further reading, consider Maurice Halbwachs's *The Collective Memory* (1925), Jan Assman's *Cultural Memory and Early Civilization: Writing, Remembrance, and Political Imagination* (2011), and Jeffrey Olick's "Collective Memory: The Two Cultures" (1999).

Chapter 3

1. Rafael Hernández Marín is also famous for another Puerto Rican songs "Preciosa." For further information on the impact of Hernandez Marín's work on Puerot Rican music, see *La Brega*'s "Preciosa: The Other Anthem."

2. Since the passing of Maria and the United States' botched response, there has been a plethora of collections that have tried to capture the various obstacles and stories of the moment. Works like *Crónicas de María: Voces para la historia* (2018), *Aftershocks of Disaster: Puerto Rico Before and After the Storm* (2019), and

Mi María: Surviving the Storm, Voices from Puerto Rico (2021), among others have tried to compile the literary and artistic expression after the storm. I chose Orsanc and Fusario Martinez because of the immediacy of the writing, where the majority of the texts were written at the end of 2017 and early 2018. The bilingual nature and political focus of Morales's collection provides a compelling addition to the analysis that is inclusive of the diaspora.

3. I use the *Tesoro lexicográfico del español de Puerto Rico* to translate the following words from a Puerto Rican–specific meaning to a general Spanish and then to English: *eñemao, envenanao.* I was assisted by my grandmother, Francisca Crespo Robles, for the following translations: *enfucaho, encaprichao, estotorlao,* and *estrasijao.*

4. I will provide loose translations of these idiomatic expressions. The gist here is "Things aren't so bad; there is no need to complain."

5. To "Sigh, because we are all in this together."

6. To "Just give up; there's no point in continuing."

7. This sentence refers to the irritation you feel when people tell you something you do not want to hear.

8. Established in 1980, Casa Pueblo is an environmental advocacy non-profit that has transformed into a mutual aid organization that works on various community-based projects. Documentation of the environmental impact in Vieques, a solar energy project, and local fair trade coffee production are just several of the ventures that the organization has embraced over the decades (Casa Pueblo). Massol-Deyá's essay makes reference to a solar energy project in the City of Adjuntas, a small community of seventeen thousand residents in the southwest mountainous region of the main island of Puerto Rico. Even prior to the arrival of Hurricane Maria, Casa Pueblo had been installing solar panels through community organization.

9. Other scholars have similarly engaged with the ongoing nature of Puerto Rican mourning. "Dancing in an Enclosure: Activism and Mourning in Puerto Rican Summer 2019" (2022) by Arnaldo Cruz-Malavé, "Cities of the Dead: Performing Life in the Caribbean" (2018) by Jossiana Arroyo, and "Necromdia, Haunting and Public Mourning in the Puerto Rican Debt State: The Case of 'Los Muertos'" (2018) by Jason Cortés provide compelling analysis on the mourning not just the lives lost in Maria but the continued devastations of colonial mismanagement.

10. While José Martí is often seen as one of the pioneers of Latin American thinking that centers the region's own cultural autonomy, his work is fraught with racial tensions. Scholars such as Juliet Hooker (2019) have noted the selective use of US racial history to obscure Latin America's own racial tensions. For further reading, see Tanya Hernández's "Envisioning the United States in Latin American Myth of 'Racial Democracy Mestizaje'" (2016), Ada Ferrer's "The Silence of Patriots: Race and Nationalism in Martí's Cuba" (1998), and Alejandro de la Fuente's *A Nation for All: Race, Inequality and Politics in Twentieth-Century Cuba* (2001).

Chapter 4

1. For further reading on the *perreo* dance and its controversy, see Fairley, "Dancing Back to Front" (2016); Baker, "The Politics of Dancing" (2009); and Rivera Rideau, "The Perils of Perreo" (2015).

2. Puerto Rico has a long history of using documentary to inform some of the most pressing issues of the day and exploring various identity questions both in the archipelago and in the United States. Some of the most notable films such as *La batalla de Vieques* (1986), *Brincando el charco: Portrait of a Puerto Rican* (1994), *La operación* (1982), and *The Heart of the Loisada* (1979) take on collection action and issues of belonging in the Puerto Rican experience. More contemporarily, films such as *Mala Mala* (2014), *Landfall* (2020), and *Serán las dueñas de la tierra* (2022) take on some of the most pressing environmental, colonial, and social issues facing Puerto Ricans today.

3. While a full genealogy of the US relationship and bombing in Culebra is not within the purview of this chapter, it is important to note the impact the movements on the island had in shifting the bombings to Vieques and the political differences in each case. For further reading, consult Katherine McCaffrey's *Military Power and Popular Protest in Vieques, Puerto Rico* (2002), in which she provides a full accounting of the history and stakes of the bombings in Vieques. It was not until 1974 that President Richard Nixon signed an executive order halting the US Navy's bombing of the island of Culebra and moving the bombing to an uninhabited island off the coast of mainland Puerto Rico. Instead, however, the military took the appropriated funds and, "with no apparent authorization," began bombing on Vieques (McCaffrey 14). This set off a crisis between the people of Vieques, the Commonwealth of Puerto Rico, the US military, and the US government that continued for the next four decades. While the navy's interest in the south side of the Vieques had been in the making since the 1960s, it was not until the 1970s that the military began using the island as a bombing site in earnest.

4. A 2018 *New York Times* article showed that the excessive deaths in the aftermath of Hurricane Maria exceeded four thousand lives while the official government toll stood at sixty-four.

Works Cited

Achugar, Hugo. "Historias paralelas/ejemplares: La historia y la voz del otro." *Revista de Crítica Literaria Latinoamericana*, vol. 18, no. 36, 1992, pp. 51–73.

Acosta, Katie. "Pulse: A Resilience, A Home for the Brave." *QED: A Journal in GLBTQ Worldmaking*, vol. 3, no. 3, 2016, pp. 107–10.

Acosta Cruz, Maria. *Dream Nation: Puerto Rican Culture and the Fictions of Independence*. Rutgers UP, 2014.

Agrelo, Justin, et al. "Puerto Ricans in Chicago: The Stories of Struggle and Survival." *Centro de Periodismo Investigativo*, 20 Mar. 2019, https://periodismoinvestigativo.com/2019/03/puerto-ricans-in-chicago-the-stories-of-struggle-and-survival-go-on/. Accessed 23 Jan. 2024.

Ahmed, Sara. *Queer Phenomenology: Orientations, Objects, Others*. Duke UP, 2004.

———. *The Cultural Politics of Emotion*. Edinburgh UP, 2014.

Alvarez, Lizette. "A Great Migration from Puerto Rico Is Set to Transform Orlando." *New York Times*, 17 Nov. 2017, https://www.nytimes.com/2017/11/17/us/puerto-ricans-orlando.html. Accessed 2 Feb. 2022.

Aparicio, Frances. "Not Fully Boricuas: Puerto Rican Intralatino/as in Chicago." *CENTRO Journal*, vol. 28, no. 2, 2016, pp. 154–79.

Arenillas, Maria Guadalupe, and Michael Lazzara. "Introduction." *Latin American Documentary Film in the New Millennium*, edited by Arenillas and Lazzara, Palgrave Macmillan, 2016, pp. 1–19.

Arroyo, Jossiana. "Cities of the Dead: Performing Life in the Caribbean." *Journal of Latin American Cultural Studies*, vol. 27, no. 3, 2018, pp. 331–56.

———. "'Roots' or the Virtualities of Racial Imaginaries in Puerto Rico and the Diaspora." *Latino Studies*, vol. 8, no. 2, 2010, pp. 195–219.

Assman, Jan. *Cultural Memory and Early Civilization: Writing, Remembrance, and Political Imagination*. Cambridge UP, 2011.

Atiles-Osorio, José M. "Neoliberalism, Law, and Strikes: Law as an Instrument of Repression at the University of Puerto Rico, 2010–2011." *Latin American Perspectives*, issue 192, vol. 40, no. 5, 2013, pp. 105–17.

Avilés-Santiago, Manuel. *Puerto Rican Soldiers and Second-Class Citizenship: Representations in Media*. Palgrave Macmillan, 2014.

Ayala, César J., and Rafael Bernabe. *Puerto Rico in the American Century: A History Since 1898*. U of North Carolina P, 2007.

Bad Bunny. "DtMF." *DeBí TiRAR MáS FOToS*, Rimas Entertainment, 2025. *Spotify*, https://open.spotify.com/track/3sK8wGT43QFpWrvNQsrQya.

———. "El apagón." *Un Verano Sin Ti*, Rimas Entertainment, 2022. *Spotify*, https://open.spotify.com/track/0UvZcEfpzVyx47QsRbjyBz.

———. "LO QUE LE PASÓ A HAWAii." *DeBí TiRAR MáS FOToS*, Rimas Entertainment, 2025. *Spotify*, https://open.spotify.com/track/1Hg0e997pObvZ91w1FCPFk.

———. "NUEVAYoL." *DeBí TiRAR MáS FOToS*, Rimas Entertainment, 2025. *Spotify*, https://open.spotify.com/track/5TFD2bmFKGhoCRbX61nXY5.

Baker, Geoff. "The Politics of Dancing: Reggaetón and Rap in Havana, Cuba." *Reggaeton*, edited by Raquel Z. Rivera, et al., Duke UP, 2009, pp. 165–99.

Baker, Peter, and Susan Glasser. *The Divider: Trump in the White House, 2017–2021*. Doubleday, 2022.

Bakhtin, Mikhail. *Problems of Dostoevsky's Poetics*, edited by Caril Emerson, U of Minnesota P, 1984.

Barradas, Efraín. " 'De lejos en sueños verla . . .' Visión mítica de Puerto Rico en la poesía neyorrican." *Revista Chicano-Riqueña*, vol. 7, no. 3, 1979, pp. 46–57.

Barreneche, Gabriel Ignacio, et al. "A New Destination for 'The Flying Bus'? The Implications of Orlando-Rican Migration for Luis Rafael Sánchez's 'La guagua aérea.' " *Hispania*, vol. 95, no. 1, 2012, pp. 14–23.

Barthes, Roland. "The Third Meaning." *A Barthes Reader*, edited by Susan Sontag, Hill and Wang, 1982, pp. 317–33.

Bay-Cheng, Sarah. "Digital Historiography and Performance." *Theatre Journal*, vol. 68, no. 4, 2016, p. 507–27.

Beltrán, Mary C. "Introduction." *Latina/o Stars in U.S. Eyes: The Making of Meanings of Film and TV Stardom*, U of Illinois P, 2009, pp. 1–16.

———, and Camilla Fojas. "Introduction: Mixed Race in Hollywood Film and Media Culture." *Mixed Race Hollywood*, NYU Press, 2008, pp. 1–22.

Berman Santana, Deborah. "Indigenous Identity and the Struggle for Independence in Puerto Rico." *Sovereignty Matters: Locations of Contestation and Possibilities in Indigenous Struggles for Self-Determination*, edited by Joanne Baker, U of Nebraska P, 2005, pp. 211–23.

———. *Kicking Off the Bootstraps: Environment, Development, and Community Power in Puerto Rico*. U of Arizona P, 1996.

Beverley, John. " 'Through All Things Modern': Second Thoughts on Testimonio." *boundary 2*, vol. 18, no. 2, 1991, pp. 1–21.

Blair, Zachary. "More Than onePULSE: Design and Dissent in Orlando." *The Avery Review*, 2019, pp. 1–7.

———. "Orlando's Rainbow Shroud." *Zachary Blair Blog*, 2022.

———. "The Pulse Nightclub Shooting: Connecting Militarism, Neoliberalism, and Multiculturalism to Understand Violence." *North American Dialogue*, vol. 19, no. 2, 2016, pp. 102–16.

———. "Pulse: How a Single Code Violation Led to One of the Worst Mass Shootings in US History." *Zachary Blair Blog*, 2021. Accessed 30 May 2021.

———. "Reimagining a Public Pulse Memorial." *Zachary Blair Blog*, 2019, https://www.zachary-blair.com/post/reimaging-a-public-pulse-memorial. Accessed 13 Mar. 2021.

Boehm, Lisa Kristoff. "Reframing, Rethinking, Remembering: Considering the Digital Harrisburg Project." *Pennsylvania History: A Journal of Mid-Atlantic Studies*, vol. 87, no. 1, 2020, pp. 233–42.

Bonilla, Yarimar. "The Coloniality of Disaster: Race, Empire, and the Temporal Logics of Emergency in Puerto Rico, USA." *Political Geography*, vol. 18, 2020, pp. 1–48.

———. *Non-Sovereign Futures: French Caribbean Politics in the Wake of Disenchantment.* U of Chicago P, 2015.

———. "Postdisaster Futures: Hopeful Pessimism, Imperial Ruination, and *La futura cuir.*" *Small Axe*, vol. 24, no. 2, 2020, pp. 147–62.

———. "Se acabaron las promesas." Episode 7. *La Brega*, WNYC Studios, 24 Feb. 2021, https://www.wnycstudios.org/podcasts/la-brega/articles/se-acabaron-las-promesas.

———. "Why Must Puerto Ricans Always Be Resilient?" *New York Times*, 10 Oct. 2022.

———, and Marisol LeBrón. *Aftershocks of Disaster: Puerto Rico Before and After the Storm.* Haymarket Books, 2019.

Bonnet, Alastair. *Left in the Past: Radicalism and the Politics of Nostalgia.* Bloomsbury Academic, 2010.

Bossi, Andrea. "How Bad Bunny Influenced Puerto Rico's 2019, 'Ricky Renuncia.'" *Forbes*, 26 Dec. 2019, https://www.forbes.com/sites/andreabossi/2019/12/26/how-bad-bunny-influenced-puerto-ricos-2019-movement-ricky-renuncia/. Accessed 1 Apr. 2025.

Boym, Svetlana. *The Future of Nostalgia.* Basic Books, 2002.

Bravmann, Scott. *Queer Fictions of the Past: History, Culture, and Difference.* Cambridge UP, 1997.

Brydum, Sunnivie. "Puerto Rico's First LGBT Monument Honors Orlando Victims." *Advocate*, 5 July 2016, https://www.advocate.com/pride/2016/7/03/puerto-ricos-first-lgbt-monument-honors-orlando-victims. Accessed 2 July 2024.

Burton, Julianne. "Toward a History of Social Documentary in Latin America." *The Social Documentary in Latin America*, edited by Julianne Burton, U of Pittsburgh P, 1990, pp. 3–30.

Butler, Judith. *Frames of War: When Is Life Grievable?* Verso Books, 2009.

———. *Notes Toward a Performative Theory of Assembly*. Harvard UP, 2015.

Cantú, Lionel. "Entre Hombres/Between Men: Latino Masculinities and Homosexualities." *Gay Latino Studies: A Reader*, edited by Michael Hames-García and Ernesto Javier Martínez, Duke UP, 2011, pp. 148–67.

Casey, Edward. "Publish Memory in Place and Time." *Framing Public Memory*, U of Alabama P, 2004, pp. 17–44.

Castillo, Luciano. "Puerto Rico." *Diccionario del Cine Iberoamericano: España, Portugal, y América*, SGAE, vol. 7, 2011, pp. 110–17.

Chansky, Rica Anna, and Marci Denesiuk. *Surviving the Storm: Voices from Puerto Rico*. Haymarket Books, 2021.

Chapman, Jane. *Issues in Contemporary Documentary*. Polity, 2009.

Chocano, Carina. "The World's Newest Superhero: Bad Bunny." *GQ*, 24 May 2022, https://www.gq.com/story/bad-bunny-june-cover-profile.

Clark, Laurie Beth. "Coming to Terms with Trauma Tourism." *Performance Paradigm*, vol. 5, no. 2, 2009, pp. 162–84.

Compañeros de lucha. Directed by Juan C. Dávila, Frútos Filimicos, 2012.

Cordero Mercado, David. "Dámatico salto en la percepción multirracial en Puerto Rico en el Censo de 2020." *El nuevo día*, 12 Aug. 2020, https://www.elnuevodia.com/noticias/locales/notas/dramatico-salto-en-la-percepcion-multiracial-en-puerto-rico-en-el-censo-de-2020/.

Cowie, Elizabeth. *Recording Reality, Desiring the Real*. U of Minnesota P, 2011.

Cintrón, Ralph, et al. *60 Years of Migration: Puerto Ricans in Chicagoland*. Puerto Rican Agenda, 2012.

Cintrón Arbasetti, Joel. "Moving Maps: Puerto Ricans Struggle for Their Place in Philadelphia." *Centro de Perdiodismo Investigativo*, 30 Nov. 2020, https://periodismoinvestigativo.com/2020/11/moving-maps-puerto-ricans-struggle-for-their-place-in-philadelphia/. Accessed 23 Jan. 2024.

Cortés, Jason. "Wounding Materiality: Oller's El velurio and the Trauma of Subaltern Visibility." *Revista Hispánica Moderna*, vol. 65, no. 2, 2012, pp. 165–80.

Craps, Stef. *Postcolonial Witnessing: Trauma Out of Bounds*. Palgrave Macmillan, 2013.

Creet, Julia. "Introduction: The Migration of Memory and the Memory of Migration." *Memory and Migration: Multidisciplinary Approaches to Memory Studies*, edited by Julia Creet and Andreas Kitzman, U of Toronto P, 2010, pp. 3–26.

Crónicas de María: Voces para la historia. Independent Publisher, 2018.

Cruz, Mariela. "Grito a la Patria." *Voices from Puerto Rico/Voces desde Puerto Rico*, edited by Iris Morales, Red Sugarcane Press, 2019, pp. 202–03.

Cruz, Wilfredo. *City of Dreams: Latino Immigration to Chicago*. UP of America, 2007.

Cruz-Malavé, Arnaldo M. "Dancing in the Enclosure: Activism and Mourning in the Puerto Rican Summer 2019." *Small Axe*, vol. 26, no. 2, 2022, pp. 1–23.

Dawson, Michael, and Megan Ming Francis. "Black Politics and the Neoliberal Racial Order." *Popular Culture*, vol. 28, no. 1, 2015, pp. 23–62.

Dávila, Arlene. "Local/Diasporic Taínos: Towards a Cultural Politics of Memory, Reality, and Imagery." *Taíno Revival: Critical Perspectives on Puerto Rican Identity and Politics*, edited by Gabriel Haslip-Viera, Centro de Estudios Puertorriqueños, 1999, pp. 11–29.

Dávila, Juan C. Personal interview. 14 June 2023.

———. Interview with Nelie Diverlus. *Vibe 105*, 18 July 2022, https://www.youtube.com/watch?v=zCndq9qmLkY.

———. Interview with Veronica Fonseca. *Diálogo UPR*, 27 June 2013, https://dialogo.upr.edu/documentar-la-resistencia-3/.

De Cesari, Chiara, and Ann Rigney. "Introduction: Beyond Methodological Nationalism." *Transnational Memory: Circulation, Articulation, Scales*, edited by Chiara de Cesari and Ann Rigney, *Media and Cultural Memory*, vol. 19, 2014, pp. 1–26.

de la Fuente, Alejandro. *A Nation for All: Race, Inequality and Politics in Twentieth-Century Cuba*. U of North Carolina P, 2001.

Delerme, Simone Pierre. *Latino Orlando: Suburban Transformation and Racial Conflict*. U of Florida P, 2020.

DeLoughrey, Elizabeth. "Tidalectics: Charting the Space/Time of Caribbean Waters." *SPAN*, vol. 47, 1998, pp. 18–38

De Onís, Catalina M. *Energy Island: Metaphors of Power, Extractivism, and Justice in Puerto Rico*. U of California P, 2021.

De Vogue, Ariane. "Supreme Court Rules Puerto Ricans Don't Have Constitutional Right to Some Federal Benefits." CNN, 21 Apr. 2022, https://www.cnn.com/2022/04/21/politics/puerto-rico-supreme-court-federal-disability-benefits/index.html. Accessed 3 May 2023.

Díaz, Junot. "Apocalypse: There Are No Natural Disasters, Only Social Ones." *Boston Review*, 1 May 2011, https://www.bostonreview.net/articles/junot-diaz-apocalypse-haiti-earthquake/.

Díaz Quiñones, Arcadio. *La memoria rota: Ensayos sobre cultura y política*. Ediciones Huracán, 1993.

Dineen, Caitlin. "Pulse Could Become the Latest Tragedy Tourism Destination: Orlando Nightclub Shooting." *Orlando Sentinel*, 27 July 2016, https://www.orlandosentinel.com/2016/07/26/pulse-could-become-the-latest-tragedy-tourism-destination/. Accessed 30 Jan. 2024.

Dinzey Flores, Zaire. *Locked In, Locked Out: Gated Communities in a Puerto Rican City*. U of Philadelphia P, 2013.

Duany, Jorge. *Blurred Borders: Transnational Migration Between the Hispanic Caribbean and the United States*. U of North Carolina P, 2011.

———. "Mickey Ricans? The Recent Puerto Rican Diaspora to Florida." *La Florida: Five Hundred Years of Hispanic Presence*, edited by Viviana Díaz Balsera and Rachel May, U of Florida P, 2014, pp. 224–38.

———. "Neither White nor Black: The Representation of Racial Identity Among Puerto Ricans on the Island and in the U.S. Mainland." *Neither Enemies nor Friends: Latinos, Blacks, Afro-Latinos*, edited by S. Ober and A. Dzidienyo, Palgrave Macmillan, 2005, pp. 173–88.

———. *The Puerto Rican Nation on the Move: Identities on the Island and in the United States*. U of North Carolina P, 2002.

———. "A Transnational Colonial Migration: Puerto Rico's Farm Labor Program." *New West Indian Guide*, vol. 84, no. 3–4, 2010, pp. 225–51.

Dugan, Lisa. *Materializing Democracy: Toward a Revitalized Cultural Politics*. Duke UP, 2002.

Dunn, Thomas. *Queerly Remembered: Rhetorics for Representing GLBTQ Past*. U of South Carolina P, 2016.

El Gran Combo de Puerto Rico. "Un Verano en Nueva York." 1975. *Spotify*, https://open.spotify.com/track/1q2J8KWeewoqOrZI4a65P9.

"Eñemado, adj." *Tesoro lexicográfico del español de Puerto Rico*, https://tesoro.pr/lema/enemado-da. Accessed 18 June 2024.

"Envenenado, adj." *Tesoro lexicográfico del español de Puerto Rico*, https://tesoro.pr/lema/envenenado-da. Accessed 18 June 2024.

Erll, Astrid. "The Hidden Power of Implicit Collective Memory." *Memory, Mind & Media*, vol. 1, no. 14, pp. 1–17.

———. "Travelling Memory." *Parallax*, vol. 17, no. 4, 2011, pp. 4–18.

Espada, Mariah. "Influencers, Developers, Crypto Currency Tycoons: How Puerto Ricans Are Fighting Back the Outsiders Using the Island as a Tax Haven." *Time Magazine*, 16 Apr. 2021. https://time.com/5955629/puerto-rico-tax-haven-opposition/.

Fairley, Jan. "Dancing Back to Front: Regeton, Sexuality, Gender, and Transnationalism in Cuba." *Popular Music*, vol. 25, no. 3, 2006, pp. 471–88.

Falconi, José Luis, and José Antonio Mazzotti. "Introduction." *The Other Latinos: Central Americans and South Americans in the United States*, Harvard UP, 2007, pp. 1–20.

Farmers of the Seas. Directed by Juan C. Dávila, Firelight Media, 2024.

Feliciano-Santos, Sherina. *A Contested Caribbean Indigeneity: Language, Social Practice, and Identity within Puerto Rican Taíno Activism*. Rutgers UP, 2021.

FEMA. *Hurricanes Irma and Maria in Puerto Rico: Building Performance, Observations, Recommendations, and Technical Guidance*. Federal Emergency Management Agency, 2018.

Fernández, Lilia. *Brown in the Windy City: Mexicans and Puerto Ricans in Postwar Chicago*. U of Chicago P, 2012.

Fernández, Mariposa. "Ode to the Diasporican." 1993.

Ferrell, Jeff. "Graffiti, Street Art and the Dialectics of the City." *Graffiti and Street Art: Reading, Writing and Representing the City*, edited by Konstantinos Avramidis and Myrto Tsilimpoundi, Routledge, 2017, pp. 27–38.

Ferrer, Ada. "The Silence of Patriots: Race and Nationalism in Martí's Cuba." *Josee Martí's "Our America": From National to Hemispheric Cultural Studies*, edited by Jeffrey Grant Belnap and Raul A. Fernandez, Duke UP, 1998, pp. 228–52.

Ferré-Sadurní, Luis. "Irma Grazes Puerto Rico but Lays Bare an Infrastructure Problem." *New York Times*, 10 Sep. 2017, https://www.nytimes.com/2017/09/10/us/irma-puerto-rico-infrastructure.html?mcubz=0.

Figueroa Cabrero, Enrique. "Un chiste a mal gusto." *Pa la posteridá: Antologia sobre el paso del Huracán María por Puerto Rico*, edited by Lucía Orsanic and Jorge Fusaro Martínez, Ediciones del Flamboyán, 2018, pp. 87–88.

Flores, Juan. *Divided Borders: Essays on Puerto Rican Identity*. Arte Publico Press, 1993.

Flores-González, Nilda. "Paseo Boricua: Claiming a Puerto Rican Space in Chicago." *CENTRO Journal*, vol. 13, no. 2, 2001, pp. 7–23.

Forte, Maximilian. "Extinction: The Historical Trope of Anti-indigeneity in the Caribbean." *Issues in Caribbean Amerindian Studies*, vol. 6, no. 4, 2005, pp. 1–24.

Franqui-Rivera, Harry. *Soldiers of the Nation: Military Service and Modern Puerto Rico, 1868–1952*. U of Nebraska P, 2018.

Gargiulo, Megan, and Monica Lugo-Velez. "Queer Bad Bunny: Gender, Nostalgia, and Coloniality in Bad Bunny's X100PRE." *Latin American Cultural Studies*, vol. 33, no. 3, 2024, pp. 407–23.

Graulau, B. [Bianca Graulau]. (2021 Dec. 28). "Are Puerto Ricans Being Pushed Out?" *YouTube*. https://www.youtube.com/watch?v=YGXtWpCOiC8.

Hernández, Tanya Katería. "Envisioning the United States in Latin American Myth of 'Racial Democracy Mestizaje.'" *Latin American and Caribbean Ethnic Studies*, vol. 11, no. 2, 2016, pp. 1–17.

Herrera, Juan. *Cartographic Memory: Social Movement Activism and the Production of Space*. Duke UP, 2022.

Hooker, Juliet. "Hemispheric Comparison in Latin American Anti-Imperial Thought." *The Oxford Handbook of Comparative Political Theory*, edited by Leigh Jenco, et al., Oxford UP, 2019, pp. 67–110.

Iasimone, Ashley. "Fans Choose Bad Bunny's 'Un Verano Sin Ti' as This Week's Favorite New Music." *Billboard*, 8 May 2022, https://www.billboard.com/music/music-news/bad-bunny-un-verano-sin-ti-new-music-poll-results-1235068374/. Accessed 30 Apr. 2025.

García, Ivonne. "Diasporic Intersectionality: Colonial History and Puerto Rican Hero Narratives in *21: The Story of Roberto Clemente* and *La Borinqueña*." *The Routledge Companion to Gender and Sex in Latin America*, edited by Frederick Luis Aldama, Routledge, 2018.

García-Moreno Barco, Francisco. "Cuerpos en sal." *Pa la posteridá: Antologia sobre el paso del Huracán María por Puerto Rico*, edited by Lucía Orsanic and Jorge Fusaro Martínez, Ediciones del Flamboyán, 2018, pp. 73–77.

García Urrutia, Laura. "Empty." *Pa la posteridá: Antologia sobre el paso del Huracán María por Puerto Rico*, edited by Lucía Orsanic and Jorge Fusaro Martínez, Ediciones del Flamboyán, 2018, pp. 69–72.

García Zambrana, Carlos. "La fila de hielo." *Pa la posteridá: Antologia sobre el paso del Huracán María por Puerto Rico*, edited by Lucía Orsanic and Jorge Fusaro Martínez, Ediciones del Flamboyán, 2018, pp. 67–68.

"Gilbert Baker: The Gay Betsy Ross." *YouTube*, uploaded by itlmedia, 16 June 2010, https://www.youtube.com/watch?v=1rx-SjnRf-c&t=150s.

Gillespie, Patrick, et al. "Puerto Rico Is Trapped in Thousands of Shipping Containers." CNN, 28 Sept. 2017, https://www.cnn.com/2017/09/27/us/puerto-rico-aid-problem/index.html.

Gillis, John R. *Commemorations: The Politics of National Identity*. Princeton UP, 1994.

Glissant, Edouard. *Poetics of Relation*. 1990. Translated by Betsy Wing. U of Michigan P, 1997.

———. *Treatise on the Whole-World*. Liverpool UP, 1990.

Godreau, Isar. "Changing Space, Making Race: Distance, Nostalgia, and the Folklorization of Blackness in Puerto Rico." *Identities: Global Studies in Culture and Power*, vol. 9, no. 3, 2002, pp. 281–304.

———. "Folkloric 'Others': Blanqueamiento and the Celebration of Blackness as an Exception in Puerto Rico." *Globalization and Race: Transformations in the Cultural Politics of Blackness*, edited by K. M. Clarke and D. A. Thomas, Duke UP, 2006, pp. 171–87.

———. *Scripts of Blackness: Race, Cultural Nationalism, and U.S. Colonialism in Puerto Rico*. U of Illinois P, 2015.

Goldman, Shifra. *Dimensions of the Americas: Art and Social Change in Latin America and the United States*. U of Chicago P, 1994.

González-Cruz, Michael. "Puerto Rican Revolutionary Nationalism: Filiberto Ojeda Ríos and the Macheteros." Translated by Alberto Marquez Sola and Lorena Terando. *Latin American Perspectives*, vol. 35, no. 6, 2008, pp. 151–65.

González Espitia, Juan Carlos. *On the Dark Side of the Archive: Nation and Literature in Spanish America at the Turn of the Century*. Bucknell UP, 2010.

Grosfoguel, Ramón. *Colonial Subjects: Puerto Ricans in a Global Perspective*. U of California P, 2003.

Gutierrez-Alea, Tomás. *Dialéctica del espectador*. Unión de Escritores y Artistas de Cuba, 1982.

Guzman, Roy. "Restored Mural for Orlando." Self-published, 2016.

Halbwachs, Maurice. *The Collective Memory*. 1925. Harper Colophon Books, 1980.

Han, Nydia, and Maia Rosenfeld. "Philadelphia Area Latinos Face Barriers to Health Insurance." *6 Action News*, 29 Sept. 2021, https://6abc.com/data-investigation-health-inequity-insurance-care/11057753/#:~:text=Philadelphia%20area%20Latino%20residents%20face,just%203.5%25%20of%20white%20residents. Accessed 7 Nov. 2023.

Hay-Brown, Matthew. "As Navy Departs Vieques, It Leaves Behind Toxic Mess." *Orlando Sentinel*, 24 Jan. 2003.

Hayward, Michele, et al. "Rock Art of Puerto Rico and the Virgin Islands." *Rock Art of the Caribbean*, edited by Michele Hayward and Lesley-Gail Atkins, U of Alabama P, 2009, pp. 115–36.

Healy, Jack, et al. "Aid Is Getting to Puerto Rico. Distributing It Remains a Challenge." *New York Times*, 3 Oct. 2017, https://www.nytimes.com/2017/10/03/us/puerto-rico-aid-fema-maria.html.

The Heart of the Loisada. Directed and produced by Mari Reaven and Beni Matias, 1979.

Hernández, Yasmín. "Lecciones Lumínicas de Liberación." *Voices from Puerto Rico/ Voces desde Puerto Rico*, edited by Iris Morales, Red Sugarcane Press, 2019, pp. 144–49.

Hernández Marín, Rafael. "Lamento Borincano." 1930.

Hirsch, Marianne, and Leo Spitzer. "Memory in Liquid Time." *Critical Memory Studies: New Approaches*, edited by Ashley Kaplan, Bloomsbury Press, 2023, pp. 107–24.

Hobart, Hi'ilei Julia Kawehipuaakahaopulani. *Cooling the Tropics: Ice, Indigeneity and Hawaiian Refreshment*. Duke UP, 2022.

hooks, bell. *Black Looks: Race and Representation*. South End Press, 1992.

Howell, Octavia. *Philadelphia's Poor: Who They Are, Where They Live, and How That Has Changed*. Pew Charitable Trust, 2017.

Huebner, Jeff. *Walls of Prophecy and Protest: William Walker and the Roots of a Revolutionary Public Art Movement*. Northwestern UP, 2019.

I Am Danny Torres. Directed by Abby Torres and Eric Melendez, Somos Society, 2022.

Ingram, Brent Gordon. "'Open' Space as Strategic Queer Sites." *Queers in Space: Communities, Public Places, and Sites of Resistance*, edited by Gordon Brent Ingram, et al., Bay Press, 1997, pp. 95–126.

Jiménez, Mónica. *Making Never-Never Land: Race and Law in the Creation of Puerto Rico*. U of North Carolina P, 2024.

Jiménez Román, Miriam. "The Indians Are Coming! The Indians Are Coming!: The Taíno and Puerto Rican Identity." *Taíno Revival: Critical Perspectives on Puerto Rican Identity and Politics*, edited by Gabriel Haslip-Viera, Centro de Estudios Puertorriqueños, 1999, pp. 75–107.

———. "Looking at that Middle Ground: Racial Mixing as Panacea?" *Wadabagei*, vol. 8, no. 1, 2005, pp. 65–79.

Jiménez de Wagenheim, Olga. *Nationalist Heroines: Puerto Rican Women History Forgot, 1930s–1950s*. Markus Wiener, 2016.

Jirau-Colón, Héctor, et al. "Toxic Metals Depuration Profiles from a Population Adjacent to a Military Target Range (Vieques) and Main Island Puerto Rico." *International Journal of Environmental Research and Public Health*, vol. 17, no. 264, pp. 1–13.

Johnson, Lauren. "Hurricane Disaster Was Faster in Texas and Florida Than Puerto Rico, Study Says." *CNN*, 29 Mar. 2019, www.cnn.com/2019/01/22/health/hurricane-maria-funding-study-trnd/index.html.

Kang, Esther Yoon-Ji. "New Census Data Confirms the Continuation of Chicago Neighborhoods' Gentrification." *WBEZ Chicago*, 19 Mar. 2022, https://www.wbez.org/stories/census-data-shows-continuing-gentrification-in-chicago/c1663c00-c3a2-41c4-845a-a76b717d8499. Accessed 7 Nov. 2023.

Kenny, Michael. "Back to the Populist Future?: Understanding Nostalgia in Contemporary Ideological Discourse." *Journal of Political Ideologies*, vol. 22, no. 3, 2017, pp. 256–73.

Klein, Naomi. *The Battle for Paradise: Puerto Rico Takes on Disaster Capitalism.* Haymarket Books, 2018.

Kuo, Christopher. "Planned Museum to Honor Pulse Nightclub Victims Canceled." *New York Times*, 2 Nov. 2023. https://www.nytimes.com/2023/11/02/arts/planned-museum-to-honor-pulse-nightclub-victims-canceled.html. Accessed 1 Jan. 2024.

La batalla de Vieques. Directed by Zydnia Nazario, Zemi Productions, 1986.

La Fountain-Stokes, Lawrence. "Gay Shame, Latina- and Latino-Style: A Critique of White Queer Performativity." *Gay Latino Studies: A Reader*, edited by Michael Hames-García and Ernesto Javier Martínez, Duke UP, 2011, pp. 55–80.

———. "Los puertorriqueños queer y el peso de la violencia." *QED: A Journal in GLBTQ Worldmaking*, vol. 3, no. 3, 2016, pp. 103–06.

———, and Yolanda Martínez-San Miguel. "Revisiting Queer Puerto Rican Sexualities: Queer Futures, Reinventions, and Un-Disciplined Archives: Introduction." *Centro Journal*, vol. 30, no. 11, 2018, pp. 6–41.

La generación del estanbai. Directed by Juan C. Dávila, Third World Newsreel, 2016.

Landfall. Directed by Cecilia Aldarondo, ITVS, 2020.

Landler, Mark. "Trump Lobs Praise, and Paper Towels, to Puerto Rico Storm Victims." *New York Times*, 3 Oct. 2017.www.nytimes.com/2017/10/03/us/puerto-rico-trump-hurricane.html

Laó-Montes, Agustín, and Arlene Dávila. *Mambo Montage: The Latinization of New York City.* Columbia UP, 2001.

La operación. Directed by Ana Maria Garcia, Latin American Film Project, 1982.

LeBrón, Marisol. *Against Muerto Rico: Lessons from the Verano Boricua.* Editora Educación Emergente, 2021.

———. *Policing Life and Death: Race, Violence, and Resistance in Puerto Rico.* U of California P, 2019.

Lennon, John. *Conflict Graffiti: From Revolution to Gentrification.* U of Chicago P, 2021.

Lloréns, Hilda. *Imagining the Great Puerto Rican Family.* Lexington Books, 2014.

———. "Ruin Nation." *NACLA Report on the Americas*, vol. 50, no. 2, 2018, pp. 153–59.

Londoño, Johana. *Abstract Barrios: The Crises of Latinx Visibility in Cities*. Duke UP, 2020.

Lothian, Alexis. *Old Futures: Speculative Fiction and Queer Possibility*. NYU Press, 2018.

Loveman, Mara, and Jeronimo Muñiz. "How Puerto Rico Became White: Boundary Dynamics and Intercensus Racial Reclassification." *American Sociological Review*, vol. 72, 2007, pp. 915–39.

Mala mala. Directed by Antionio Santini, Killer Films, 2014.

Maldonado, A. W. *Boom and Bust in Puerto Rico: How Politics Destroyed an Economic Miracle*. U of Notre Dame P, 2021.

Martínez-San Miguel, Yolanda. "Colonialismo y decolonialidad archipelágica en el caribe." *Tabula Rasa*, no. 29, 2018, pp. 37–64.

———. "Taíno Warriors?: Strategies for Recovering Indigenous Voices in Colonial and Contemporary Hispanic Caribbean Discourses." *CENTRO Journal*, vol. 23, no. 1, 2011, pp. 197–215.

———, and Michelle Stephens. "Introduction: 'Isolated Above, but Connected Below': Toward New, Global, Archipelagic Linkages." *Contemporary Archipelago Thinking: Toward New Comparative Methodologies and Disciplinary Formations*, Rowman and Littlefield, 2020, pp. 1–44.

Massol-Deyá, Arturo. "Nuestra Insurrección Energética." *Voices from Puerto Rico/ Voces desde Puerto Rico*, edited by Iris Morales, Red Sugarcane Press, 2019, pp. 216–21.

Mazzei, Patricia. "Former Puerto Rico Education Secretary Is Sentenced to Prison." *New York Times*, 17 Dec. 2021, https://www.nytimes.com/2021/12/17/us/ puerto-rico-education-corruption-keleher.html.

———. "Protest in Puerto Rico Over Austerity Measures Ends in Tear Gas." *New York Times*, 1 May 2018, www.nytimes.com/2018/05/01/us/puerto-rico-protests.html.

McCaffrey, Katherine. "Las Playas son del Pueblo: The Struggle for Puerto Rico's Coast." *Beach Politics: Social, Racial, and Environmental Injustices on the Shoreline*, edited by Setha Low, NYU Press, 2025, pp. 243–62.

———. *Military Power and Popular Protest: The U.S. Navy in Vieques, Puerto Rico*. Rutgers UP, 2002.

———, and Sherrie Baver. "Ni una bomba más: Reframing the Vieques Struggle." *Beyond Sund and Sand: Caribbean Environmentalisms*, edited by Sherrie Baver and Barbara Deutsch Lynch, Rutgers UP, 2006, pp. 109–28.

Meléndez, Edwin. "The Politics of PROMESA." *CENTRO: Journal of the Center for Puerto Rican Studies*, vol. 30, no. 3, 2018, pp. 43–73.

———, and Charles Venator-Santiago. "Puerto Rico Post-Hurricane Maria: Origins and Consequences of a Crisis." *CENTRO: Journal of the Center for Puerto Rican Studies*, vol. 30, no. 3, 2018, pp. 1–10.

Meléndez-Badillo, Jorell. *Puerto Rico: A National History*. Princeton UP, 2024.

Mercer, Kobena. "Black Hair/Style Politics." *Welcome to the Jungle: New Positions in Black Cultural Studies*, Routledge, 1994, pp. 97–130.

Mitchell, Chip. "Mural Restoration Heartens Puerto Ricans." WBEZ Chicago, 21 Sept. 2011, https://www.wbez.org/stories/mural-restoration-heartens-puerto-ricans/ee354e11-13e6-44f1-ad90-91b1aaf5e3c0. Accessed 23 Jan. 2024.

Molina, Alejandro. "The Restoration of *La Crucifixión de Don Pedro*." The Puerto Rican Cultural Center, 4 Oct. 2010, https://prcc-chgo.org/2010/10/04/the-restoration-of-la-crucifixion-de-don-pedro/. Accessed 23 Jan. 2023.

Mora, Marie, et al. "Migration, Geographic Destinations, and Socioeconomic Outcomes of Puerto Ricans During La Crisis Boricua: Implications for Island and Stateside Communities Post-Maria." *CENTRO Journal*, vol. 30, no. 3, 2018, pp. 208–29.

Morales, Ed. *Fantasy Island: Colonialism, Exploitation, and the Betrayal of Puerto Rico*. Bold Type Books, 2019.

Morales, Iris. *Voices from Puerto Rico/Voces desde Puerto Rico*. Red Sugarcane Press, 2019.

Moreno, Marisel. *Family Matters: Puerto Rican Women Authors on the Island and the Mainland*. U of Virginia P, 2012.

Morse, Tal. "'We Are One': Mediatized Death Rituals and the Recognition of Marginalized Others." *International Journal of Communication*, vol. 17, 2023, pp. 1302–29.

Murphy, Kaitlin. *Mapping Memory: Visuality, Affect, and Embodied Politics in the Americas*. Fordham UP, 2018.

Murphy-Marcos, Coral. "Puerto Rico Approves Electricity Rate Increase Weeks After Massive Blackout." AP News, 1 July 2024, https://apnews.com/article/puerto-rico-electricity-rates-blackout-53f96091f59738b79af3be515b8e6915.

Muñoz, Andre Lee. *Vida y Hacienda: The Life and Legacy of Dr. Pedro Albizu Campos*. Remembering Don Pedro, 2022.

Muñoz, José Esteban. *Cruising Utopias: The Then and There of Queer Futurity*. 2009. NYU Press, 2019.

Neil, Emily. "'Sanctuary City, Sanctuary Neighborhood' Mural Unveiled in Fairhill." *Al Día*, 29 Aug. 2019, https://aldianews.com/en/culture/heritage-and-history/sanctuary-neighborhood. Accessed 1 Mar. 2024.

Negrón Muntaner, Frances. *Boricua Pop: Puerto Ricans and the Latinization of American Culture*. NYU Press, 2004.

———. "Puerto Rican Women Directors: Of Lonesome Stars and Broken Hearts." *Jump Cut: A Review of Contemporary Media*, no. 38, 1993, pp. 67–78.

Nixon, Rob. "Introduction." *Slow Violence and the Environmentalism of the Poor*. Harvard UP, 2013, pp. 1–44.

Nora, Pierre. "Between Memory and History: Lieux de Mémoire." *Representations*, no. 86, 1989, pp. 7–24.

Olick, Jeffrey. "Collective Memory: The Two Cultures." *Sociological Theory*, vol. 17, no. 3, 1999, pp. 333–48.

Omi, Howard, and Michael Winant. "Colorblindness, Neoliberalism, and Obama." *Racial Formation in the United States*. 3rd ed., Routledge, pp. 211–44.

O'Neill-Carrillo, Efraín, and Miguel Rivera-Quiñones. "Energy Policies in Puerto Rico and Their Impact on the Likelihood of a Resilient and Sustainable Electric Power Infrastructure." *CENTRO: Journal of the Center for Puerto Rican Studies*, vol. 30, no. 3, 2018, pp. 147–71.

One Orlando Collection. "Javier Jorge Reyes." *Keep the Pulse: The One Orlando Collection*, 2024, https://oneorlandocollection.com/tile-22/. Accessed 5 Mar. 2024.

———. *Keep the Pulse: The One Orlando Collection*, 2024, https://oneorlandocollection.com. Accessed 5 Mar. 2024.

Orangias, Joseph, et al. "The Cultural Functions of Social Potential of Queer Monuments: A Preliminary Inventory and Analysis." *Journal of Homosexuality*, vol. 65, no. 6, 2018, pp. 705–26.

Orsanic, Lucía, and Jorge Fusaro Martínez. *Pa la posteridá: Antologia sobre el paso del Huracán María por Puerto Rico*. Ediciones del Flamboyán, 2018.

Ortiz, Jen. "Bienvenido a Bad Bunny's Puerto Rico." *The Cut*, 18 Feb. 2025, https://www.thecut.com/article/bad-bunny-new-album-debi-tirar-mas-fotos-interview.html. Accessed 1 Apr. 2025.

Pedreira, A. S. *Insularismo: An Insight into the Puerto Rican Character*. 1934. Translated by Aoife Rivera Serrano. Ausubo Press, 2005.

Pelet, Valeria. "Puerto Rico's Invisible Health Crisis." *The Atlantic*, 3 Sept. 2016, www.theatlantic.com/politics/archive/2016/09/vieques-invisible-health-crisis/498428/.

Pérez, Gina. *The Near Northwest Side Story: Migration, Displacement, and Puerto Rican Families*. University of California Press, 2004.

Phillips, Karin. " 'El Centro de Oro' Section of Philadelphia Gets $4-Million Makeover." CBS Philadelphia, 20 June 2011, https://www.cbsnews.com/philadelphia/news/el-centro-de-oro-section-of-north-philadelphia-gets-4-million-makeover/. Accessed 23 Jan. 2024.

Portnoy Brimmer, Ana. "A Julia Keleher, Secretaria de Educación de Puerto Rico, Quien Se Encontraba en el mismo Vuelo de American Airlines Que Yo, Cuatro Meses Después de María." *Voices from Puerto Rico/Voces desde Puerto Rico*, edited by Iris Morales, Red Sugarcane Press, 2019, pp. 159–60.

"Preciosa: The Other Anthem," season 2, episode 1, hosted by Alana Casanova-Burgess, *La Brega*, WNYC Studios, 26 Jan. 2023, https://www.wnycstudios.org/podcasts/la-brega/articles/preciosa-other-anthem.

Puar, Jasbir. *Terrorist Assemblages: Homonationalism in Queer Times*. Duke UP, 2017.

"The Puerto Rican Cultural Center." 14 Feb. 2025, https://prcc-chgo.org/prcc/.

Quijano, Anibal. "Colonialidad del poder, cultural, y conocimento en América Latina," Quijano, Aníbal. "Colonialidad del poder, eurocentrismo, y América Latina." *Colonialidad del saber, eurocentrismo y ciencias sociales*. Buenos Aires: Consejo Latinoamericano de Ciencias Sociales (CLACSO), 2000.

Ramirez, Johanna, et al. "'Invisible During My Own Crisis': Responses of LGBT People of Color to the Orlando Shooting." *Journal of Homosexuality*, vol. 65., no. 5, 2018, pp. 579–99.

Ramos Ortiz, Maite. "Pos-Huracán María." *Voices from Puerto Rico/Voces desde Puerto Rico*, edited by Iris Morales, Red Sugarcane Press, 2019, pp. 136–37.

Ramos-Perea, Roberto. "Una Nueva Dictadura se ha Instaurado en Puerto Rico." *Voices from Puerto Rico/Voces desde Puerto Rico*, edited by Iris Morales, Red Sugarcane Press, 2019, pp. 167–69.

Ramos-Zayas, Ana. *National Performances: The Politics of Class, Race, and Space in Puerto Rican Chicago*. U of Chicago P, 2003.

Randall-Moon, H. "Mediations of Security, Race, and Violence in the Pulse Nightclub Shooting: Homonationalism in Anti-Immigration Times." *GLQ*, vol. 28, no. 1, 2022, pp. 1–28.

Recuber, Timothy. "The Prosumption of Commemoration: Disasters, Digital Memory Banks, and Online Collective Memory." *American Behavioral Scientist*, vol. 56, no. 4, 2012, pp. 531–49.

"Resultados Censo 2020: Puerto Rico no se quedó en blanco." *Colectivo Ilé*. https://www.colectivoile.org/blog-1/resultadoscenso2020.

Reyes, Israel. *Embodied Economies: Diaspora and Transcultural Capital in Latinx Caribbean Fiction and Theater*. Rutgers UP, 2022.

Rice Kerr, Andrew. *A Disembodied Shade: Vieques, Puerto Rico at the Intersection of Empire and Environmentalism in the Twentieth Century*. 2009. University of California Davis, PhD dissertation.

Ricourt, Milagros, and Ruby Danta. *Hispanas de Queens: Latino Panethnicity in a New York City Neighborhood*. Cornell UP, 2003.

Riggle, Nicholas Alden. "Street Art: The Transfiguration of the Common Places." *Journal of Aesthetics and Art Criticisms*, vol. 68, no. 3, 2010, pp. 243–57.

Rivera-Rideau, Petra R. "From Carolina to Loíza: Race, Place, and Puerto Rican Racial Democracy." *Identities: Global Studies in Culture and Power,* vol. 20, no. 5, 2013, pp. 616–32.

———. "The Perils of Perreo." *Remixing Reggaeton: The Cultural Politics of Race in Puerto Rico*, Duke UP, 2015, pp. 53–80.

Rivera Figueroa, Luis Enrique. "Bad Bunny's Transgressive Gender Performativity: Camp Aesthetics and Hegemonic Masculinities in Early Latin Trap." *Journal of Latin American Communications Research*, vol. 8, no. 1–2, 2020, pp. 86–108.

Robinson, Emily. "Radical Nostalgia, Progressive Patriotism and Labour's 'English Problem.'" *Political Studies Review*, vol. 14, no. 3, 2016, pp. 378–87.

Robles, Frances, et al. "Official Toll in Puerto Rico: 64. Actual Deaths May Be 1,052." *New York Times*, 9 Aug. 2018, https://www.nytimes.com/interactive/2017/12/08/us/puerto-rico-hurricane-maria-death-toll.html. Accessed 15 Jan. 2024.

Rodríguez, Gamaliel. *Correctional Faith*, Colby College Museum of Art, Waterville, Maine, 2022.

———. *(In)hospitable*. Center of Maine Contemporary Art, Rockland, 2022.

Rodriguez-Muñiz, Michael. "Riots and Remembrance: Puerto Rican Chicago and the Politics of Interruption." *CENTROL Journal*, vol. 28, no. 2, 2017, pp. 204–17.

Rodriguez Rabin, Rose. "Vejigantes." *The Oxford Encyclopedia of Latinos and Latinas in the United States*, edited by Suzane Obeler and Deena Gonzalez, Oxford UP, 2005.

Rodríguez Ramos, Reniel. *Rethinking Puerto Rican Precolonial History*. U of Alabama P, 2010.

Roman, Ivan. "Study: Vieques' Cancer Rates Higher than Puerto Rico's." *Orlando Sentinel*, 10 May 2003.

Roque Antonetty, Anaís Delilah. "Historicizing Puerto Rico's Energy Present: A Political and Environmental Justice Approach to Energy Production in Puerto Rico." *CENTRO Journal*, vol. 35, no. 1, 2023, pp. 57–80.

Rosa, Alejandra. "Grietas." *Pa la posteridá: Antologia sobre el paso del Huracán María por Puerto Rico*, edited by Lucía Orsanic and Jorge Fusaro Martínez, Ediciones del Flamboyán, 2018, pp. 29–33.

Roscoe, Jane, and Craig Hight. *Faking It: Mock-Documentary and the Subversion of Factuality*. Manchester UP, 2001.

Rothberg, Michael. *The Implicated Subject: Beyond Victims and Perpetrators*. Stanford UP, 2019.

———. *Multidirectional Memory: Remembering the Holocaust in the Age of Decolonization*. Stanford UP, 2009.

Rúa, Mérida. "Coloa Subjectivities: PortoMex and MexiRican Perspectives on Language and Identity." *CENTRO Journal*, vol. 13, no. 2, 2001, pp. 117–33.

Ruiz, Sandra. *Ricanness: Enduring Time in Anticolonial Performance*. NYU Press, 2019.

Sánchez, Luis Rafael. "La guagua aérea." *La guagua aérea*, Editorial Cultural, 1994, pp. 11–22.

Sanderson, Hans, et al. "Civilian Exposure to Munitions-Specific Carcinogens and Resulting Cancer Risks for Civilians on the Puerto Rican Island of Vieques following Military Exercises from 1947 to 1998." *Global Security: Health, Science, and Policy*, vol. 2, no. 1, 2017, pp. 40–61.

Santich, Kate. "Pulse Memorial and Museum Design Tranquil and Towering." *Orlando Sentinel*, 31 Oct. 2019, A1.

Schachter, Jason, and Antonio Bruce. "Estimating Puerto Rico's Population After Hurricane Maria: Revising Methods to Better Reflect the Impact of Disaster." 19 Aug. 2020, United States Census, https://www.census.gov/library/stories/2020/08/estimating-puerto-rico-population-after-hurricane-maria.html. Accessed 23 Apr. 2023.

Schneider, Mike. "After Pulse Attack, Gay Latino Community Seeks Strength." *The Gleaner* [Henderson, KY], 9 June 2017, A6.

Schwartz, Pam, et al. "Rapid-Response Collecting after the Pulse Nightclub Massacre." *The Public Historian*, vol. 40, no. 1, 2018, pp. 105–14.

Serán las dueñas de la tierra. Directed by Juanma Pagán Teitelbaum, Producciones Libélula, 2022.

Serrano, Maria. "Osceola County to Break Ground on 40-Foot Pulse Tribute Sculpture. *Spectrum News* (Kissimmee, FL), 06 May 2024.

Sharpe, Christina. *In the Wake: On Blackness and Being*. Duke UP, 2016.

Silver, Patricia. "'Asking as a Citizen': Navigating Ambiguity in the Interest of Community." *The Latin Americanist*, vol. 65, no. 1, 2021, pp. 123–41.

———. *Sunbelt Diaspora: Race, Class, and Latino Politics in Puerto Rican Orlando*. U of Texas P, 2020.

———. "'You Don't Look Puerto Rican': Collective Memory and Community in Orlando." *Memory Studies*, vol. 9, no. 4, 2015, pp. 405–21.

Simulacros de liberación. Directed by Juan C. Dávila, República 21 Media, 2021.

Sion, Bridgitte. *Death Tourism: Disaster Sites as Recreational Landscapes*. U of Chicago P, 2014.

Solanas, Fernando, and Octavio Getino. *Cine, cultura, y descolonización*. Siglo XXI, 1973.

Sontag, Susan. *On Photography*. 1973. Farrar, Straus, Giroux, 2005.

Soto-Crespo, Ramón. *Mainland Passage: The Cultural Anomaly of Puerto Rico*. U of Minnesota P, 2009.

Spade, Dean. *Mutual Aid: Building Solidarity During This Crisis (and the Next)*. Verso, 2020.

Stoler, Ann Laurie. "Introduction: 'The Rot Remains': From Ruins to Ruination." *Imperial Debris: On Ruins and Ruination*, Duke UP, 2016, pp. 2–35.

Sturken, Marita. *Tangled Memories: The Vietnam War, the AIDS Epidemic, and the Politics of Remembering*. U of California P, 1997.

Szeman, Imran, and Darin Barney. "Introduction: From Solar to Solarity." *The South Atlantic Quarterly*, vol. 120, no. 1, 2021, pp. 1–11.

Talbot, Jessica, Cristina Poleacovschi, and Sara Hamideh. "Socioeconomic Vulnerabilities and Housing Reconstruction in Puerto Rico After Hurricanes Irma and Maria. *Natural Hazards*, vol. 110, 2022, pp. 2113–2140.

Thompson, Lanny. *Imperial Archipelago: Representation and Rule in the Insular Territories Under U.S. Domination*. U of Hawaii P, 2010.

Tinsley, Meghan. "Revisiting Nostalgia: Imperialism, Anticolonialism, and Imagining Home." *Ethnic and Racial Studies*, vol. 43, no. 13, 2020, pp. 2327–55.

Tomkins, Cynthia. "Introduction: Mise-en-scéne, a Seemingling International Staging." *Experimental Latin American Cinema: History and Aesthetics*. U of Texas Press, 2023, pp. 1–46.

Torres, Julie. "'We Are Orlando': Silences, Resistance, and the Intersections of Mass Violence." *Meridians: Feminism, Race, Transnationalism*, vol. 22, no. 2, 2023, pp. 446–74.

Torres Ramos, Rafael. "Toque de queda." *Pa la posteridá: Antologia sobre el paso del Huracán María por Puerto Rico*, edited by Lucía Orsanic and Jorge Fusaro Martínez, Ediciones del Flamboyán, 2018, pp. 93–94.

Torres-Vélez, Victor M. "Reification, Biomedicine, and Bombs: Women's Politicization in Vieques' Social Movements." *Disability Studies and the Environmental Humanities: Toward an Eco-Crip Theory*, Nebraska UP, 2017, pp. 313–37.

Traverso, Enzo. *Left-Wing Melancholia: Marxism, History, and Memory*. Columbia UP, 2017.

Unites States Congress. *Public Law 114-187: Puerto Rico Oversight, Management, and Economic Stability Act*. Government Printing Office, 30 June 2016, https://www.govinfo.gov/app/details/PLAW-114publ187.

Urciuoli, Bonnie. *Exposing Prejudice: Puerto Rican Experience of Language, Race, and Class*. Westview Press, 1996.

Valcárcel, Xavier. *Aterrizar no es regreso*. Ediciones Alayubia, 2019.

VanHaitsma, Pamela. "Digital LGBT! Archives as Sites of Public Memory and Pedagogy." *Rhetoric and Public Affairs*, vol. 22, no. 2, 2019, pp. 253–80.

Vázquez-Hernández, Victor. *Before the Wave: Puerto Ricans in Philadelphia, 1910–1945*. Centro Press, 2017.

Vidal, Teodoro. *El vijugante ponceño*. Universidad de Puerto Rico, 2004.

Vieques: Una batalla inconclusa. Directed by Juan C. Dávila, Patas Ariba Media Project, 2018.

Walcott, Derek. "The Antilles: Fragments of Epic Memory Nobel Lecture, 7 December 1992." *The Georgia Review*, vol. 49, no. 1, 1995, pp. 294–306.

Waclawek, Anna. *Graffiti and Street Art*. Thames and Hudson, 2011.

Whalen, Carmen Teresa. *From Puerto Rico to Philadelphia: Puerto Rican Workers and Postwar Economies*. Temple UP, 2001.

Wherry, Frederick. *The Philadelphia Barrio: The Arts, Branding, and Neighborhood Transformation*. U of Chicago P, 2011.

Widrich, Mechtild. "Moving Monuments in the Age of Social Media." *Future Anterior: Journal of Historic Preservation, History, Theory, and Criticism*, vol. 15, no. 2, 2018, pp. 133–44.

Williams, Raymond. "Structures of Feeling." *Structures of Feeling: Affectivity and the Study of Culture*, edited by Devika Sharma and Frederick Tygstrup, De Gruyter, 2015, pp. 20–25.

Zaezae, Y. "Dismembered Bodies of Color: U.S. Imperialism in the Pulse Shooting." *Queer Cats*, vol. 3–4, 2019, pp. 57–85.

Zambrana, Rocio. *Colonial Debts: The Case of Puerto Rico*. Duke UP, 2021.

Zimmerman, Marc. "The Flag and Three Puerto Rican Artists." *Defending Their Own in the Cold: The Cultural Turns of U.S. Puerto Ricans*, U of Illinois P, 2011, pp. 21–49.

Index